Franco A BIOGRAPHY

J. W. D. Trythall

Rupert Hart-Davis LONDON 1970

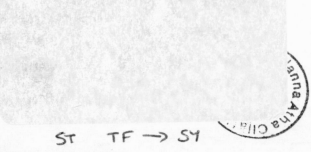

ST   TF → SY

First published 1970
Rupert Hart-Davis Ltd
3 Upper James Street, Golden Square,
London, W1.

Printed in Great Britain by
Cox & Wyman Ltd,
London, Fakenham and Reading

SBN: 246 63981 4

To JO

No queremos panegiristas de nuestra obra, sino hombres que la aprecien y la calibren en lo que vale, . . .

We do not want panegyrists of our work, rather men who will value it and assess it at what it is worth, . . .

(Speech of H.E. the Chief of State at the Extraordinary Session of the Spanish Cortes, 22 November 1966)

Contents

List of Illustrations

The photographs of Franco in Morocco, the visit of the French War Minister to Zaragoza, and Franco with Eisenhower are reproduced by the great courtesy of the Subdirector General de Información, Madrid.

Foreword

by Professor Raymond Carr

The problem with General Franco is not how he attained supreme power in Spain but why he still possesses it. His biographers, excellent as some of them are, have been specially concerned with his rise to power and his ambivalent diplomacy in the Second World War. Mr Trythall is the first to trace in more detail the trajectory after 1945.

A supremely competent regimental and staff officer, the youngest general in Europe, he stood out in an old-fashioned army as a moderniser. His political theory came from Spanish history as taught in military academies and from the officer's conception of order. Party politicians had lost the remnants of the Spanish empire in Cuba in 1898 and blamed the army: *ergo* party politics were bad for Spain. Generals, in military political theory, are like Rousseau's legislator; they interpret the real will of the nation when others are incapable of seeing it. It is the first duty of a government to keep the people (the troops) in order: if it fails then those who understand order must intervene. This is the simple model of society with which political soldiers worked until recently.

General Franco's mess-room political theory was common to most officers — though it is an oversimplification to imagine them all as anti-Republicans in 1936, only two generals with command of an organic division in Spain supporting the movement. Franco came to the top, not only, as I have argued, because the African Army he commanded was the best army in the Civil War or, as others have argued, because of his seniority in the army list, but because he was clearly recognised by his military peers as indisputably the ablest man on the Nationalist side. What surprised his creators was his rapid acquisition of the political talent and ruthlessness that he first demonstrated in the crisis of April 1937 and his Cromwellian capacity for the assumption of a providential mission. Too late monarchists like General Kindelán realised he was there to stay on his own terms. He had become indispensable.

On the middle and later stages of Franco's career Mr Trythall is excellent. In his treatment of Franco's response to pressure from Germany 1939–45 he shows that Franco wanted a German victory and a place in the sun of the New Order, but that he set too high a price for his co-operation. The lesson after 1945 is that ostracism by world opinion does not pay except against tottering regimes. The efforts to start a guerrilla rising in 1944–5 merely reinforce the words of the Duke of Wellington on the perils of revolutionising a country. 'I always said, if they rise of themselves, well and good. But do not stir them up; it is a fearful responsibility.'

In any case, in the end, the strategic necessities of the United States overcame President Truman's Baptist dislike of Catholic authoritarianism. The Allies had always seen Franco as a symbol; the photograph of Hitler and the Caudillo on Hendaye station remained in the mind even when the reality of German–Spanish relations were known. Now the photograph was replaced by another: President Eisenhower, leader of the Crusade in Europe, embracing General Franco, leader of the Crusade in Spain. After 1957 the warmth — if it ever existed — went out of this peculiar special relationship.

After the lean years of the late forties and early fifties Mr Trythall describes General Franco's progress from the dream of economic autarchy, state control and imperialism to the reality of foreign aid, indicative planning and material prosperity as a substitute for Great Spain. His Moroccan policy was ill-conceived, but Mr Trythall emphasises a point that must be rammed home in this country. Gibraltar is not a relic of the Falange Great Spain; it is the demand of every Spaniard and any successor regime, right or left, will continue to demand the return of the Rock.

General Franco's rule will never be acceptable to Western liberals and they will never understand the source of his strength. To General Franco the art of politics is to avoid by force and by subtlety the polarisation of opinion, the clash of ideas that is the life of liberalism. Rightly Mr Trythall emphasises General Franco's successes with the forces that have no alternative but to support his regime: the political manipulation by which, as Mr Trythall shows, no element is driven to absolute opposition nor so satisfied that it can dispense with the Caudillo. His capacity to jettison his ministers, to keep cool in crises such as those in 1944–1946, in 1956–1957, or even in 1969, is astonishing. He never loses his political nerve.

Yet still one must always wonder how long it can all last. Has General Franco, by choosing Juan Carlos as his political heir, shown a political narrowness, a fear of the 'particular demons' of political debate, that imperils his whole work? Certain problems he refuses to face; Mr Trythall perhaps says too little of the opposition. But he does make one wise observation. It is hard to see how a monarchic successor can solve those problems the solution of which Franco himself has postponed.

I have listened to two generations of Spanish liberal friends predicting the downfall of General Franco. He is still there. What is the quality which has given him power for longer than any other statesman in the West? Partly, of course, he benefits from the horror of a relapse into civil war; this is a diminishing asset. But, as in the case of Louis XIV, there is something else, a sort of personal embarrassment in opposing the will of the ruler in his self-created hieratic court. Men stand in awe of him not merely because he commands and will use the instruments of repression; there is no arguing with him. Even Hitler found this out. Convinced of his mission, he is not troubled by tactical failures; he can ride unruffled crises which would unbalance a more sensitive man — perhaps his genuine retreats into bourgeois family life and his faith give him a strength denied to politicians concerned with images, for he does not have to bother about polls and elections. 'I do not find the burden of rule heavy,' he once remarked. 'Spain is easy to govern.' This is an astonishing remark for the ruler of a twentieth-century state, even for an absolute ruler. Mr Trythall's quotations are short but always illuminating. Perhaps, as in 1936, General Franco still believes 'Spaniards are tired of politics and politicians.' I wonder.

RAYMOND CARR,
Oxford.
October, 1969.

Preface

There have been biographical studies of Franco before this one and there will without doubt be many to follow it. One day historians will have the private papers of the generalissimo, the minutes of his Councils of Ministers, and doubtless he will remain a far from straight-forward character. Myself, I have used little material that was not either published or readily available, though some sources had seemingly escaped previous attention. I am very much a dwarf on the shoulders of giants. My subject has given rise to much passion on either side, but I have tried to be dispassionate. I have to differ from those who believe that historians should in honesty not only admit but even flaunt their prejudices. I believe that I can only be excused for writing if I can strip away more encrusted cant and prejudice than I contribute by ineradicable preconceptions. I hope that I have been helped to achieve this by being a non-Spaniard, without strong political convictions, and born at a date after most of the action of this book had taken place. For such offensive views and ignorant errors as appear in the book no one but myself is to blame, certainly none of those too numerous to name, both in England and in Spain, who have helped me in the researching or writing of this book. I am most grateful to them all, but should like to single out Raymond Carr, Warden of St Antony's College, Oxford, without whom this book would not have been started, and my wife without whose secretarial and other assistance I doubt if it would have been finished.

J.W.D.T.,
York.
October, 1969.

Chronological Synopsis

<table>
<tr><td>1892</td><td>Birth of Francisco Franco at El Ferrol.</td></tr>
<tr><td>1898</td><td>War between Spain and the United States. Spain loses Cuba, Puerto Rico and Philippines.</td></tr>
<tr><td>1902</td><td>Majority of Alfonso XIII.</td></tr>
<tr><td>1907</td><td>Franco goes to Toledo Infantry Academy.</td></tr>
<tr><td>1909</td><td>First of the series of Moroccan campaigns which lasted until 1926.
The 'tragic week' of revolutionary violence in Barcelona.</td></tr>
<tr><td>1912</td><td>Franco posted to Morocco.</td></tr>
<tr><td>1914</td><td>Outbreak of First World War. Spain was neutral throughout.</td></tr>
<tr><td>1917</td><td>March Franco posted to Oviedo.
June Military Juntas movement.
August General strike.</td></tr>
<tr><td>1919–1923</td><td>Wave of strikes and violence in Catalonia.</td></tr>
<tr><td>1920</td><td>October Franco joins the Legion.</td></tr>
<tr><td>1921</td><td>July Disaster at Annual.</td></tr>
</table>

<table>
<tr><td>1923</td><td>June Franco given command of Legion. Promoted Lieutenant Colonel.
September Primo de Rivera's coup d'état.
October Franco's marriage.</td></tr>
<tr><td>1926</td><td>February Franco promoted Brigadier-General. Leaves Morocco.</td></tr>
<tr><td>1927</td><td>May Final pacification of Morocco.</td></tr>
<tr><td>1928</td><td>October Inauguration of the General Military Academy.</td></tr>
<tr><td>1929</td><td>November Wall Street stock crash. The peseta had already been falling rapidly on the exchanges against sterling.</td></tr>
<tr><td>1930</td><td>January Resignation of Primo de Rivera. Succeeded by Berenguer.</td></tr>
<tr><td>1931</td><td>February Government of Admiral Aznar.
April Fall of the Monarchy. Broadly based Provisional Republican government under Alcalá Zamora.
June General Military Academy closed.
September The pound sterl-</td></tr>
</table>

15

1931 ing goes off the gold standard. *October* Azaña becomes Prime Minister of a Radical government with Socialist support.

1932 *March* Franco posted to Corunna. *August* Rising of Sanjurjo. Institution of British Imperial Preference by Ottawa agreements hurts Spanish trade.

1933 *January* Hitler comes to power in Germany. *March* Franco posted to Balearics. Roosevelt inaugurated as President of the USA. The 'New Deal'. *November* Rightist victory in elections. Lerroux government with CEDA support.

1934 *February* Dollfuss suppresses Austrian Socialists. *March* Franco promoted Major-General. *October* CEDA joins the government. Asturias revolt.

1935 *January* Franco appointed Military C-in-C in Morocco. *May* Appointed Chief of General Staff. Gil Robles War Minister. *October* Outbreak of Italo–Abyssinian war. *December* Gil Robles leaves War Ministry. Portela becomes Premier.

1936 *February* Victory of the Popular Front. Azaña Premier. *March* Franco posted to the Canaries. Hitler's troops re-enter the Rhineland. *May* Azaña becomes President, Casares Quiroga Premier.

July Assassination of Calvo Sotelo. Outbreak of Civil War in Spain. *Aug–Sept* Franco's armies approach Madrid from the south. *October* Franco becomes Head of State. *November* Failure of the Madrid offensive. Franco recognised by Germany and Italy.

1937 *Spring* Continued failure on Madrid front. Success in the south. *April* Unification decree. Carists and Falangists welded together. *Summer* Basque country, Santander fall to Nationalists. *Autumn* Asturias campaign. *December* Republican offensive at Teruel.

1938 *January* Ministerial government formed in Nationalist Spain. *Spring* Maestrazgo and Levante campaigns. Germany's Anschluss with Austria. *July* Franco promoted Captain-General of Land, Sea and Air Forces. Beginning of the Battle of the Ebro. *September* The Czech crisis. The Munich settlement. *December* Catalan campaign launched.

1939 *April* The end of the Civil War *August* Spanish Cabinet reshuffle. Hitler–Stalin pact. *September* Outbreak of Second World War. Spain strictly neutral. Seat of government returns to Madrid. *November* Russo–Finnish war breaks out. (Ends March 1940.)

1940 *April* Denmark and Norway conquered by Germany.
May Benelux countries fall to Germany. British Army withdraws to Dunkirk.
June Italy enters the war. Spain becomes 'non-belligerent.'
Franco draws up Spain's demands. Franco–German armistice.
September Battle of Britain. Serrano Súñer visits Berlin.
October Franco meets Hitler at Hendaye.
Italy invades Greece.
November Serrano Súñer summoned to Berchtesgaden.
December German plans for bringing Spain into war shelved.

1941 *February* Franco meets Mussolini, then Pétain.
April German conquest of Yugoslavia and Greece.
May Lt. Col. Galarza fills the vacant Ministry of the Interior, whose control is thus removed from Serrano.
June Germany invades USSR. Blue Division recruiting begins.
November INI founded.
December Japan and USA enter the war.

1942 *February* Franco meets Salazar.
Japan triumphs in the Far East. Singapore falls, though Corregidor holds out until May.
May Arrese supplants Serrano in Falange hierarchy.
August Affray in Bilbao results in the fall of Serrano— and of Varela.
November Battle of Alamein. Allied landings in N.W. Africa. Germans occupy the re-

mainder of France. The turning point at Stalingrad.

1943 *March* First meeting of the Cortes.
May Franco speaks in favour of peace.
June Surrender of Italy.
July Generals petition for the Restoration of the Monarchy.
October Spain discards 'non-belligerency', declares herself neutral.

1944 *Spring* Spanish–Allied dispute over embargo on wolfram exports to Germany.
June Allied landings in France.
October Franco proposes Anglo–Spanish understanding to Churchill.
December Abortive Republican invasion of Spain.

1945 *March* Pretender's Lausanne manifesto.
April Death of Roosevelt. Truman President of the USA.
May Surrender of Germany.
June Issue of the Spaniards' Charter.
San Francisco Conference condemns Franco's regime.
July Labour government formed in Britain.
August At Potsdam the Big Three confirm ostracism of Spain.
September Hiroshima and Nagasaki. The end of the war in the Far East.
Bevin makes it clear that Britain will not intervene in Spain.
Republican Spanish Government set up in exile.

1946 *March* The Paris Conference of Foreign Ministers reveals increasing divisions of the World War victors. Churchill's

B

1946 'iron curtain' speech at Fulton, Mo.
December UNO recommends withdrawal of ambassadors from Spain.

1947 *June* Announcement of Marshall Aid.
July Referendum confirms Franco as Head of State for life, formally makes Spain a kingdom without a king.
August Independence of Britain's Indian Empire opens the age of decolonialisation.

1948 *March* Communist *coup d'état* in Czechoslovakia.
April Franco–Perón protocol.
May Foundation of the State of Israel.
June Beginning of an eleven-month Russian blockade of Berlin.
August Spanish monarchists and Socialists conclude the Pact of St Jean de Luz. Franco and the Pretender meet on the *Azor*

1949 *April* Signature of NATO Treaty.
September First Soviet atom bomb test.
October Proclamation of the Chinese People's Republic.

1950 *April* Marriage of Franco's daughter.
June Outbreak of Korean War.
November UN formally rescinds 1946 condemnation of Spain.

1951 *May* Nationalisation of Iranian oilfields.
July Sherman's visit to Spain. Spanish Cabinet changes.
October Churchill returns to power in Britain.

1952 *April* Martín Artajo's tour of the Middle East.

November Spain readmitted to the administration of Tangier.

1953 *January* Inauguration of President Eisenhower.
Death of Stalin.
July Armistice ends the Korean war.
August French depose the Sultan of Morocco.
Concordat between Spain and the Holy See.
September The Pact of Madrid. USA granted bases in Spain.

1954 *July* Geneva agreements on Indo-China.
September Paris agreement on West German rearmament.
December Franco meets the Pretender near Cáceres. Decided that Juan Carlos should receive training for all three fighting services.

1955 *April* Bandung conference of Afro-Asian states.
July Summit meeting at Geneva.
December Spain admitted to the United Nations.

1956 *February* Falangist threat to public order. Dismissal of Fernández Cuesta and Ruiz Jiménez. Arrese set to propose new structure for the Movement.
March Independence of Tunisia.
April Independence of Morocco.
October Anglo–French invasion of Suez Canal zone.
November Russian suppression of Hungarian revolution.

1957 *February* Major Cabinet reshuffle in Spain. Castiella to Foreign Ministry. Opus mem-

1957 bers to Finance and Commerce.
March Signature of the Treaty of Rome, creating EEC with effect from January 1958.
October Launching of the first Sputnik.
November Spanish involved in Ifni war until February 1958.

1958 *June* De Gaulle comes to power in France, his chief mission to overcome the crisis of the Algerian War.
July Spain joins IMF.

1959 *January* Castro comes to power in Cuba.
July Devaluation of the peseta, stabilisation the watchword.
December Eisenhower visits Franco.

1960 *March* Franco again meets the Pretender, near Cáceres.
May Khrushchev withdraws from summit conference following the capture of a U-2 spy pilot.

1961 *January* Inauguration of Kennedy as President of the USA.
March Kennedy announces the Alliance for Progress.
April Bay of Pigs invasion.
December Franco injured in a shooting accident.

1962 *February* Spanish approach to the EEC.
March France agrees to Algerian independence.
April Wave of strikes begins in Spain.
July Cabinet reshuffle. Captain-General Muñoz Grandes Vice-Premier.
October Cuban missile crisis.
December Anglo–American

Nassau agreement on nuclear armaments.

1963 *January* De Gaulle vetoes British entry to EEC. Franco–German treaty signed.
April The Grimau affair.
September Renewal for five years of the Bases Agreement between Spain and the USA.
October Gibraltar on the UN agenda.
November Assassination of President Kennedy.

1964 *January* Beginning of Spain's Four-Year Development Plan.
October Fall of Khrushchev. Labour government in Britain. 'Confrontation' at Gibraltar.

1965 *January* Johnson becomes President in his own right.
During this year he quadruples US forces in South Vietnam from 50,000 to 200,000.
July Changes in Spanish Ministry. López Rodó enters the cabinet.

1966 *January* Collision of US military aircraft over Palomares in Almería province. One hydrogen bomb lost in the sea.
April A liberalisation in Spanish Press laws. Prior censorship replaced by 'self-censorship'.
December Formation of the 'Great Coalition' in West Germany.
Referendum endorses Franco's constitution proposals for Spain.

1967 *May* 'Kennedy Round' agreements on liberalisation of world trade.
June Arab–Israeli Six Days War.

19

1967   *September* Admiral Carrero becomes Spanish Vice-Premier.
November Devaluation of sterling, and of the peseta.

1968   *May* Serious unrest in France.
August Soviet invasion of Czechoslovakia.
September Salazar replaced as Portuguese premier.
A 'state of exception' proclaimed in Guipúzcoa.
October Independence of Equatorial Guinea.

1969   *January* Spain agrees to cede Ifni to Morocco. State of exception extended to all Spain.
March State of exception lifted.
May Resignation of De Gaulle.
June Two-year extension to lease of US bases in Spain.
Isolation of Gibraltar from Spain.
July First American moon-landing.
Franco nominates Juan Carlos as Heir to the Crown, his successor as Head of State.
October Large cabinet reshuffle in Spain.

1 Youth

El Ferrol is a town in the far north-west of Spain situated on a peninsula within one of the *rías* or firths which are a feature of the Galician coastline. It is a remote place and looks towards the sea which gives it its livelihood, rather than to its hinterland. Madrid is 375 miles away, and the provincial capital, Corunna, though only 12 miles as the crow flies, is 40 miles by road round the jagged coastline. For generations Ferrol remained just a fishing village. Only in the eighteenth century was the potential of its wonderful natural harbour realised. In 1726, Philip V chose it as the headquarters of a naval *departamento* or command, and half a century later Charles III, Spain's enlightened despot, raised it to the first rank of naval ports by building its arsenal and dockyard. Since then it has always been, with Cádiz and Cartagena, one of the three great Spanish naval bases.

Named El Ferrol after the old lighthouse (*farol*) that showed seamen the entrance to the *ría*, the town has more recently acquired another claim to historical fame. On 30 September 1938 it was decreed that the town should henceforth be known as El Ferrol del Caudillo on account of the birth there, on 4 December 1892, of Don Francisco Franco Baamonde, 'the Caudillo' and Head of the Spanish State.

The Franco family arrived in El Ferrol from the south early in the eighteenth century, and they soon established a family tradition of service in the Naval Administrative Corps. Don Nicolás

Franco, Francisco's father, became the fourth in the direct male line to become an officer in it when he was commissioned in 1878. He saw overseas service in the Philippines but mostly he served in his home town, where he seems to have been more than adequate in the arranging and auditing of naval pay, supplies and victualling. Rapid promotion was quite impossible in the Administrative Corps, but when he finally retired in 1924, he had served seven years in its highest rank and had been awarded the Grand Cross of the Order of Naval Merit for his service.

In 1890 he married the daughter of a senior officer of his corps, María del Pilar Baamonde y Pardo de Andrade. Socially she was a good match, for the Baamondes were certainly a nobler family than the Francos (Baamonde is a village in the province of Lugo), while his mother-in-law's family figured in the medieval history of Ferrol, the King of Castile having in 1371 granted the lordship of the town to a Pardo de Andrade. Emotionally, however, it is difficult to see the couple as compatible. Nicolás was 34, ten years older than his bride, and had gained the reputation of being an easy-going man of the world, a rake even. Pilar, on the other hand, was a convinced Catholic with a strong feeling of Christian duty. Charity and moral example were not for her just another hobby in a crowded social calendar, but coloured her whole life with a certain austerity and seriousness. Yet such a contrast between husband and wife was, and is, quite a common feature of Spanish marriages, and while procreation is a more important end of marriage than companionship it presents no great problems.

The eldest child of the Francos was born on 1 July 1891 thirteen months after their marriage, and was christened Nicolás after his father. Francisco was the second child, and he was followed by Pilar, Ramón and finally Pacita, who died in 1903 at the age of five. Francisco was quite adventurous as a child, fishing, swimming, kicking a football about, and generally running wild through Ferrol with his young companions. Yet he was of a serious nature, taking after his mother, and he early showed himself stoical in the face of pain. When he was sent to the small private School of the Sacred Heart he worked conscientiously; he was intelligent but not an outstanding student. At twelve, however, he was sufficiently promising to follow his brother to the Naval Preparatory Academy, which was run by an unemployed naval lieutenant named Suanzes. The pupils there were destined for the executive branch of the Spanish Navy and studied the syllabus of the entrance examination to the Naval Training Ship: geography, World and Spanish history, arithmetic, algebra, geometry, drawing and French. The standard appears to have been roughly equivalent to the GCE at Ordinary Level in England today, though the examination was of course competitive.

As an executive officer, Paquito, as the young Franco was known, would have climbed one rung higher than his paymaster father in the intricate hierarchy of the naval port. Instead of a bureaucrat, with at least half his allegiance due not to the Navy but to the Treasury and to the Court of Accounts, he would have been a combatant officer, lord of Ferrol society. But the foundations of this introspective society had been eroded by events in the world beyond, and Francisco Franco was prevented from entering on the naval career which had always been planned for him.

The Ferrol into which Francisco Franco had been born had been prosperous and optimistic. It was undergoing expansion, rebuilding, modernisation. All Spain seemed on the surface to be tranquil. The beneficent constitutional rule of the Queen Regent presided over the alternation in power of the comfortably moderate and oligarchic Conservative and Liberal parties: even the Republicans and the Carlists, parties who had previously opposed the dynasty by force of arms, seemed content to remain placidly on the margin of political life. The colonial rebellion in Cuba was a dark cloud perhaps, but one with the silver lining that a war, and in particular a distant war, brought profitable activity to a naval port like Ferrol. Then in 1898, the rebellion widened into a conflict with the United States; war was popular with the people in Spain as in America, though both governments had sought to avoid it. Both sides were unprepared for such a war, but the United States had vastly shorter lines of communication and vastly greater resources. The Spanish Navy, through causes almost wholly outside its control, was at an even greater disadvantage than the Spanish Army. Its two battle fleets were utterly destroyed in circumstances which amounted to cool-headed self-immolation.

23

Defeat in 1898 underlined for Spaniards what had been recognised north of the Pyrenees for a century: that Spain, however great she had been in her Golden Century, was no longer a power of the first rank. She had lost the last of the overseas possessions which she had conquered and evangelised, and lost them to a country of brash, materialistic parvenus. Her people were forced to take stock of the national situation. Some hoped for a new course in which Spain would forget her past and look resolutely to the future, which usually meant to contemporary Britain, France and Germany. But in Ferrol, where they had many men and many ships to mourn, they were more apt in their grief to look for those responsible. They were proud that their sons and husbands had died so gallantly, but their pride was mingled with shame at the uselessness of their deaths. They had been betrayed by politicians. And if they were well-instructed Catholics, it was clear to them that Spain had been slipping downhill since the ideas of the Enlightenment and the mysteries of Freemasonry crossed the Pyrenees. It seemed logical, after all, that the freemasons in their implacable hostility to the Church should scheme to undermine the nation which was the Church's eldest daughter, the domain of His Most Catholic Majesty the King of Spain. This attitude was certainly early ingrained in Franco.

The Spanish-American War was not just a psychological blow to Ferrol. It also meant a serious economic recession there, for Spain had lost the majority of her fighting ships, and without ships there is no work for a dockyard. It had to be faced, furthermore, that without ships there is less need for naval officers. The Administrative Corps colleges were closed in 1901, and cadetships in the executive branch were restricted to ten a year, so Nicolás did very creditably to win one in 1905 when he was only just fourteen. Even now there were still too many men for too few ships. The Conservative government of Antonio Maura, which came into office in January 1907, planned to restore the right proportion by building new ships, some of the smaller ones at Ferrol, at the same time entirely suspending officer entry to the Navy. In February the 1907 examinations for naval cadetships were cancelled, and there was little prospect of their resumption for several years.

Unable therefore to enter the Navy, Francisco decided to sit the examinations for the Infantry Academy at Toledo, for this was admitting as many cadets as ever. Many years later he said that this decision had not pleased his father,[1] but Don Nicolás did not actually forbid it, possibly because his interest in family affairs had now been dwindling for some years. Tears and spiritual devotions were now the solitary comfort to which Doña Pilar resorted more and more, for she was left increasingly on her own in bringing up the children while her husband's behaviour shamed her and scandalised the neighbours. When he was posted to Cádiz in 1903 and stayed there for nine months, he did not take his family with him, nor did they accompany him to Madrid when he served at the Ministry of Marine in the winter of 1908–9. Finally, in January 1912, he was appointed to a committee at the Ministry on the revision of his branch's working rules, after which he never served in Ferrol again nor did he ever rejoin his wife.

Of his sons, Nicolás and Ramón were too easy-going and extrovert to take the family atmosphere to heart, and Francisco was too shy of emotion to express the full sympathy he felt for his mother. But that he was very much on her side is quite apparent from his later attitude towards his parents. He remained constantly dutiful to his mother, saw her whenever he was on leave, and wrote or telegraphed to her frequently while he was on active service. With his father, on the other hand, he had as little as possible to do, and the father seems to have retained less affection for him than for his brothers. In an interview with the newspaper *ABC* he spoke of all his other children but scarcely mentioned Francisco, although he was already well-known.[2] When the old man died in 1942, he was buried with no more honours than befitted his naval rank, though Hitler sent a wreath.

Having successfully passed into the Toledo academy, Franco entered the King's service on 29 August 1907. One of 382 new entrants, he was one of the youngest and smallest of them all: the majority of his fellows were about two years older. Seeing how frail he looked, the authorities offered to let him drill with a cut-down rifle; the offer was rejected with cold indignation. His high-pitched voice and his small stature made him a natural butt for the

[1] Interview published in *Estampa* 29 May 1928.
[2] *ABC* 5 February 1926.

institutionalised bullying that was a feature of the place, while his shy sensitivity and cold dignity can have done little to improve the position. But he was prepared to stand up for himself, and he never 'sneaked' on his tormentors.

The curriculum at Toledo was broad, but too much confined to the classroom, and the cadets were taught more of strategy than of tactics. Moreover, the Spanish Army was unsure of its role. While in reality it was inadequate for a European war, and its major functions were to be colonial warfare and auxiliary police work in Spain, a fact recognised in that cadets were taught the Law of Public Order in their first term, before the Constitution,[3] technical instruction was based on the assumption that they would take part in large scale operations. In the problems of colonial warfare they were given little or no guidance. One subject was taught which is of universal military application, and it was that which Franco most enjoyed—topography. In later life his appreciation of ground was his most remarked quality as a military commander. He also took great interest in the history of Spain, and wistfully compared Spain's great past with her undistinguished present. His career at the Academy was one of persevering study but not of outstanding brilliance. Unlike his brother Ramón, he never became a cadet under-officer (*galonista*), and he passed out in July 1910 about half way down his term, but Toledo had anchored in him the uncomplicated patriotism of his childhood, and fostered his fervent hope that Spain might again enjoy her rightful prominence in the world. He had become there part of a community, the Infantry, which might depend on the other arms of the Army to some extent, but which felt it owed nothing but betrayal and frustration to civilians. The Infantry was the real, uncorrupted Spain. 'You will still have your faithful Infantry', their song told the King.

Franco's first posting as a commissioned officer was back to his home town, to the Infantry Regiment of Zamora, No 8 (Under the Monarchy all Army units had both a name and a number.) Although he was still short, even by Spanish standards, photographs of the 17-year-old Franco show him as a handsome-looking young officer with a pencil moustache extending the length of his upper lip in the style favoured by the young Alfonso XIII. Still his uni-

[3] *La Academia de Infantería en 1909: Recuerdo* (Toledo 1909)

form did not carry the same cachet as that of his naval brother, and doubtless it often embarrassed him to be his father's son. Meanwhile he undertook the normal duties of a young officer, taking his turn as officer of the day, training the conscripts in elementary soldiering, but he longed to be away. Some of his contemporaries at Toledo were to spend their entire careers in the same garrison town, and he was far from typical of officers in regarding the Army as a potential adventure rather than as a steady job. The Galician is famous as a migrant, and Francisco Franco longed to escape from his family history and to prove himself in the service of Spain.

In 1909 a colonial war had broken out in Morocco, and the Spanish Army was sending more and more of its number to fight there. For a young officer who did not shun hardship and danger, a passage to Morocco was greatly to be desired, for there was a thirty per cent supplement (from 1911 fifty per cent) on the basic pay of those who served in Africa. Decorations were not hard to win, either—Franco was later awarded the Cross of Military Merit 'for three months on active service without award'[4]—and they too carried a monetary allowance. Apart from financial considerations, a keen soldier who takes his profession seriously must welcome the practical experience of war service, particularly if, as obtained in the Spanish Army at that time, training manœuvres are few and far between. Second Lieutenant Franco was nothing if not serious about his profession, and he would rather have been almost anywhere but Ferrol; so it was small wonder that he asked to be transferred to Africa. His first request, in 1911, was refused on the grounds that he was too young; but in February 1912 Colonel Villalba, who had been the Director of the Academy at Toledo in his time, and who was taking command of a regiment at Melilla, arranged for him to be allotted to the reserve pool of officers there.

When the time came for him to leave, Galicia was having wet, stormy weather. The route by road to the railhead at Corunna was impassable for mud, and the journey by sea crossed a notoriously rough patch of sea and was considered to be too dangerous. But young Franco could not wait to be on his way, and somehow

[4] *Diario Oficial del Ministerio de Guerra* (1912) No. 160.

prevailed on the ship captain to abandon caution and leave for Corunna with him and the two young officers who were accompanying him. On 12 February he arrived safely in Melilla and within a week he was attached as a supernumerary to Colonel Villalba's Regiment of Africa, No 68, and went into preparation for the summer campaign.

2 Franco Africanus

The Sherifian Empire of Morocco was almost the last corner of the African continent to receive the attentions of European colonialists. Its disposition was difficult. It faced Spain, and Spain already possessed as enclaves the *presidios* of Ceuta and Melilla, and several rocky islets off the coast. Yet Spain was not strong enough to back any claim. France had the largest commercial interests, and adjoining territory in Algeria, but England was opposed to seeing the coast opposite Gibraltar in anyone's hands but her own, while acknowledging her own possession to be out of the question. By 1912 the Powers had agreed that Morocco should be divided between Spain in the north and France in the South, but the arrangement was far from satisfactory for Spain. She already owned two of the three viable ports on the Moroccan Mediterranean coast, while the third and most important, Tangier, was specifically excluded from the control of any single power. She did not command the Straits, and so could be cut off from her Moroccan possessions at any time she lacked English naval support. This was particularly dangerous, since, owing to the unfriendliness of both the terrain and the inhabitants, her zone in Morocco could not become self-sufficient for many years, if at all.

Spain was divided on the issue. There were those who regarded the assumption of power in Morocco as an essential safeguard to Spain's security, as a last chance for her 'to keep a place in the concert of Europe worthy of her history'[1], and those who were eager to fulfil the will of Isabella the Catholic with a crusade in North Africa. Others simply dreamed of riches from the iron mines of the Rif. There were on the other hand those who thought it was high time Spain accepted the fact that she was not a first-class power and started to live within her means. In November 1912 the Government accepted the challenge and signed the Protectorate Treaty with France, by which Spain was to watch over the tranquillity of her zone, and to take such steps, military or administrative, as might be necessary to ensure it.

She already had a considerable military commitment, and Second Lieutenant Franco had been in Africa less than a month when she undertook a further advance towards the mouth of the Kert. The Regiment of Africa took the heights overlooking Sammar and Franco saw his first action. In mid-May came the long-awaited clash with the Berber warlord El Mizián, and once again the Regiment of Africa were on active service. But the campaign was a short one, for it petered out after El Mizián was killed on 15 May in a skirmish with Spain's Regular Native Forces (known as *Regulares*). It became increasingly firm policy to rely heavily on such locally raised forces, and to avoid as far as possible offending home opinion by the recruitment of Spánish conscripts for Africa. Their officers and NCOs were selected from among Spanish volunteers, and once their reliability was proved they were used more and more as shock troops. Front-line fighting was just what Franco was looking for, and in April 1913, now a First Lieutenant, he obtained a transfer to the Melilla *Regulares*.

That June there was a crisis in the western part of the zone; Tetuán, the Protectorate capital, was threatened by hostile Yebala tribesmen, under El Raisuli, a classic compound of brigand and politician. The *Regulares* were summoned and marched in such haste to embark at Melilla that two of their number died of exhaustion on the way. The succeeding two years were filled with endless small actions: clearing hostile tribesmen from the Beni Hosmar massif overlooking Tetuán; protecting communications

[1] Conde de Romanones: *Notas de una vida, 1912–1931* (Madrid 1947) p. 36.

30

between Tetuán, Ceuta and Tangier: convoying food and water to outlying posts. In these engagements Franco served a full military apprenticeship. He was frequently commended for his courage, several times decorated, and in March 1915 he became the youngest captain in the Spanish Army at the age of twenty-two. He was given the seniority of 1 February 1914, which was the date of an action near Tetuán in which he had been particularly conspicuous.

He lived entirely for his profession, showing no interest in cards, women or the bottle, those traditional diversions of the Spanish officer later said by wits to be emblazoned on the shield of General Primo de Rivera. 'When we went into town in search of longed-for relaxation,' recalled a colleague, 'he used to stay in the barracks or in his tent with books and plans.'[2] He did not show much interest in religion either, for all the piety with which his mother had brought him up; as at the Infantry Academy his chief love was topography. He also paid more attention to the welfare of his troops than was often the case with officers, with the result that his company got a good reputation among the Moors for its food. When, early in 1916, his battalion (tabor) required a paymaster, a job requiring probity and tedious additional work for no extra pay, Franco was the obvious choice. On the other hand, he never became a very good Arabist, and was not one of those rare Spaniards like Riquelme or Beigbeder, whom Moors felt understood them. Perhaps this was because his job did not call for the same absorption in the daily life of the natives as that of, for example, an officer in the Native Police or in the Department of Native Affairs at Tetuán; perhaps because he was simply concerned with military technicalities; or again, perhaps he lacked the imaginative sympathy necessary to understand different kinds of people.

Not that Franco was without friends despite his disdain for the usual social diversions. Serious-minded he may have been, but he was far from gloomy. If on the one hand he was not the man to make a boon companion, he was nevertheless a respected comrade of officers who shared with him a real interest in the profession. Emilio Mola and Jorge Vigón, who became prolific writers on

[2] Quoted in F. Salvá Miquel & J. Vicente: *Francisco Franco: Historia de un Español* (Barcelona 1959) p. 101.

military topics, both got to know Franco at this time. Franco also had a reputation for astonishing luck. There is a story that a cork of a canteen from which he was drinking was once shot from between his fingers. He continued to drink, and then called out 'Better shot next time!'[3] The Moors believed that he had divine protection, *baraka*, for none was bolder in battle and yet in dozens of fierce engagements he had never been scratched.

His luck could not last for ever. On 29 June 1916 his unit took part in operations at El Biutz to capture that strong point as a demonstration of Spanish strength in the Anyera, their column having as its objective a parapet being used to harass the advance and endanger the lines of communication. After one company had lost all its officers in a vain attempt at frontal assault, Franco led in his company for a further attempt. During this assault he was hit. He felt as if he had suddenly been 'clapped with a fiery plaster that was burning me up, cutting short my breath'.[4] The medical officer feared that the intestine was punctured, and doubted that he would live. He was kept at the advanced post of Federico, and for a fort-night his condition was too critical for him to be moved to the military hospital at Ceuta. Yet even in this luck did not desert him; the path of the bullet had missed his vital organs, and his fitness and youth enabled him to make a full recovery.

For what the High Commissioner described as his unsurpassable valour, gifts of command and energy,[5] he was recommended for the *Cruz Laureada de San Fernando* (Cross of St Ferdinand with laurel leaves), Spain's highest decoration for gallantry. It was eventually decided, however, that his feat was not worthy of this, for his company had suffered heavy casualties and he himself had been wounded while the outcome of the action was still undecided. A recommendation that he be promoted to major was also rejected; instead, together with seven other officers of the Melilla *Regulares,* he was awarded the Cross of the Order of María Cristina.[6]

[3] Joaquín Arrarás: *Franco* (San Sebastián 1937), p. 32.
[4] Quoted in Arrarás: *Francisco Franco* (London 1938) p. 26.
[5] Lt. Gen. Gómez Jordana's report quoted in Luis de Galinsoga (with Lt. Gen. Franco Salgado): *Centinela del Occidente: Semblanza biográfica de Francisco Franco* (Barcelona 1956) p. 2.
[6] *Diario oficial del Ministerio de Guerra* (1916) No. 212.

Franco was not satisfied, and as was his right, stated his case for promotion in a petition to the King. The King was favourably disposed, and Franco was eventually made major with seniority of 28 June 1916. By this time the posts of the three field officers of *Regulares* killed at El Biutz had been filled, and there was no vacancy for the young Major Franco. His first spell in Africa was therefore at an end, and on 4 March 1917 he went on three months' further sick leave, after which he took up his post in the Prince's Regiment No. 3 at Oviedo.

The three years that followed were quiet ones in Franco's military career.

'I believe', he was to say later, 'that the soldier's life has two sections: one is war and the other is study.... Earlier war was simple. A bit of courage that was all. Now it has become more complicated. It is perhaps the most difficult of sciences.'[7] Therefore he devoted much time in Oviedo to studying the art and science of war in broader terms than those to which he had been accustomed in Africa. He tried to get himself admitted to the Staff College (*Escuela de Guerra*), but was too senior—it was open only to captains and lieutenants. Nevertheless he lectured to his brother officers on the current European war; he also studied accountancy, the better to fit himself for the duties of an adjutant, and his general reading was wide. Also in Oviedo he met and became engaged to a young girl of good Asturian family named Carmen Polo y Martínez Valdés. Her family had at first opposed the match, for not only was Franco of less good family and of modest means, he was also a man with a dangerous calling, and eager for combat in Africa, while Señor Polo and his family were 'anti-militarists'.[8] But consent was forthcoming eventually and the wedding was arranged for the autumn of 1920.

It had to be postponed. In September Franco received a telegram asking him to accept the position of second-in-command of the newly created Spanish Foreign Legion (*Tercio de Extranjeros*). In keeping with the policy of avoiding the use of Spanish troops,

[7] Interview with Juan Ferragut, *Nuevo Mundo* (Madrid), 26 January 1923.
[8] Arrarás: *Franco*, p. 38 (San Sebastián ed.)

33

it had finally been decided to imitate France's Foreign Legion, which had over eighty years of varied and useful service behind it. As its founder the authorities had chosen José Millán Astray, a man with great experience of fighting, and festooned with decorations for gallantry, a man whose speeches to his men were like caricatures of Shakespeare's Henry V before Agincourt in their ardent enthusiasm for martial glory. It was he who coined the Legion's slogan: *Long Live Death*! He had met Franco on a course in September 1918, and had immediately been struck by his dedication to the military life, as complete as his own, but utterly different, as tight-lipped and austere as his own was vociferously passionate. Franco's imagination had been caught by Millán Astray too, so despite his wedding arrangements he accepted with alacrity the post he was offered in the Legion.

On 10 October he arrived in Africa again. Much more of the Protectorate was subdued than when he had left. The High Commissioner, Berenguer, who had been Franco's first CO in the *Regulares*, was pursuing an energetic forward policy in the West, where the holy city of Xauen was about to fall into Spanish hands; while Fernández Silvestre was encountering little opposition in his westward penetration in the Melilla zone. It would be months, though, before Franco's legionaries could take part in any operations, for they had first to be trained and moulded as a unit.

The first characteristic of the Legion was that it was tough, and if any of the officers had joined simply to pay their card debts with the extra allowance, as Arturo Barea suggests,[9] they had quickly to harden themselves. To handle soldiers, who were neither young nor unsophisticated, but mature, often violent men with minds of their own, required the exercise of great force of personality, or failing that, physical force. It is no surprise that the officers attracted to the Legion were usually men of strong will who found satisfaction in running risks. Many of them afterwards joined the Aviation Service. Others found notoriety in political life: Jesús Rubio rose against the Government on St John's Day 1926, and was imprisoned; Fermín Galán and Angel García Hernández died for the Republican cause in December 1930. These were extreme examples

[9] Arturo Barea: *The Forging of a Rebel*, tr. Ilsa Barea (New York 1946) p. 364.

of the sort of personality the Legion attracted and developed—
passionate men of action for whom courage was the greatest virtue
and inaction was akin to cowardice. Though the circumspection
that was so characteristic of him in later years was in 1920 not so
evident, Franco was far from reckless. Yet he differed little from
his colleagues, for he too experienced self-fulfilment in using the
example of his courage and the force of his personality to bend
others to his will.

The raw material was varied. There were Latin American political exiles, discharged German professional soldiers ill at ease in a
world at peace, an American negro boxer, a former circus clown;
many of the recruits were Spanish volunteers. They had it in
common that they were, in Franco's own words, 'shipwrecked
from life',[10] and the shore on which they were cast up was by no
means hospitable. Their first camp was at Riffien. 'The hutments
...' British volunteers reported, 'were of stone with earth floors.
They were infested with fleas. The men had each a straw mattress
which it was wise not to use.... There were no latrines, no arrangements for washing. There was one doctor for 3,000 men. Cases of
venereal diseases were so common that none or few of the affected
sought medical aid.'[11] As the organisational machine got into gear,
the barracks life of the Legion became more comfortable, and the
standards of food and accommodation came to eclipse those of
other units. Their pay had always been much higher, but in return
they had to undergo for indefinite periods the discomforts of
soldiering in Africa, which the conscript had only to endure briefly.
They had to manœuvre on foot in the African high summer, and
later sleep out in the freezing November nights. They had to drink
brackish water; they might die slowly of wounds or of malaria.
This was what the Legion volunteered for; and, even if officers
had more comfortable accommodation and rode while other ranks
marched, it was essentially what Franco also volunteered for and
accepted with more foreknowledge than most.

In November, three companies organised under Franco's command as the First 'Banner' (*Bandera*) marched to Uad-Lau camp
in the Gomara. It was a more pleasant place than Riffien, in a

[10] Franco: *Diario de una Bandera* (Madrid 1922) p. 19.
[11] *The Times* (London) 26 November 1921.

35

green sub-tropical valley, though wells had to be dug especially. On the other hand it was remote, and though there were long hours of intensive training what leisure there was was difficult to spend. The visit of a little gunboat was a big occasion. Special chits had to be obtained in order to buy liquor; gambling was prohibited. Athletic pursuits were encouraged, and Franco records that the olive groves near the camp were frequently 'mute witnesses of legionary gallantry'[12] with Moorish women; but after five months everybody was longing to leave, and there had been desertions. Discipline was extremely harsh, and Franco was notable among the officers for the harshness as well as for the justice of his punishments, but there is no doubt that a considerable *esprit de corps* was created. The desperation of men with nothing to lose was canalised into a crude Spanish patriotism and into the proud contempt for death, their own and that of others, which Millán Astray had admired in the code of the Samurai. If, in years to come, legionaries died with '*Viva España*' on their lips in a foreign accent this was partly the legacy of Franco's training. If they were never hesitant to kill, often in cold blood, and customarily mutilated the bodies of their enemies to take proof of their prowess, this too was partly Franco's responsibility.[13]

In April 1921 the Legion was finally used for the first time. After a promenade through the Gomara, they joined a column advancing up the valley of the Lau. They saw their first action on 4 May in an operation to establish some blockhouses near Xauen, but for the moment garrison duty was their primary task. During June they took part in Sanjurjo's punitive expedition in the Beni Lait, but Franco was constantly disappointed that his men were not placed in the front line. Their only serious engagement was on 29 June, when they suffered their first casualties. The next stage in the campaign was a large operation in the Beni Arós, designed to

[12] Franco: *Diario*, p. 46.
[13] See for example the account of a patrol led by Franco from Dar Drius, of which each member brought back the head of a Moorish warrior. *El Correo Gallego* (Ferrol) 20 April 1922 quoted in Rudolf Timmermans: *General Franco* (Olten, Switzerland 1937), p. 135. Also the anecdote in Franco's *Diario*, p. 177.

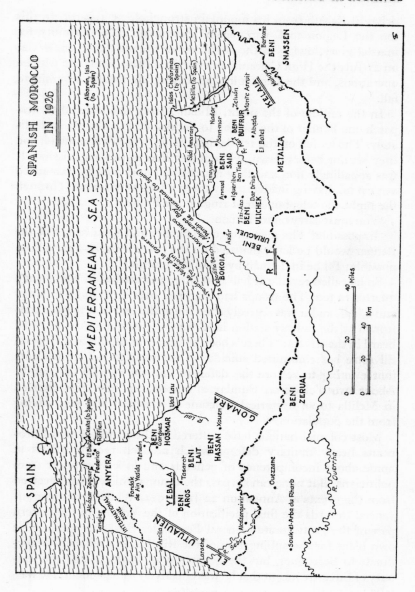

SPANISH MOROCCO IN 1926

drive El Raisuli from his mountain stronghold at Tasarot. In this too the Legion took part, again without much opportunity for martial glory, owing to the slightness of the resistance. However, on 21 July the High Commissioner arrived from Tetuán to witness operations, and the Legion looked forward to Tasarot's imminent fall.

In the middle of the night, Millán Astray was ordered to despatch one Banner of the Legion to Fondak de Ain Yedida immediately. The lot fell on the 1st Banner under Franco's command, and they set out before dawn, without any idea as to their mission. It was appallingly hot, and they marched all day, arriving exhausted at 11 p.m., having inadvertently taken a long way round. Through the night the telephone kept ringing for Franco:

'You must carry on to Tetuán...'

'Impossible! The men can go no farther and need rest; half the Banner would be left exhausted on the road. I'll arrive as soon as possible; I'll be in Tetuán by 10 in the morning.'

So he called reveille at half past three and arrived in Tetuán at a quarter to ten. The troops had marched over sixty miles in a day and a half, and it was scarcely cheering at the end of it to have confirmed at the railway station in Tetuán the rumour that they had heard in the streets: 'There's been a disaster in Melilla and General Silvestre has committed suicide.' They were to sail from Ceuta that evening to restore the defences and the morale of Melilla. About two o'clock on Sunday afternoon, 24 July, they arrived in Melilla to an hysterical welcome of cheering and flag waving from the population.[14]

Most colonial nations have suffered at the hands of non-Europeans heavy military defeats which aroused recriminations at home about incompetence of generals and lack of support from politicians. But none can surpass the trauma which Spain received from the events at Annual on 22 July 1921. While Berenguer advanced towards the final pacification of the Yebala, in the eastern part of the protectorate General Fernández Silvestre pursued his own plans for the subjugation of the Rif. He was officially subordinate to Berenguer, but the geography of Morocco and the jealousy of Silvestre meant that he was effectively independent. He was,

[14] This episode is recounted in Franco's *Diario*, pp. 99–102.

however, unable to obtain the reinforcements in men and material that were necessary to his plans, and he was equally unwilling to shelve them and allow the Melilla zone to become an insignificant sideshow. At the time, hostility to Spain was mounting, fostered by the Beni Uriaguel and their leader Abd-el-Krim. The advanced Spanish positions were extremely vulnerable, and when in July the provisioning of the post of Igueriben was prevented, Silvestre collected as large a force as possible and went to its relief. The action was not successful, and Igueriben fell to the Rifis on the 21st.

That evening it was decided to retire from Annual, where the lines of communication were now seriously threatened. But the planning was terrible and the morale worse; it must be remembered that most of Spain's conscript army had not had any training at all for active service. The withdrawal turned into headlong flight, interrupted occasionally by fruitless feats of heroic resistance which are the more striking against the background of cowardice and incompetence. The officers who meet with praise in official reports on 'the disaster'—as it was simply known—are generally those who had committed or attempted suicide in expiation of failure. As he returned over the ground during the reconquest Franco noted: 'The more one advances the less explicable is what happened.'[15] In three days at least 16,000 Spaniards had been killed, and Spain had lost the territorial gains of 12 years.[16] When the Legion arrived in Melilla the town was open to the enemy; only the exhaustion of the Rifis and their satiety with loot explain its survival.

Spanish national pride, and probably any hope of retaining a position in Morocco at all, demanded energetic plans to retrieve the situation. For the troops this involved more than just policy; their combativeness was sharpened by the desire for revenge. But at first they had to maintain the defensive. They even had to watch Nador, seven miles from Melilla, sacked and burned before their eyes, without risking an attempt to relieve it. Until mid-September most of the Legion's work involved the convoying of provisions columns to outposts; but the fighting was none the less fierce nor the casualties less heavy for their unglamorous circumstances. The

[15] Franco: *Diario*, p. 244.
[16] This number was quoted by W. B. Harris as that officially acknowledged. *France, Spain and the Rif* (London 1927) p. 73.

Legion was making a name for itself for 'indomitable courage, admirable patriotism, incomparable skill'.[17] Franco himself also had the opportunity to show his skill as a commander, particularly on 15 August, when, in the absence of Millán Astray, he commanded two Banners in an operation at Sidi Amarán. In his published diary he writes that 'the advance turned out beautifully; as if it had been an exercise', and how he describes it is perhaps revealing as to the nature of the war:

'At midday I get authorisation from the General to punish the villages in which the counter-attack started and from which the enemy is engaging us. The job is difficult but pretty; on our right broken ground falls away to the beach and at the foot there is a wide belt of small settlements. While one section opens fire on the houses to cover the manœuvre, another slips down by a small cutting, surrounds the villages and puts the inhabitants to the sword; the flames rise from the roofs of the houses and the Legionaries pursue their residents.'[18] After that comes the *razzia* or authorised pillage of the place. Looting was in any case a recognised leisure activity of the Army in Africa.

The advance started in mid-September and Spanish forces pushed forward gradually and at great cost, but relentlessly; the Legion were to see plenty of examples of the barbarity of their opponents. They had killed all except the most valuable prisoners: when the Army recaptured Monte Arruit they buried at least eight hundred putrid corpses of their slaughtered compatriots.[19] At Abada Franco thought it wise to halt his men outside the village rather than let them see the enemy atrocities and so rouse their lust for revenge as to put the political officers' pacifying work at risk. In 1926 Franco-Spanish negotiations with Abd-el-Krim would be considerably protracted by the latter's reluctance to reveal that of nineteen Spanish officers taken prisoner since 1923 not one was left alive. Moreover, most Rifis lacked interest in the trappings of

[17] From an Army Order of the Day of 10 September 1921, published in Franco: *Diario*, p. 150.
[18] ibid., pp. 127–8.
[19] 800 is the figure given in an official account (C. Hernández de Herrera and T. García Figueras) *Acción de España en Marruecos, 1492–1927* (Madrid 1929–30), Vol. I, p. 384.

civilisation; they destroyed rather than occupied the houses the Spaniards had abandoned. They did not recognise any debt to Spain for the introduction of European civilisation, and this, to Franco's mind, was astonishing in a way that their actual hatred of Spain was not. In fact Franco pays tribute to the *Regulares* because 'they fight for Spain against their own house', but says 'it is inexplicable how resistant these peoples—the Beni Buifrur— are to civilisation.'[20] Yet, in the midst of the brutality, there were moments of almost fraternal behaviour, as when during the great retreat of 1921 the oasis of El Batel was besieged, and each day the tribesmen bartered food for its water. The Spanish soldier, indeed, had a great respect for the tribesman as a fighting man, and often a good deal of affection for the country.

This undoubtedly had a bearing on the Army's judgement that there was no half-way house between total withdrawal and total pacification. When the reconquest started the Government had intended only to regenerate Spanish prestige in Morocco with the expense of as little blood and treasure as possible, and to recover territory only as far west as the line of the Kert. This was achieved in January 1922 with the recapture of Dar Drius, but the Army wished to press forward. Franco expressed a widespread view when he wrote that 'while the Beni Uriaguel—Abd-el-Krim's tribe—is not subdued, the Moroccan problem must continue in being.'[21] The Sánchez Guerra ministry, which replaced Maura's in March, refused to consider a landing in Alhucemas Bay and ordered that at least 20,000 troops be repatriated by the end of May. Nevertheless they permitted Sanjurjo to proceed with the operations against the Beni Said which had been agreed in February, and the main advance accordingly began on 18 March.

Meanwhile Franco had gone to the peninsula on leave, first to his fiancée's home in Asturias and then to his own home. Since his last visit he had become a legend, 'the ace of the Legion', 'not only an officer but a national figure', and he was greeted by bands and flower-decked streets. His reaction was that of his shy nature; he blushed, and projected the image he felt to be in keeping, the image of the officer who seeks no glory greater than the fulfilment

[20] Franco *Diario*, pp. 112, 179.
[21] ibid., p. 278.

of his duty. In October he had replied to the Mayor of Ferrol's greeting: 'The Legion feels honoured by your greetings. I only fulfil my duty as a soldier. Greetings to the town from the legionaries. Franco, Major.'[22] At a banquet given him in Oviedo in February he struck the same aloof disdainful note: 'To command officers and men who are going to their death is no merit. It is no more than simply fulfilling one's duty. The merit is due to them alone.'[23] At these public occasions, as in his Diary, then about to be published, he apparently preferred a glow of glory reflected on him as a founding officer of the Legion to an embarrassingly personal adulation as a hero in his own right.

A further, if not wholly welcome, tribute came when he was specially recalled from leave in order to take part in the second stage of Sanjurjo's offensive on 29 March. The first stage had been hesitant, but within a fortnight of the renewal of operations the occupation of Timayast achieved the last objective. Meanwhile, in the west of the zone, Tasarot finally fell in May, and Berenguer felt that now he could honourably resign a post which mounting political criticism and deteriorating health made daily more unwelcome to him. He left in July, demanding that his responsibility for Annual be tried at law, and was succeeded by General Burguete. The New High Commissioner's orders were to hold the line and, if possible, to arrive at a political settlement. Nevertheless on 26 October he started large scale operations in the Beni Ulichek, and on the 28th he took the salient of Tizi-Aza, where Franco won another special commendation for untiring enthusiasm and singular skill. But the Government, horrified by the casualties, immediately ordered the curtailment of the operation, so Tizi-Aza was virtually the last action Franco saw that year.

On 12 January, 1923, at a ceremony at Dar Drius in which the Foreign Legion was presented with a collective Medalla Militar, Major Franco received an individual one. Shortly afterwards he left Africa; it was with a heavy heart he parted from his Legionaries, but on the other hand 'the war had been transformed into a job of work like any other, only more exhausting. It was just

[22] *El Correo Gallego* 19 October 1921, quoted in Timmermans, op. cit., pp. 117–18.
[23] *El Carbayón* (Oviedo) 26 February 1922.

vegetating now.'[24] He was perhaps disappointed that he had not been appointed to succeed Millán Astray in command of the Legion, but, rejoining the Prince's Regiment at Oviedo he was able to resume his plans for marriage. On behalf of Francisco, his elder brother Nicolás formally asked Don Felipe Polo for the hand of his daughter in marriage, and the wedding was arranged for 15 June.

But Franco's sojourn in the Asturias was to be too brief. On 5 June 1923, the commanding officer of the Legion, Rafael Valenzuela, was killed in an heroic attempt to relieve Tizi-Aza, which had been left seriously exposed by the cancellation of the Beni Ulichek offensive, but which for some reason had not been evacuated. The King now chose Franco for the vacant command, and on 8 June he was promoted. This was a triumph for the officers of the colonial Army over the elements who wished for a system of promotions strictly by seniority. Franco was for the 'African' officers a symbolic figure, an example of how talent was being held back by the promotion system.[25] Now, at least, he was a Lieutenant-Colonel, at 30 the youngest in the Army. But for the second time he had to postpone his wedding and leave for Madrid.

As in January he was given a banquet in the capital, in which many of the great names of Spain participated. An old Galician alarmed guests by speaking of the arrangements he would like to see for Franco's burial in the event of his death in action. It is unlikely that the indiscretion troubled Franco much; he was not the man to be superstitious or fearful of death. 'Have you ever had any feeling of fear?', a journalist once asked him. He smiled, and replied, 'I don't know — Courage and fear, one doesn't know what they mean. For the soldier it all turns on something different: sense of duty, love of country.'[26]

He found the situation in Morocco far from satisfactory. Abd-el-Krim had held the initiative all the year, and was at liberty to wear away the Spanish Army by intermittent harassing. Franco and most of his colleagues felt that, in terms of human and financial

---

[24] *Nuevo Mundo*, loc. cit.
[25] See for example *El Debate* (Madrid) 26 January 1923: 'Had Franco been born in another age, he would have been a general: he is a major ...'
[26] *Nuevo Mundo*, loc. cit.

waste, this indefinite continuance of a low-keyed war was as bad as an outright defeat. They could derive little comfort, moreover, from the *coup d'état* of the Military Directory on 13 September 1923. On the one hand it had swept away parliamentary democracy, and replaced it with military rule, so averting the scandal which had been about to break over the Army with the publication of the parliamentary report on the Annual disaster. On the other hand, although General Primo de Rivera, who took over the Government, had fought with distinction in Morocco, he was certainly no partisan of a forward policy there. Indeed in 1917 he had lost his post as Military Governor of Cádiz by publicly advocating the exchange of Ceuta for Gibraltar, and in 1921 he had been instantly dismissed as Captain-General of the Madrid region for suggesting to the Senate a complete withdrawal from the Rif. Each time he had managed to salvage his career, and he had never recanted his views.

Now in his manifesto he said: 'We wish to live in peace with all peoples.... We are not imperialists and we do not believe that the honour of the Army, daily vindicated by its courageous conduct, depends on stubborn perseverance in Morocco.... We shall seek a quick, worthy and sensible solution to the Moroccan problem.'[27] He himself still wished to abandon Morocco altogether, but, with the temper of the Army and of the King as they were, this was not practical politics. He therefore worked out a compromise plan by which Spain would retain only the major towns—Ceuta, Larache, Melilla and Tetuán—and their hinterlands, and would withdraw from the interior, whose subdual he reckoned beyond Spanish means.

Franco's new command actually entailed less sustained fighting than his previous posts in Africa, for he had to look after the Legion's headquarters in Ceuta and to divide his time between the various Banners. Apart from the relief of the besieged outpost of Tifarauín on 22 August, in which he played an important part, he saw little action in what was admittedly a quiet summer. He had the opportunity therefore to return to Oviedo on leave, and to be married there on 22 October. It was a glittering occasion, with the

[27] The Manifesto is printed in C. González Ruano: *Miguel Primo de Rivera* (Madrid 1933) pp. 74–81.

bride entering under a canopy borne by uniformed officers, and the King himself being sponsor (*padrino*) for the groom; though actually General Losada, the Military Governor of Oviedo, acted as proxy for the King. Congratulatory telegrams poured in from all over Spain and Morocco; there was even one from the 'Legionaries convicted by courts martial, but not for desertion, and imprisoned in the Hacho fortress'![28] Sadly though, the reception was a quiet one owing to the serious illness of an uncle of Carmen's, but they had a month's honeymoon before Francisco had to return to duty.

In the spring of 1924, however, the conflagration which the pessimists had predicted had occurred. Talk of withdrawal and the tribes' observation of Spanish war-weariness had lowered Spain's prestige all over Morocco, and Abd-el-Krim found it correspondingly simpler to wrest the leadership of the Yebala tribes from El Raisuli, now pro-Spanish but a physical wreck. In June the Yebala rose; the Beni Hosmar was captured by the insurgents, and Tetuán itself threatened. Reinforcements, among them the Legion, were rushed from the Melilla zone and from the peninsula, but, though their presence prevented disaster, it did not retrieve the situation. Many posts remained completely cut off, some fell, communications with others were uncertain in the extreme.

Franco meanwhile took every opportunity to press his project for a landing in Alhucemas Bay, even raising the matter with the King and with the Dictator (as Primo de Rivera was referred to, even by his friends).[29] He did not hesitate to berate Government policy in the military journal which he and certain brother officers had founded the previous summer. He drew on the knowledge of Moorish psychology he had acquired in the *Regulares*, reminding his readers of the changeability of Berber behaviour. 'It only needs a respected leader or a bearded miracle-worker to throw villages and areas into confusion and to lead straight to revolt. With the resignation of the Koran they admit the mastery of the stronger, but they take every opportunity to regain their

[28] *El Carbayón* 23 October 1923. The Hacho fortress is at Ceuta.
[29] See George Hills: *Franco, the Man and his Nation* (London 1967) pp. 133–5.

independence.'[30] Despite possible appearances to the contrary, therefore, the war would only be over when the natives were disarmed.

In the middle of July, the Dictator came to Morocco on a flying visit of inspection. On 19 July he came to a luncheon at Ben Tieb, which was a stronghold of the military opposition (the 'hawks' in modern terminology). They made no secret of their conviction that the proposed withdrawal was motivated by cowardice, and General Sanjurjo feared that they would offer their visitor violence. Franco, as their spokesman, again raised the question of Alhucemas and told the General that the hard-won territory he intended to abandon was endued with a special value by the blood of the comrades shed on it. 'It should not be abandoned by our country before she has fulfilled the civilising mission which of her free will she undertook,' he said. This speech was greeted with applause, while Primo de Rivera's reply, explaining and justifying his plans, met with a cool response; Major Varela even greeted it with 'Very bad, General'.[31] Primo de Rivera later said that he had set out deliberately to sound out reactions, and doubtless expected little different. He confined his reaction to an oblique remark to Franco on the importance of 'blind obedience'; but that evening he received from him on the telephone an assurance of the Legion's complete loyalty.

Early in September Primo de Rivera came to Morocco again and began to take a more and more detailed interest in the conduct of the war, finally having himself appointed High Commissioner for the Protectorate. The first operation in which he was personally involved was one in mid-September to clear the enemy from Gorgues in the Beni Hosmar massif to the south of Tetuán. It was not a success, and many of the officers felt that the unintelligent planning and lack of a clear chain of command were to blame; that Primo de Rivera was in fact responsible. On 21 September, accord-

---

[30] Francisco Franco: 'Pasividád e Inacción, in *Africa: Revista de Tropas Coloniales* (Ceuta), April 1924.
[31] There are many accounts of this lunch. See, in particular, José Calvo Sotelo, *Mis servicios al Estado* (Madrid 1931) p. 239; Francisco Javier Mariñas: *General Varela* (Barcelona 1956) p. 36; Arturo Barea, op. cit. p. 416.

ing to General Queipo de Llano, Franco went to see him and proposed that he should lead a rebellion and that the Military Directory should be locked up.[32] Whether or not this interview actually happened, there is no doubt that if opposition to the Dictator's policy had kept resentment simmering, doubts about his military competence caused it to seethe—particularly, despite Franco's pledge of loyalty, in the Legion. Primo de Rivera was not imprisoned, but he felt it necessary on 22 September to remove Queipo from his command and on 3 November to issue instructions that the slightest questioning of orders was to be punished with draconian severity.

Worse might have befallen him had it not been a moment at which Spain patently could not afford to show the weakness of disunity. If Xauen were not soon evacuated another Annual would be the result. Large forces were assembled to cover the complicated operation of withdrawal, Franco and the Legion being assigned to the column of General Castro Girona. Fighting their way through Beni Hassan, the Legion reached Xauen on 29 September and spent the following month pulling out the garrisons from the outposts and concentrating them in Xauen. Meanwhile the detailed plans for the final retreat were made.

The operation posed the gravest problems. A large column, including many hangers-on, would have to pass through hostile territory where the baggage train would often be able to proceed only in single file, for the Spanish had not in their four years of occupation built a proper road. It was certain that the Berbers, ably led by Abd-el-Krim's brother M'hamed, were for the time being only using delaying tactics. When the retreat itself got under way they would harass it in earnest, for they had not forgotten any more than the Spaniards how the retreat from Annual had been turned into a rout. Moreover the year would be far advanced, and the column might well encounter very unfavourable weather conditions. It was certainly a challenge to the planners, Franco among them, to take every possible precaution; they would not hope to avert a severe mauling, but by attention to detail they could perhaps avoid a disaster.

[32] G. Queipo de Llano: *El General Queipo de Llano persequido por la Dictadura* (Madrid 1930) p. 105.

During November Xauen began to take on a ghost town's appearance. Everyone knew that it would be pillaged by the Rifis when the Spanish left, and tried to unload their possessions at any price and leave. Meanwhile details of soldiers removed the Spanish street names to save them from the indignity of defacement. Others made dummies and, dressing them in old uniforms, left them to defend the battlements after the legion, the last of the rearguard, left under cover of darkness on the morning of 17 November. The ruse probably did not deceive the Rifis, who preferred anyway to avoid fighting in the holy city of Xauen and to attack the column on the march while it was more vulnerable.

The conditions of the retreat were as bad as could have been feared. Heavy mist enabled the enemy to swoop down on the Spanish column and disappear before his position was pinpointed; it also played havoc with Spanish communications. Meanwhile continuous rain made the route a sea of mud in which guns and wagons became frequently bogged down. Everything the Army possessed became soaked and filthy, and supplies of food and provender often failed to reach the troops and their animals. Casualties mounted, reaching 18,000 all told,[33] and those killed included a number of high-ranking officers, among them, it was once falsely reported, Lieutenant-Colonel Franco. The effect on morale, which had never been good, was alarming; according to an American witness, 'the army bordered on mutiny and panic.'[34] But it was in anticipation of this that the hardened troops of the Legion had been placed in the rear, and despite the terrible conditions of the retreat, the survivors reached Tetuan on 10 December in military order.

There was great enthusiasm in Tetuan. Primo de Rivera publicly congratulated the Army as if on a great victory, and the censored Spanish press could only echo him. In private he suffered from no such illusions. During the retreat he said: 'Abd-el-Krim has defeated us. He has the immense advantages of the terrain and a fanatical following. Our troops are sick of the war and have been for years. They don't see why they should die for this strip of

[33] Harris, op. cit., p. 147.
[34] W. Miller: *I found no Peace: The Journal of a Foreign Correspondent* (London, 1937) p. 150.

Lt.-Col. Franco, in command of the Spanish Legion in Morocco, with
his brother, Ramón, hero of the Plus Ultra

Franco surveys the enemy lines, Morocco 1922

worthless territory.'[35] He felt that Spain was spending her blood and treasure simply to gratify Britain's wish not to see the French opposite Gibraltar. But he was unfortunately committed to retaining the major towns. The withdrawal planned was now virtually complete in the Western half of the Protectorate, and the following summer the emphasis would be shifted to the Melilla zone.

Still, pressures to revert to a forward policy continued. In March 1925 an amphibious landing was made at Alcázar Zeguer to secure communications between Ceuta and Tangier; and Franco, a full Colonel since February, was encouraged to believe that this operation, in which he took part, might be a rehearsal for a landing at Alhucemas. In April, indeed, a memorandum was drawn up for the Military Directory on the project, while plans for withdrawal in the East progressed simultaneously. But the Dictator told a French journalist that month that the occupation of the Rif would require 200,000 men and 'that is a sacrifice Spain cannot allow herself.'[36]

Then in that same April the whole outlook was changed, for Abd-el-Krim, who until then had operated only in the Spanish zone, struck out against the French. Although his early successes were remarkable and at one time brought Rifi raiders to within 15 miles of Fez, this was the beginning of the end for him, and he took the step reluctantly. The Beni Zerual, who lived in the Ouerrha Valley, had however come to blows with the French, and Abd-el-Krim was bound in honour to come to their aid. Moreover, the Ouerrha valley had been used by his people as a granary and as a supply route for smuggled arms. A forward policy by the French in this area meant that he was encircled. To break out he must hope to smash the French as he had smashed the Spanish, and after all the task did not look so impossible now that Spain was on the defensive.

The French reaction was strong and perhaps rather surprising in the light of the strained history of Franco-Spanish relations. Marshal Pétain, after an inspection of the situation, advised his goverment to negotiate an alliance with Spain against the Rif, and

[35] Miller, op. cit., p. 148.
[36] J. & J. Tharaud: *Spain and the Riff: Political Sketches* tr. A. S. Moss-Blundell (London 1926) p. 29.

c

agreement was rapidly reached. Pétain had envisaged a joint offensive from the south and east, but Primo de Rivera was now determined on the prestige of an amphibious operation in Alhucemas Bay, since French naval reinforcement and a simultaneous push northwards by their land forces would greatly reduce the risks involved. The landing was accordingly scheduled to begin on the morning of 7 September; and Franco was concerned both with the planning and, even more, with the special training of the shock troops for amphibious warfare.

The nine thousand men of General Saro's brigade embarked at Ceuta on 5 September to begin their journey down the coast, but on the morning of the 7th the convoy was scattered over miles of coastline owing to the strong current, and after postponements and delays it was not until noon of the 8th that the first wave, led by Franco, went ashore. It had been hoped that armoured vehicles would go first and provide cover for the infantry, but since the landing craft went aground fifty yards from the shore they could not be used. They had nevertheless the advantage of surprise by landing on La Cebadilla beach. Abd-el-Krim had expected them farther east and as near as possible to his capital at Axdir, while the sector of the actual landing was in the territory of the Bokoia, who did not enjoy his complete confidence. Moreover, such guns and fortifications as there were in the area were the other side of the Morro Nuevo (New Headland), commanding the beach where the Spaniards had in fact originally planned to land. The result was that the Franco column was able quickly to establish a bridgehead with well-chosen defensive lines at small cost in casualties.

Up to this point the operation had been most successful, but its underlying weaknesses were to be exposed by the advent of stormy September weather, and it was not helped by the postponement of the French offensive. There were considerable periods when supply and reinforcement were impossible, and in the calm periods there were not enough small craft available. Reinforcements under Colonel Goded were landed on the 11th and further troops on the 13th and 17th, but it was not until the 22nd that supplies of food, water, ammunition and pack animals could be landed in sufficient quantities for an enlargement of the bridgehead. Notwithstanding, the Spaniards' initial advantage of surprise at Alhucemas

Abd-el-Krim could have made his major counter-attacks before the landing of reinforcements, and so pushed the invaders into the sea, had it not been for one error of judgement. He had at the moment of the landing launched an offensive in the Beni Hosmar, but, although this successfully diverted forces from the main theatre, it deprived Abd-el-Krim of the strategic reserve which he could commit to the main battle with decisive results. So the Spaniards were able to hold out, though at great cost, against an enemy superior both in numbers and firepower. Once their supplies were landed their advance went ahead, though casualties were heavy; by 2 October they had taken the intermediate hills and were poised for the capture that day of Abd-el-Krim's capital Axdir.

As so often before, Franco was highly praised by his superiors for his part in the operations, for he had once again displayed the tactical skill and cool judgement in battle that he had developed over the years of campaigning. Even his judgement on the strategic plane seemed borne out by the success of Alhucemas, though in fact the closeness of the decision, even with French help, calls in question his wisdom in advocating a purely Spanish landing for so long. All the same there is no denying his enormous experience of colonial warfare, and he had thought about its problems and embodied his solutions in the training of the Legion. He was an excellent commander—brave, resourceful and a leader who inspired trust if not affection. It was therefore no surprise that Franco was on 3 February 1926 made Brigadier-General. This meant that he had fought his last African campaign, for final pacification was in prospect and his promotion took him away from the Legion and from Africa. At the age of 33 one career, that of a front-line officer had ended, and another was about to begin.

3 The Youngest General

Seven other colonels were promoted to Brigadier-General for their war merits at the same time as Franco, including Fanjul and Goded, who were to be shot by the Republic in 1936 for their leadership of unsuccessful risings in Madrid and Barcelona. But Franco was easily the youngest and probably the best-known of the eight: in fact he was probably the youngest officer of his rank in Europe. Yet his new triumph was not attended with a blaze of publicity, for all Spain could think of nothing but the flight of the *Plus Ultra* and of the glory its heroic crew had brought to Spain.

A Spanish seaplane, setting out like Columbus himself from Palos in the province of Huelva, had in four hops crossed the South Atlantic Ocean and on 2 February 1926 reached Pernambuco in Brazil, smashing all speed and endurance records for seaplanes. The conquest of the air was, in the twenties, as prestigious and exciting as the space race today, so Spain was jubilant at having shown herself among the world leaders. Primo de Rivera was particularly glad that the main impact was made in South America, where he was anxious to reinforce Spain's cultural influence and the sense of *Hispanidad* (Spanishness). The *Plus Ultra* continued her triumphal progress from Brazil into Uruguay and Argentina, the best possible ambassador for Primo's policy; and the hero of the hour, the captain of the seaplane, was Francisco Franco's younger brother, Major Ramón Franco.

Ramón was just over three years younger than Francisco, having been born in February 1896. He had been a rowdy, mischievous child, and seemingly the favourite of his father, whom he took after. In 1911 he went to the Infantry Academy and, according to his father, had an exemplary career there, though later he seems to have been a very wild young man. In the early 1920s many of Spain's most adventurous officers were volunteering for the Aviation Service, the shock troops (the *Regulares* and the Legion) losing particularly many in this way. Lieutenant Ramón Franco was one of the early volunteers and became one of Spain's original military seaplane pilots, using these craft for reconnaissance and for tactical support of ground forces, in the Alhucemas operation for instance. It was around this time that he formed the idea of attempting a transoceanic flight which would put Spain on the map in aviation, and incidentally give him some of the limelight to gratify his exhibitionism and help his career. Eventually, the Government was persuaded to meet the very considerable cost of the project, and its fruition in February 1926 made Ramón world-famous overnight.

The adulation that surrounded him went rapidly to his head: he was rude to the Spanish Ambassador in Buenos Aires and refused to show himself in Jerez de la Frontera, the Dictator's home town, on his way home. Despite the shower of decorations that descended on him, including the especially struck *Medalla Plus Ultra*, his career suffered a setback, and the urge to recapture the centre of the stage seems to have played a leading and disturbing part in his life thereafter. He had, however, completely upstaged Francisco, and his fame continued to eclipse his brother's for years. Finally, after a period on the extreme Left politically, he rallied to his brother in 1936 and was killed on active service in 1938.

Franco's first post as a general would have been a plum for a man more interested in advancement than in military affairs. He was to be commander of the 1st Brigade of the 1st Division with head-quarters in Madrid. The job itself was not arduous, since his forces were used only for the routine ceremonial duties of the capital's garrison, and most of the administration connected with this devolved on the regimental commanders anyway. What remained could be conscientiously discharged in a fraction of the time Franco had devoted to the command of the Legion. But it was not the light duties that were the principal attraction of the post; it was rather the opportunity to be often at the King's side, the leisure to play the courtier and the political intriguer. Any officer who could win the friendship of the King might look forward to a successful career, for Alfonso took a great personal interest in service problems and particularly in service appointments. General Franco already enjoyed the royal confidence; and was a Gentleman of the Bedchamber, and he wore a holy medal that Alfonso had sent him as a mark of esteem and for his protection. But this confidence stemmed from his obvious gifts rather than from charming companionship or from the advocacy of influential friends, so he had no need to be in Madrid to preserve his position.

In fact, Madrid threatened him with boredom. He moved a certain amount in Madrid society, and, always fascinated by cinematography, appeared with a number of fashionable people in an amateur film about himself,[1] but he had neither the financial resources nor indeed the inclination to play a leading role in the frivolities of the civilian world. Despite his promotion, his aggregate pay and allowances were less than two-thirds of what he received as a Colonel, when he had large special allowances for serving in the Legion and in Africa; and while his wife probably had private income she hardly had a great fortune. Besides, he was too serious to have much aptitude or sympathy for the graces of high society, the ready, shallow wit and the small gesture. As in Oviedo in 1917 he filled his idle hours with study, and acquainted himself with political history and with political theory. He was beginning to equip himself, perhaps not deliberately, for what was traditionally the second profession of the Spanish general, politics.

If there was one lesson pointed by the direction of Spanish politics during Franco's adult life up to 1926, it was that Spain was never more quiet nor more prosperous than when it was under the government of generals. Under the Military Directory all was peace at home; while, after a false start, victory in Africa seemed assured as well. Before 1923 the professional politicians had been helpless in the face of social and national disintegration. The parliamentary

[1] S.F.A. Coles: *Franco of Spain* (London 1955) p. 26.

regime had ceased to work and Spain had been saved by the military.

The Conservative and Liberal parties had never been genuinely representative of the country. They broadly corresponded to two political tendencies within the landed, business and professional classes, and on account of their moderation and the common ground between them were able to make the system work so long as the country as a whole continued to stomach a 'democratic' system in which the Government never lost an election. The illusion of universal democracy was preserved, only by trading on the political apathy of most voters and by corrupt practices of every kind. During the early years of the twentieth century the unrepresented elements in the political system were growing to appreciate the injuries done them, to find voices to complain, and to sense their power. Catalans resented the politicians of Madrid who were concerned only with Madrid and did not consult Barcelona; others had equivalent resentments but they lacked the wealth, organisation and sense of cultural identity which enabled the Catalans to express their protests and their threats articulately. Socialism was growing, but Anarchists, many of them recent immigrants to industrial Catalonia from Andalusia, made their protest more strikingly and less subtly with bombs and revolvers.

Perhaps inevitably, violence called forth not concession but repression. The Army as the most national of institutions stood four-square for centralism against the growth of Catalan nationalism, while the bulk of the employers came to view the class struggle only too literally in terms of warfare. They resisted every labour demand, however moderate and reasonable, to the last, and did not hesitate to foment unrest so that they could meet their class enemy on ground of their own choosing. They were supported by military men, who tended to view society as analagous to a military hierarchy with the working classes in the place of the enlisted men. Since a large proportion of officers were the sons of servicemen, in many cases of NCOs, they were not concerned with the defence of economic privileges of their own; but they would always spring to the defence of order, for without the concept of order their whole lives would be meaningless. Moreover, the knowledge that the Army distrusted change naturally aroused the hostility of the Left to the Army itself, and this hostility equally naturally aligned the Army more firmly than ever with the Right.

Meanwhile, as the elements unrepresented in the old politics became politically conscious and organised, the artificial two-party system ceased to suit even those classes on whom it had previously rested. Some of them, like Maura, looked for a more genuine popular representation, but they assumed that the mass of the people stood for nation, Church and Monarchy, though in fact successive elections showed that anti-centralist, anti-clerical and Republican parties were growing in strength as the old system broke down. The King himself disliked the rigidity of party politics, and liked to build his own coalitions of supporters of the dynasty, so undermining and complicating parliamentary government more than ever. Each governmental crisis turned the minds of more people to favour simple, radical solutions, the descriptive metaphors for which they tended to draw from surgery. The malignant growths on Spanish society would be removed, and the essentially healthy body politic would be reinvigorated. While the Left looked for a thoroughgoing social revolution, the Right looked for continuity of government, and clear united leadership.

The First World War compounded these internal problems notwithstanding Spain's neutrality. Catalan businessmen made great profits out of the war, for it caused the prices of their textiles to soar, and the attempts of the Romanones government in 1916 to introduce a mild profits tax whipped up renewed outrage in Catalonia. In some areas of Spain the workers' real income had fallen despite rises in money wages, and even where they were absolutely better off they felt that they deserved a larger share of profits—whose size they doubtless overestimated. This was a source of smouldering discontent.

Another disgruntled group were those Army officers who were stationed in the peninsula, living off basic pay without the numerous allowances and perquisites available to their colleagues in Morocco. They had seen the purchasing power of their pay seriously eroded, for there had been no change in most rates since the 1890s and Infantry officers had the additional grievance that their career was less secure than that of Artillery and Engineers. These specialist arms were promoted only according to strict seniority, and had therefore a steady job assured until a late age of retirement from the moment they were commissioned. The Infantry aspired to an equal security, so the rapid promotion of royal favourites and the Government's decision in 1917 to impose tests of fitness and competence particularly enraged them.

At the end of May 1917 the attempt of the Government to break up the illegal Infantry Defence Junta led to an officers' strike. This was a fairly serious crisis, for the Army was used to getting its way in politics: in 1905, for instance, anti-military newspaper articles had resulted not only in the Army breaking up the offender's presses but also in a law that thenceforth insults to the Army would be tried under martial law. What made the incident so serious that it rocked the very regime, however, was the Junta's manifesto of 31 May in which it claimed that the Army was intolerably weakened by politicians' parsimony and royal favouritism, and in which it expressed a vague aspiration for a political change. This manifesto struck a resounding chord throughout Spain, and placed the Junta movement, whose principal end was the maintenance and extension of bureaucratic restrictive practices on the part of sedentary Army officers, at the forefront of a campaign to sweep away the old politics once and for all. The mediocre Colonel Marquez, the Infantry Junta's leader, gained the stature of a national hero, as people mistook his naïveté for uprightness.

It was on the day after the manifesto's publication that Francisco Franco joined the Prince's Regiment; which must have been a little awkward since he had twice been promoted out of turn and some of his juniors had been officers before he was born. However, the Junta does not appear to have regarded him as an enemy. Years later, when he was promoted to Brigadier-General, the old *junteros* grudgingly recognised that he deserved the promotion, and comforted themselves that it was not Millán Astray, who had in 1922 resigned from the Army in a blaze of notoriety as a protest against the Junta's activities. Franco had expressed the Legion's solidarity with him in a telegram. At that stage, though, the Junta had become a purely military phenomenon; their zeal for political reform had been cooled by the decision to grant them official recognition and to make promotions except in strict seniority very much more difficult.

The summer of 1917 held more for Spain than the renovation movement of the officers. The rank and file of the Socialist UGT (General Workers' Union) had been fired with a new militancy by the apparent ease with which revolution had toppled the Tsar in March. They shared the general confidence of all classes at that period in the effectiveness of the revolutionary strike, and at the local level leaders often felt the need to outdo the Anarchist CNT (National Confederation of Labour) in militancy. Consequently, it was not surprising that a bitter industrial dispute with the *Compañía de Caminos de Hierro del Norte de España* (Northern Railway Co.) broadened on 10 August into a general strike. The Government lost no time in suspending the constitutional guarantees of free speech and assembly and in declaring martial law. The strike was by no means complete, and Pablo Iglesias, the founding father of Spanish Socialism, had seen that it was doomed from the start. Nevertheless, in Asturias it was both well-supported and dangerous because the leading industry there was coal-mining, and miners could both lay hands on explosives and use them effectively for offensive purposes.

Major Franco was placed on security patrol duty in charge of a small force of men comprising an infantry company, a machine gun platoon and a platoon of Civil Guards. Leaving Oviedo on 16 August, he moved around the outlying areas of the provinces to areas of disturbance or threatened unrest. The strike movement lasted longer in Asturias than elsewhere in Spain, and Franco's mission lasted nearly a fortnight; but it was hardly a hazardous operation in military terms, for although arson and sabotage were fairly widespread, casualties throughout Spain amounted to only a handful outside Barcelona. His most important task was the administration of martial law; that is to say, seeing to the detention, but emphatically not the shooting, of the strikers' leaders. It was his first close contact with the life of the lower orders in Spain, an instructive experience but a bewildering one. The miners were clearly not monsters or savages, yet they had not that respect for patriotism or hierarchy which was necessary for decent men. It was in his search for a resolution of this paradox that he first turned his energy to the study of social and political questions.

While he was in Africa the technical business of war absorbed him to the exclusion of such studies, but back in Madrid in 1926 he again had time to let his intellect range widely. He continued to be fascinated by military history, devouring all the books on Napoleon he could find, and he also read economics and political theory. Perhaps the Dictator heard of Franco's studies and felt that his political education should be directed along the right lines, for he later gave him a subscription to the *Bulletin de l'Entente Internationale contre la Troisième Internationale*, a militant anti-Comintern organisation based in Geneva. The bulletin directed the attention of its readers to the machinations of the Communist International, and concerned itself particularly with pacifism and anti-imperialism, which it regarded as especially insidious menaces. Much of its material was drawn from the vainglorious boastings of the Communist International's own sources, for they scorned concealment except in the smaller details of their tactics, and always planned their operations on a grander scale than was justified by their strength. Franco read the Bulletin right up to the Civil War and was thus well-informed on the aspirations of the Comintern. In common, however, with many others who were concerned about the fragmentation of social structures and values, he was led to attribute too many of society's ills to Communist machinations: he tended to take Communists at their own valuation, to join them in their overestimate of the threat they posed to capitalist society.

In 1926, however, the Spanish Government's most pressing problem concerned not the minuscule Communist Party but the unity of the Army. Primo de Rivera had assailed the Artillery officers' proudly guarded privilege of accepting promotion only in strict seniority. Up until 1918, they had been able to accept the Cross of María Cristina in lieu of a promotion without incurring loss, for a monetary allowance equivalent to a promotion went with that decoration. Then the allowance was abolished, but war merit promotions were anyway so restricted that Artillerymen remained scarcely worse off than Infantrymen. With the coming of Primo de Rivera, however, there was a growing flood of promotions on war merit, and the Artillery were therefore at a great disadvantage even before June 1926 when the final insult was delivered. It was declared that officers would no longer be offered any decoration in lieu of promotion, and awards on that basis since 1920 were cancelled. The Artillery lost any recompense, monetary or honorary, for war services just at a moment when Infantry promotions for war merits were being made on an unprecedented scale. They decided to go on strike, but this was a failure. Primo de Rivera simply suspended the corps *en bloc*, and despite widespread misgivings in other sections of the Army nobody came to their aid, not even the King, who had promised to do so. The Artillery was embittered, the Army divided; the wide support which Primo de Rivera had enjoyed in 1923 was beginning to ebb away.

It was against this background that the Dictator conceived the creation of a single Military Academy at which officer cadets of all arms of the Army would be trained together for three years. Only after that would Engineers and Artillerymen go on to their own Academies for their necessary specialised training. Loyalty to the corps would thus be subjected at the formative stage to loyalty to the Army as a whole; little by little inter-corps bitterness would disappear. The Academies of the various arms were commanded by colonels, but the director of the Academia General Militar was to be a Brigadier-General, for Primo de Rivera had a particular man of that rank in mind. Franco protested that a better choice would be Millán Astray, who had taught at Toledo and had written manuals of instruction besides gaining vast experience in the field. But in vain, for Millán Astray was as widely hated as he was respected, while Franco had as yet won only golden opinions. Accordingly on 14 March 1927, he was appointed Chairman of the committee charged with the planning and organisation of the new Academy. In January 1928 he was named Director, and went to Zaragoza to take charge of the nucleus of his staff and to oversee the construction of the Academy buildings.

The first entrance examinations were held in June 1928 at a secondary school in Zaragoza and 215 candidates were accepted and told to present themselves on 1 October. The Academy was subject to the usual building delays and when Franco arrived back from his summer leave on 5 September he found that the municipal authorities had made no progress with the sewerage arrangements. Nevertheless they assured him all would be ready in time and set to work with such a will that the main Madrid-Barcelona road was blocked by their work. In the end the term started only a day late, and on 5 October the Academy was ceremonially opened by Primo de Rivera.

The recruits found themselves in a quite different atmosphere from that in which the young Franco had been a cadet. Though the formal subjects were the same, the teaching methods were very different and so up-to-date that cinema was used as a teaching aid. During 1927 General Franco had been abroad for the first time, visiting the Ecole Militaire at Saint-Cyr and the Infanterieschule at Dresden to glean ideas. Not that a copy of one of these institutions would have been at all satisfactory at Zaragoza. The Germans, after all, had separate schools for each branch of the Army and concentrated the loyalties of their officers on the traditions of a regiment, which was just the sort of thing Spain wanted to avoid. And at Saint-Cyr they concentrated their military teaching on the paramount importance of firepower, while Franco was an early advocate of the war of movement. 'Woe to the officer who finds himself in Morocco with modern methods and training, against a resourceful and manœuvrable enemy!' he had written, 'It should not be many years before time proves us right and units in the Peninsula, particularly Infantry, efface the bad habits of trench warfare from their organisation and regain their mobility and flexibility.'[2]

Mobility indeed was a keynote of his teaching methods. He was not going to have his cadets tied to classrooms to read Clausewitz; for one thing his estimates did not allow him enough money to buy textbooks. Instead, the mountains of Aragon were used for constant practical training in the use of ground and for development of physical stamina, self-reliance and discipline, while training for winter warfare took place round Canfranc in the Pyrenees. The instructors were for the most part fighting men rather than academic staff officers. Franco's deputy, Colonel Campins, had commanded a column at Alhucemas, and the more junior staff included no fewer than eleven Legion veterans out of 34 Infantry officers and a total of 79 teaching staff. A number of other officers had fought with Moorish shock troops, but very few, particularly among the Infantrymen, had any experience of military instruction. This was to the satisfaction of Franco who wanted to make a

[2] *Africa: Revista de Tropas Coloniales,* November 1926, p. 241.

new start in the pedagogic aspects of military training. He was also closely concerned with the physical health of the cadets, insisting, for example, that each man always carry at least one contraceptive, which he might have to produce for inspection at any time. This order had the desired effect, it seems, for when Franco took his leave of the Academy in 1931, he was able to boast of the cadets' unprecedented freedom from venereal diseases.

On the other hand, he did not want the ethos of the place to be very different from that he had known at Toledo. He did, it is true, outlaw the institutionalised bullying from which he had himself suffered so much as a cadet, but he urged his cadets 'not to forget that he who suffers conquers'. 'Be a volunteer for every sacrifice, asking—and wishing—always to be used in the riskiest and most arduous circumstances. Be a lover of responsibility and firm in decision.'[3] These were two of the 'ten commandments' he handed down to the cadets at the beginning of the course to encourage them to patriotism, faithfulness to the King, care to maintain a good reputation, exact and unquestioning obedience to orders, comradeship and courage.

These commandments were from time to time supplemented by Orders of the Day or by polished orations delivered by the Director before the whole Academy on the parade ground. When Queen María Cristina died in February 1929 Franco penned a fulsome eulogy of her, finishing: 'We shall always make it a rule that faithfulness is the most prized quality of the gentleman and ought always to rule the heart of a good soldier.'[4] At the beginning of the second year he spoke to the cadets of the purpose of their education at the Academy. They were to be 'the paladins of that longed-for renascence, of that struggle which you will have to carry on against the positivism of the present day ... Winds of pacifism,' he went on, will blow across your path, utopian illusions in contradiction to the history of the World and to laws which nature obeys ... Fine utopias which will not be able to temper your ideals!'[5]

With ideals like monarchism and the rejection of modern 'positivism', it is hardly surprising that the cadets of the Academy were on

[3] Galinsoga, op. cit., pp. 134–5.
[4] ibid., p. 138.
[5] ibid p. 139.

very bad terms with the students of the University of Zaragoza, since Republicanism, rampant in the country at large, was nowhere more vocal and radical than in student and literary circles. The Dictator could afford to ignore intellectuals, whom he despised, but the Government was at the same time facing an economic recession and a steady fall of the peseta on the foreign exchange markets, and even in the Army and in the Palace the feeling was growing that he had outstayed his usefulness in office. Finally in January 1930 he resigned and went into exile, perplexed by the ingratitude of his erstwhile political friends.

The monarchy did not long outlast Primo de Rivera. It was seriously implicated in, if not responsible for his rape of the Constitution, so the problem of a return to normal political life was virtually insoluble within its framework. General Berenguer's government vacillated between repression and tolerance of political opposition. Eventually they decided to hold elections for the Cortes in March 1931, but the Republicans threatened to boycott them unless new municipal councils were first elected. The Republicans were now so influential that Berenguer had to resign, and his successor Admiral Aznar called municipal elections for 12 April. These resulted in anti-monarchist victories in all Spain's largest cities and Republicans immediately took over in Barcelona and Seville. On the evening of the 14th the King left Madrid for Cartagena and exile, realising that only civil war could save him, although a majority of monarchist councillors had been elected in Spain as a whole. Sanjurjo had refused to guarantee the loyalty of the Civil Guard, of which he was commander, and Berenguer had telegraphed to the regional military commanders, asking them to let the country 'follow ... the logical course imposed on it by the supreme national will'.[6] The Army's leaders would not stir to save the monarchy, and, as Brigadier-General Franco was not the man for a quixotic gesture, he too stood by and let Alfonso go.

So long as the King had been on the throne, however, he had remained his loyal subject. He had done his best to dissuade his brother Ramón from his feverish plotting against the monarchy, dining with him far into the night on 10 October 1930, but unable to alter his resolve. When his former subordinate, Captain Galán,

[6] Julián Cortés Cavanilles: La Caída de Alfonso XIII (Madrid 1932), p. 206.

63

stationed in the Pyrenean garrison town of Jaca, declared himself in rebellion on the following 12 December, he was captured within hours. Yet Franco had acted with such energy that a company of cadets had already moved out to guard the main Jaca-Zaragoza highway. He was in fact a great deal more zealous in the service of the Monarchy than the majority of his colleagues, who forbore to swim against the rising tide of Republicanism, and who were in consequence in a less delicate situation on the morrow of the revolution.

The King had not abdicated, only suspending the use of his prerogative, and expecting to be called back to rescue Spain from the consequences of Republican rule. Meanwhile, he encouraged his supporters to stay at their posts and make what terms they could with the new government. Franco was Monarchist in sentiment and too proud to pretend to any opportune conversion, so after 14 April he simply stayed in Zaragoza and followed instructions, while impressing on his cadets the need for calm and orderly behaviour. Then on the 18th a rumour appeared in the Press that Franco was to be given preferment to the post of High Commissioner in Morocco. He had heard nothing about it and, fearing that such a report would discredit him with his predominantly Monarchist colleagues, he wrote an involved denial to the Monarchist newspaper *ABC*.

'I should be grateful if you would correct this erroneous news, since the Provisional Government which now directs the nation cannot have considered my appointment, nor could I, if it was in my power to refuse, have accepted any post which could be interpreted by anyone as a previous agreement between me and the regime just installed, or as a consequence of my having shown the slightest lukewarmness or reserve in the fulfilment of my duties or in the loyalty which I owed and rendered to those who until so recently embodied the representation of the nation in the monarchical regime. On the other hand, it is my firm intention to respect and observe, as I have up to now, the national sovereignty and my own desire that this may express itself through adequate legal channels.'[7]

[7] *ABC* 21 April 1931.

This circumspect letter did not save his job. Manuel Azaña, who had become Minister of War in the Provisional Government was best known as a man of letters and as President of the *Ateneo*, Madrid's leading literary club, but had long been a student also of military affairs, about which he had decided views. In 1918 he had published a book in which, taking the French military system as his *point d'appui*, he criticised the alienation of the Spanish Army from society. He was particularly hostile to 'the boarding system of Military Academies where an anaemic middle class shelters its sons and orphans instead of throwing them into the concourse of social life'.[8] He therefore lost no time in decreeing on 25 April 1931 the cancellation of the entrance examinations to the Zaragoza Academy which were due to take place that summer. On 30 June the Academy was suppressed altogether, and, while it would exaggerate Franco's importance at this time to suggest that the decision was specifically intended to wound him, the closure certainly had that effect.

Four years he had laboured to create an institution which the French War Minister André Maginot (after whom the Line was named) had called 'not a model organisation, but the most modern centre of its kind in the world … the last word in military technique and instruction.'[9] Now it had been closed with a stroke of the pen by a man whose attitude to the military Franco considered compounded of ignorance and prejudice, and who had certainly no first-hand experience whatsoever of the Army's affairs. Bitterness was only too apparent from the text of his final speech to the Academy as director made on 14 July. 'At this time,' he said 'when military reforms and new policies are closing the gates of this Centre, we should rise above these circumstances, repressing our deep sorrow at the disappearance of our work, and thinking with altruism that, though the machine is dismantled, its product remains. You are our product … you who will constitute a great nucleus of the professional Army, and will no doubt be paladins of loyalty, honour, discipline, duty and self-sacrifice for the Father-

[8] Manuel Azaña: *Estudios de política contemporánea francesa: La política militar* (Madrid 1918): quoted Joaquín Arrarás: *Historia de la Segunda Republica Española* (Madrid 1956–68) Vol. I, p. 117.
[9] *Historia de la Cruzada Española* (Madrid 1939–43), Vol. I, p. 377.

land.' He went on with a paean of praise to the 'sublime virtue' of discipline, 'which takes on its real value when one's thoughts counsel the opposite of what one is ordered, when the heart battles to rise rebellious within one, or when the action of the command partakes of arbitrariness or error',[10] Azaña did not fail to see the irony of this speech and ordered him to be formally censured for it. When Franco left Zaragoza he was left without an appointment, at the disposal of the Minister.

While Franco remained without employment he devoted himself as usual to study, this time concerning himself particularly with the defence of Spain in the context of modern warfare, for which he drew up his personal plan. Meanwhile the Government was making wide changes in every aspect of government and nowhere were its reforms more far reaching than in the military field. A basic weakness of the Army was that it was trying to be much larger than the country could afford. There were far too many units, all with their complement of officers, but almost all below strength in other ranks and in equipment. Azaña planned straight away to bring the number of officers and units down into balance with Spain's real needs and resources. His method was bold in its simplicity, and it tackled another of the Republic's problems at the same time. Worried that many Monarchists would not give loyal service to the Republic, Azaña gave all officers the option of retiring on full pay. To the surprise of his critics, there were five thousand retirements, and the officer corps was reduced by forty per cent at a stroke.

The War Minister also enhanced the status of non-commissioned officers, constituting them a separate corps and making commissions more easily attainable by them. He wanted to draw officers as far as possible from the lower classes, and so to create an Army that was Republican from conviction and not simply from convenience. He abolished the jurisdiction over certain civilian offences which the military had previously enjoyed, and he discontinued military courts of honour. He instituted instead of the Supreme Court of Military Justice a Military Division of the High Court in charge of which he placed a civilian, Carlos Blanco, previously the

[10] The speech is printed in full in Arrarás: *Franco* (San Sebastián ed.), pp. 170–74.

Director General of Security. He suppressed newspapers produced by serving officers, some of which had been outspokenly hostile to the Government. (*Ejército y Marina* even proclaimed itself at the masthead as an 'organ of constitutional revisionism.') Though Azaña's policy was usually reasonable, his every move aroused hostility, the more so because of his obvious vindictiveness towards the old Army. But unlike some of his colleagues Franco did not speak out again after his farewell to the cadets; he pledged his allegiance to the Republic and remained on the active list, waiting hopefully in Madrid for employment.

Finally, at the beginning of February 1932, in a wide-spread redistribution of senior posts in the Army, Franco was posted to Corunna as commander of the 15th Infantry Brigade. It was hardly a post of great prestige or influence, but it was to be preferred to idleness. He took up his post on the 17th and was joined a couple of days later by his wife and three year-old daughter Carmencita. Franco's work in the months at Corunna followed the pattern by which he usually approached a job. He studied its demands thoroughly, first at Corunna itself, where his forces consisted of Infantry Regiment No 8, in which he had served as a newly commissioned officer, and which was now under the command of the staunchly Republican Rogelio Caridad Pita. Then in April he made a tour of inspection of the other Regiment under his command, Infantry Regiment No 12 with a battalion each for garrison duty in Lugo and Orense. As at Madrid in 1926 his scope for constructive action was limited by the small administrative area in which a brigade headquarters operated in peacetime conditions, but he discharged his routine duties conscientiously and played his part in the official social life, appearing for instance among the dignitaries photographed with Azaña, now Prime Minister, on his visit to Corunna in September 1932. In March 1933 his patience and competence met with their due reward. Although a decree of the previous January had, by annulling seniority due to war merit promotions under the Dictatorship, placed Franco among the most junior, he was appointed to command the military forces of the Balearics, a post usually given to a Major-General.

When, on arrival in Palma de Mallorca, Franco took stock of his new command, it became apparent to him that, in a situation of growing international rivalry in the Mediterranean, one of the greater powers—Italy for instance—might attempt to seize a naval base in the Balearics; Menorca, after all, had for half the 18th century served Britain well in that capacity. To meet this threat, which was not negligible if not immediate, he found in existence no defensive plan worthy of the name. Immediately he set about drawing one up. He discharged the essential routine work of his command early in the morning, and then set out by motor car or on horseback to study the coastal defences of the island of Mallorca, arriving back after six or more hours to lunch late even by Spanish standards. Later he visited the other islands to set similar studies in hand there.

Perhaps his most important success, however, as far as his career was concerned, was the impression he made on Diego Hidalgo, the new Minister of War, in the spring of 1934. Franco had come to Madrid for medical treatment and to escort his mother to the coast on her way to Rome on a pilgrimage. Unfortunately, the old lady died before setting out, and Franco had to stay for the funeral. While he was there he met Hidalgo, who formed a favourable judgement of him which was to be enhanced when he came to inspect the military installations of the Balearics. Before leaving the islands the Minister was anxious to mark his visit with an act of clemency and asked whether there were any military prisoners whom he might amnesty. Franco said that there was indeed an officer under close arrest, but that he would rather not release him unless the Minister insisted, for he had committed the worst crime an officer can commit: he had slapped a private.[11] Hidalgo was immensely impressed, and certainly Franco must have set aside in Mallorca his memories of Africa; in the Legion it was quite normal for slackers to be chivvied into action with a blow or two across the face with a switch.

At all events under Hidalgo's patronage, Franco went from strength to strength. In March 1934 a vacancy occurred in the Major-Generals' list and Franco was selected to fill it. In September the Army held major manœuvres in the province of León, and Franco was invited by the Minister to attend them as his personal adviser. At their conclusion he returned to Madrid before going on

[11] *Sunday Express* 15 May 1938.

68

leave, and it was there that he met with the perhaps greatest opportunity of his career. The Minister of War called on him to organise the suppression of the proletarian rising in Asturias.

The immediate cause of this insurrection was the entry into the government on 4 October 1934, of José María Gil Robles's Catholic group, the Spanish Confederation of Autonomous Parties of the Right or CEDA, an event which the parties of the Left regarded as a provocation and as a sure preliminary to fascism in Spain. The Left coalition which had governed the country from 1931 had broken down internally in the course of 1933, and in November of that year elections were held for the Cortes. The Right gained heavily. The Left failed to make adequate electoral pacts, the Anarchists boycotted the ballot altogether, and moderate voters were too shocked by the anti-clericalism of the Left, or too disillusioned by its failure to quieten social unrest, to give them much credit for their enlightened labour legislation or for their mass education programme. Of the two largest parties in the new Cortes, Lerroux's centre-right Radical party formed the government, but it was far from having an absolute majority and depended on the benevolence of the CEDA. This party, modelled on the German Centre Party, was formally committed to the liberal Catholic social programme of Pope Leo XIII, and formally uncommitted to the Republic or to the Monarchy. But a section of its members, with financial leverage perhaps out of proportion to its numerical strength, was secretly, or even openly, monarchist; and the suspicion that the party planned to betray the Republic was heightened by its proclaimed intention to revise the Constitution, purging it of its anticlerical content.

Meanwhile, throughout Europe, the Left was obsessively frightened of the upsurge of fascism. In February 1934 the Austrian Chancellor Dollfuss suppressed left-wing political opposition by armed force, using artillery against the working-class quarters of Vienna. The previous year, Hitler had banned the millions-strong Social Democrat Party with hardly a murmur raised against him. In February it seemed that the extreme Right had come within an ace of taking power illegally in France. Even in England Fascism was making strides, and there were grounds too for the feeling that the CEDA did not feel much love for democracy either. Its green-shirted youth movement, the *Juventudes de Acción Popular* (JAP) increasingly took on the aspect of paramilitary organisation familiar from Germany and Italy. Gil Robles himself was built up as a leader, and encouraged his followers to use the rhythmic cry of 'Jefe! Jefe! Jefe!' in imitation of the Italian 'Duce! Duce! Duce!' At a mammoth meeting at El Escorial in April 1934 which the Left tried to have banned, a lecture was given by the youth leader Ramón Serrano Súñer, entitled 'Anti-parliamentarianism'.

The working-class parties decided that, if Gil Robles, whose political standpoint seemed very similar to that of Dollfuss, were to take office, the possibility was remote of the democratic process being allowed to return his opponents to power again. And the fact that, for them too, there were principles and purposes more sacred than democracy made them all the readier to defend it with revolutionary violence in the guise of a preemptive strike against fascism.

At the beginning of the Cortes' long summer recess Gil Robles gave notice that his party would no longer support the centre-right government of Ricardo Samper. When the Cortes re-assembled in October, therefore, President Alcalá Zamora would have either to dissolve, or to find a government acceptable to Gil Robles, that is to say one including CEDA members. If he dissolved, Alcalá would face the possibility that the elections would bring about no change in the situation, or even that they would increase Gil Robles's power. On the other hand, if the CEDA entered the government, the ominously united Left threatened to unleash a revolution; while Catalonia threatened to settle by outright secession her quarrel with the central government over the working of the regional devolution she had been granted.

On 4 October 1934, Alejandro Lerroux formed a government which included three ministers from the CEDA. A general strike was proclaimed forthwith, but Lerroux lost no time in declaring martial law; in most of Spain the revolution collapsed immediately. Many workers had exhausted their militant energy in the long and bitter economic disputes of the previous year. In Asturias, however, and in Catalonia the authority of the Government was badly shaken. By the night of 5 October the Asturian miners, united in a Workers' Alliance comprising all the working class parties, controlled virtually all the coal-mining area of Asturias and were on the road to Oviedo.

Meanwhile in Madrid the new cabinet had met and had decided to call on the Legion and the *Regulares* for service against the rebels in Asturias. Spain's home forces were scattered in small detachments throughout the peninsula so that they were difficult to mobilise in a crisis of this kind. Besides, the general unrest might erupt into disturbance anywhere, so it was difficult to know what troops could be spared. To bring over troops from Africa was the logical solution, and one which Azaña had used against General Sanjurjo's abortive rising on 10 August 1932. To command the forces collected to suppress the rising, Hidalgo, still Minister of War, suggested Franco; but Lerroux preferred to send Eduardo López Ochoa, who might be less brilliant militarily but whom he considered more loyal to him politically. Hidalgo was not dismayed, and continued trying to find out whether Franco was still in Madrid or whether he had already left for his leave in Oviedo. Eventually, about nine o'clock in the evening of the 6th Franco arrived at the Ministry of War, and immediately joined a meeting with the Minister and the senior generals in the Ministry. This led to no definite conclusions and in the interests of quick decision Hidalgo put the coordination of operations in the Asturias entirely into Franco's hands.

Franco trusted almost nobody. He took over the communications centre of the War Ministry with a staff of only four (two naval officers, his cousin and ADC., Major Francisco Franco Salgado, and a telegraphist), and from there coordinated operations against the Asturian rebels. He summarily dismissed from their posts any officers whom he suspected might harbour sympathies for them. He had the cruiser *Cervantes* put into Ferrol to land Lieutenant-Colonel López Bravo, and he removed his own cousin Ricardo de la Puente from command of the airfield at León. At the same time he issued the orders necessary to muster columns to converge on Asturias from all sides, saving valuable time by his mastery of the details of the Army's deployment. First on the scene were to be the expeditionary forces from Africa, commanded by Lieutenant-Colonel Yagüe, who joined them by autogiro on the beach at Gijón. From the west, General López Ochoa was to arrive at

Oviedo from Lugo on the 11th. General Bosch was to come from León through the mountains into the coalfield area, while Colonel Solchaga would join him from the east. Once these columns were organised and moving, the rebels could not hope to resist successfully. They were completely isolated, since the 'Catalan State within the Spanish Federal Republic' had lasted only one night after its proclamation on the 6th, and all resistance outside Asturias was at an end.

After little more than a week the struggle was prolonged only by suspicion, all too often well-grounded, that death in battle was preferable to the treatment accorded to prisoners by the Legion and the *Regulares*. Franco, of course, was not a battlefield commander but a long-range coordinator, and if valid charges can be levelled against his conduct of the Asturias campaign, they must be of inefficiency rather than of brutality. It seems that he ordered the victualling of the Army in Asturias in such a fashion that tons of food simply rotted, while on the other hand the troops remained extremely short of blankets.[12] But such shortcomings did not prevent his wife's home town of Oviedo making him its adopted son on 26 October, nor did they deter the Prime Minister from creating him a Knight Grand Cross of the Order of Military Merit for his services. He was one of the heroes of the hour, of the victors in a war altogether more serious than those in Morocco, one in which 'the fronts are socialism, communism, and the other formulae which attack civilisation to replace it with barbarism.'[13]

[12] According to José Martín Blásquez: *I helped to build an army* (London 1939), pp. 15–16, 19–20.
[13] *Cruzada*, Vol. II, p. 263.

4 Rising to Power

Franco remained in Madrid until the end of the year and went back to Palma only briefly before in February 1935 he was posted to Morocco. The Prime Minister had thought of making him High Commissioner, or head of the civil administration, but did not press the idea against the President's objection, and named him simply Commander-in-Chief of the military forces there.[1] When Franco left Madrid on 5 March to take up the post, his journey was the first he had made to Africa since, in October 1927, he had accompanied the King and Queen on a victory tour of the newly subdued Protectorate.

Since then Spanish security in Morocco had, he felt, been seriously impaired. In February 1933 he had broken a long silence in columns of *Africa*, the colonial army's magazine, to sound a warning note. 'It is no secret to anybody the interest and attention which Communism devotes to creating a situation ripe for insurrection in countries subject to protectorates and mandates,' he wrote. 'In the cities of Morocco Communist money and activities have already combined with the complicity of fanatics and the constant intrigues of petty religious leaders to produce incipient nationalisms.'[2] In these circumstances he thought it vital to maintain a

[1] Alejandro Lerroux: *La pequeña historia: Apuntes para la Historia Grande vividos y redactados por el autor* (Buenos Aires, 1945) p. 354.
[2] General Franco: 'Ruud ... Balek' in *Africa: Revista de Tropas Coloniales*, February 1933.

high standard of military preparedness. He was worried that the Army of Africa had been allowed to run down both in quantity and quality. In 1927 it had consisted of some 92,000 men of all arms: in 1933 the complement was only 37,481. Although the Legion had not suffered in proportion, its complement had nevertheless been halved from 8,000 to 4,000.[3] And by 1935 the capability of Spanish forces in Morocco had been further eroded by cuts in the military and Protectorate budgets.

In the prevailing economic depression of those years, the task facing Franco as Commander-in-Chief was one of making bricks without straw, but his stay there was too short for him to achieve much in any circumstances. In May 1935, after governing precariously for a month without his support, Lerroux called Gil Robles to the Ministry of War, and Gil Robles appointed Franco to be his Chief of the General Staff.

Franco found the Army in the Peninsula yet more run down than that of Africa. The military budget was even smaller than under the Azaña regime, and there was not enough ammunition to sustain the Army through a single day's fighting. Gil Robles was determined to make the Army effective, even if this meant additional expenditure, and perhaps he alone carried sufficient political weight to force such a proposal through a Cabinet which was struggling to balance the budget. He and his advisers drew up a programme of re-equipment which would involve extra expenditure of 1100 million pesetas (£44m or $212m at par) over the period 1936–8. Foreign licences were sought for the construction of military aircraft. New artillery was to be constructed and the old refitted. Steel helmets were to be provided for the troops. A respectable level of military stocks was to be built up in everything from medical stores to aerial bombs.

But it was not just the economics of the Republic that came under scrutiny. Mola was told to draw up a plan for general mobilisation. Other changes, like the restoration of military Courts of Honour and the reopening of the Zaragoza Academy, were of a more political nature. Azaña, and to a lesser extent his successors, had advanced only staunchly Republican officers and left unem-

[3] Statesman's Yearbook 1928, p. 1304; *Enciclopedia Universal Ilustrada*, Appendix Vol. 10, p. 1425; *Africa*, February 1933, loc. cit.

ployed those whose devotion to the regime was suspect. Gil Robles proclaimed that henceforth only merit would determine appointments in the higher ranks of the Army. Of course, the assessment of merit is largely subjective, but while it is easy to agree that Franco was a more capable Chief of Staff than Masquelet, and that Mola's talents had been wasted by the Republic on account of his secret police work for the Monarchy, Gil Robles made certain other appointments which laid him open to charges of political bias. Miaja and Riquelme, for example, whom Gil Robles left unemployed, had surely been as distinguished in the past as Orgaz and Fanjul, who were now given important posts despite their well-known hostility to the Republic. The allocation of awards for the Asturias campaign of 1934 was also reconsidered, and the hostility of the Left was further aroused by the award of the Medalla Militar to Lt. Col. Yagüe, whom they regarded as the 'hyena of Asturias'.

The strengthening of the Army was widely supposed to be aimed at the preservation of the established order rather than at the needs of the external defence, and Gil Robles's selection of personnel did not dispel the illusion. Nor was it reassuring that he decided to hold summer manœuvres whose scenario assumed a need to supply Oviedo, with the enemy (presumably revolutionaries) in possession of its port of Pajares. The Minister's enthusiasm for parliamentary government was regarded as co-extensive with the advantages it might bring to his party, and he had chosen the War Ministry at a time when any portfolio except the premiership was within his grasp. In such a key office he might hope to build a personal position which he could use the Army to maintain. The only surprise as 1935 wore on was that a Gil Robles coup did not materialise.

Then the autumn of the year produced major scandals implicating Lerroux's Radicals in financial corruption, and proposals by Chapaprieta to raise progressive taxes which were unacceptable to the Right. First Lerroux and then Chapaprieta resigned, leaving in ruins the coalition of Centre-Right and Right wing which had ruled Spain since 1933. Now it seemed as if Gil Robles must achieve the premiership by impeccably constitutional means and so justify that unwillingness to appeal to force for which so few, friends or enemies, had been prepared to give him credit. Only a predominantly CEDA ministry could hope to manage the Cortes in the present circumstances.

However, President Alcalá Zamora feared that a frankly right-wing government would cause the breakdown of the parliamentary regime by the reactions of others if not by its own act. He spent a week in trying to find a centre government before finally persuading the moderate Portela to take office with a government which could be no more viable in the Cortes than the last. Gil Robles was furious at being passed over. He felt that the President had violated the spirit of the constitution by refusing to call on the leader of the largest party in the Cortes when he could clearly form a workable ministry. Even if he did not now prepare a *coup d'état* on his own behalf, he looked benignly on the Rightist generals who did. Only he told them that they must first consult with the Chief of the General Staff.

Franco was opposed to any such adventure. Some generals, mostly personal friends of the King, had never ceased to plot against the Republic from its inception, while others like Sanjurjo, whose refusal to guarantee the loyalty of the Civil Guard to the King had made him one of the midwives of the new regime, supported it at first only to become quickly disillusioned with it. They were dismayed by the anticlericalism written into the Constitution and by Azaña's treatment of the Army; and Sanjurjo had probably hoped for better recompense than the Inspectorate of Frontier Guards. By the summer of 1932 he was ready to accept a major part in a military rising. Franco, on the other hand, was not a conspirator by temperament; he refused Sanjurjo's invitation to join, and persuaded others not to risk their careers in such an adventure either.[4] The failure of the rising was so total that it not only vindicated his prior advice but also amply justified his later description of it as 'more a romantic flash in the pan than a proper rising'.[5] It did not dispose him to change his mind about the undesirability of rebellion, and by October 1934 he was in so important and prestigious a position that, when he said he did not

[4] Timmermans, op. cit., p. 222; J. A. Ansaldo: ¿ *Para Qué? De Alfonso XIII a Juan III* (Buenos Aires 1951) p. 51.
[5] *Cruzada*, Vol. III, p. 58.

think it was 'the moment to act', a new scheme for insurrection was dropped forthwith. It had been planned to use the forces brought to Asturias to deal with the proletarian rising as the shock troops of a Monarchist counter-revolution.[6]

But if Franco did not encourage conspirators, neither did he betray them, for he thought them misguided rather than wicked. He preserved a watchful neutrality towards the Republic, refusing to join the clandestine UME (Spanish Military Union) or to expose himself to the risks of plotting, but he nevertheless always professed himself ready to draw the sword in defence of Spain against the enemy within should it be necessary. He would remain the judge of when that necessity arose, and he was able to convince his colleagues that the moment had not come in December 1935. The national situation, if serious, was not critical, and the Army had no right to intervene in what must be seen as essentially a party political dispute, considering Gil Robles's constitutional correctness up to that point. So, lacking the support of Franco and his colleagues, the Minister had no choice but bitterly to accept his dismissal.[7]

His opportunity for redress came soon. By the end of the year it was clear that Portela could not go on unless the President used his power of dissolution of the Cortes, and on 8 January 1936 he did so. He hoped that the Prime Minister would be able to form a Centre bloc strong enough in the new Cortes to bridge the growing gap between the implacably hostile parties of Right and Left. The CEDA hoped for an overall majority. They used the large funds at their disposal in a huge poster campaign urging voters to return their *Jefe* or Chief, Gil Robles, to full power.

Against them were ranged the united strength of Azaña and the Left Republicans, the Socialists, the Catalans and the small Communist and Trotskyite parties. They had learned the lesson that under the 1931 Constitution parliamentary strength depended on effective collaboration in the constituencies, and had therefore formed an alliance known as the Popular Front. Their rallying point was an amnesty for those still suffering for their part in the

---

[6] Ansaldo, op. cit., pp. 91–2.
[7] For Gil Robles' attitude at this time, see J. Gutiérrez Ravé: *Gil Robles, Caudillo Frustrado* (Madrid 1967), pp. 144–7, and José María Gil Robles: *No fue posible la paz* (Barcelona 1968), pp. 364–7.

October revolution of 1934. It was agreed that the Government should be formed without the participation of the working class parties, and a programme was drawn up. Many of the commitments contained in it were to restore what had been dropped or repealed since 1933. The clauses in the Constitution directed against Church education, for instance, would again be enforced; Catalan autonomy would be given the scope which the Statute had originally intended; minimum wage rates would be reintroduced in the countryside. None of this may seem particularly radical, but the Right were nevertheless scared.

They hurried into negotiations for the formation of a rival electoral alliance, a National Front. More and more their propaganda played on middle class fears, and not on any future programme — let alone their past record. They feared the appeal of the Popular Front to Spain's millions of Anarchists, who usually abstained from the parliamentary struggle, but who, it was reported, would go to the polls in support of a political amnesty. Most of all they feared what the Popular Front manifesto did not say but the Socialists of the Left did. Even at his coolest their leader Largo Caballero rejected any suggestion of collaboration with bourgeois parties after the elections. In a speech at Alicante on 26 January he promised 'social transformation' following a leftist victory, and threatened that 'if the right wins ... we shall have to go straight into civil war'.[8] Largo Caballero's followers had dubbed him 'the Spanish Lenin', and Azaña seemed only too well cast in the role of Kerensky. No wonder the Right was afraid.

At the height of the campaign, the death was announced of King George V of England, who had been Honorary Colonel-in-Chief of Franco's first Regiment, and Franco went to London to represent Spain at the funeral on 29 January. He had not been abroad since November 1930 when, at Maginot's invitation, he had gone to France for a senior officers' course at the École Supérieure de Guerre. In England he was able to extend his knowledge of military educational establishments by visits to Sandhurst and Camberley, but he did not cease to ponder the disturbing situation of Spain. He was particularly disturbed at the apparent growth of Communist influence in Spain. He had as Chief of Staff set in train

[8] *ABC* (Madrid), 28 January 1936.

investigations into the political affiliations of conscripts, and found that twenty-five per cent of them were members of one or other of the working-class parties, a proportion which shocked him. Confiscated leaflets confirmed that the subversion of the Army was a priority task for the extreme Left. If the Government once relaxed its vigilance, Army discipline might be superseded by soldiers' soviets and the election of officers—despite the patriotic instruction given in some garrisons on the dangers to Spain from the secret enemy within. Public order would be soon at the mercy of the Revolution. If the Popular Front won the elections, could it be relied upon to protect the Army from this creeping destruction? Was it not itself a creature of Moscow?

Its very name, Popular Front, was an invention of the Communist Party. In August 1935 the seventh meeting of the Comintern had ordered the tactics of collaboration with all anti-fascist parties. 'Comrades', Dimitrov had said, 'you will remember the ancient tale of the capture of Troy. . . . The attacking army was unable to achieve victory until, with the aid of the famous Trojan horse, it managed to penetrate to the very heart of the enemy camp'.[9] He was advocating infiltration of nazi organizations, but could not these tactics be used to subvert the Popular Front? If overt Communists were few in Spain, many more left-wing politicians were doubtless the tools or dupes of Moscow. Franco hoped that his fears might be exaggerated, telling Gregorio Marañon in Paris at the beginning of February that the excitement in Spain would blow over in a few weeks and denying any intention to mount a *coup d'état*. But shortly before he had told Major Barroso, the Military Attaché in Paris that the Army must be prepared to intervene 'if the worst came to the worst'.[10] He was carefully but certainly moving away from the aloof, political stance he had taken in December.

The country went to the polls on Sunday 16 February, and though there were a number of disturbances, most commentators were agreed that the elections had been conducted in satisfactory

[9] G. Dimitrov; *The Working Class against Fascism (London 1935)* p. 47.
[10] Hugh Thomas: *The Spanish Civil War* (London 1961) p. 95; Hills, op. cit., p. 210.

calm and fairness. The polls closed at 6 pm, and it was only a few hours before the word was out that the Popular Front had won a massive victory in the large towns. It was the last Sunday before Lent—a carnival day in many places—and it was in a festive mood that the populace took to the streets to celebrate their victory. Their actions, according to some reports, were not so jocular in spirit; at Oviedo the promised amnesty was anticipated by the opening of the gaol, and in other places churches and convents were burned. Yet, however superficially alarming the situation might be, it was strikingly parallel to many other occasions in Spanish history, the last of them at the fall of the Monarchy, when the populace hurried to expunge the relics of the bad old world from the new and beautiful one they imagined to be dawning. In April 1931 General Franco had ordered his subordinates to remain calm, but on this occasion he was himself quick to become excited.

At two o'clock in the morning of the 17th he telephoned General Pozas, an old African comrade of his, who was Inspector-General of the Civil Guard. He asked him what he intended to do, and expressed his fear that post-election disturbances would get out of hand and would lead on to social revolution, for which the elections could not have given any mandate. Pozas replied that he did not think there was 'any foundation for fearing anything serious'. Franco was not satisfied. At three, he woke up General Molero, the caretaker Minister of War, and painted a lurid picture of the disturbances across the country. He asked Molero to propose the declaration of martial law in the cabinet the following morning. That Monday Franco spent in making the necessary plans to put martial law into effect, only to hear that it would not be declared; the President of the Republic had turned down Portela's request. In December, Franco had considered that any attempted *coup d'état* would be doomed to failure, but now he decided that one was both possible and desirable to forestall the entry into office of a Popular Front government and the chaos which would ensue from it.

He did not, however, feel that a *coup* could succeed without respectable political backing. He certainly did not expect the Army as a whole, let alone Pozas and the Civil Guard, to follow a lead from him. The military, he said, lacked 'the moral unity necessary to undertake the task'. His best hope was that he might persuade

Visit of André Maginot to the Academia General Militar under Franco's command, October 1930

General Franco in the field during the Civil War (Mansell Collection)

Portela to declare martial law even without Alcalá Zamora's approval. Through Natalio Rivas, a liberal politician and a friend of many years' standing, he arranged an interview with the Prime Minister, and put his case. Portela pointed out that a declaration of martial law would mean 'revolution within two hours of its proclamation'. 'Yes', replied Franco, 'but with a force able to fight and defeat it. The other course means revolution too, but revolution unchecked.'[11] Not without apprehensions for the future, Portela paused at this; but unwilling as he had been to take up the burden of the premiership, he was all the more unwilling to assume the responsibility for a revolution. He put Franco off with promises to consider it, but the General left with the knowledge that he had failed. Later that day, Goded, Fanjul and General Rodríguez del Barrio called on Franco at the War Ministry. They persuaded him to investigate whether after all a purely military coup might be possible. But the response from the garrisons was discouraging. It was now inevitable that Azaña must take office, and Franco could only hope that the new Government would prove able after all to withstand the revolution.

His personal position was now very unsure, for his dissatisfaction with the political situation was common knowledge. On the evening of the 18th, Pozas and General Núñez del Prado, the commander of the Assault Guards (whose role was primarily urban crowd and riot control) told Portela that Franco and Goded were planning a *coup d'état* and assured him of their own support for the government. It had been assumed that Portela would remain in office until second-round elections had, in accordance with the law, been held in those constituencies where no candidate had polled forty per cent of the first-round vote. But the populace was already vociferous in its demands for the immediate transfer of power to the Popular Front, which, it seemed clear, must in any event hold a majority in the new Cortes. It had won less than fifty per cent of the overall vote, but it had a comfortable majority over the National Front, and its constitutional position was apparently virtually unchallenged.

Little could be gained in the circumstances by Portela staying,

---

[11] The direct speech used in this account of the 17 and 18 February 1936 is taken from Arrarás: *Franco* (San Sebastián ed.), pp. 231–5.

and the threat of popular insurrection on his Left and of military revolt on his Right made him only too anxious to hand over to Azaña, so he resigned on the afternoon of Wednesday the 19th. That morning he had told Franco of his intention, and had been roundly abused for what the General regarded as his treachery. Nevertheless Portela did what he could to shield Franco, not only denying the rumour that he was under arrest but also stating publicly that he had done his duty.

The testimonial hardly disguised from Azaña the dangers of retaining Franco at the centre of affairs. Coming into office on Wednesday 19 February, the following Saturday he published a decree transferring General Franco to the command of military forces in the Canary Islands with headquarters at Santa Cruz de Tenerife. Goded was sent to Franco's old post in the Balearics. It was Azaña's policy at this time to keep the Army firmly under control without creating unnecessary martyrs, to give suspect officers rope but always to ensure that their heads were in a noose. The gilded exile of the Canaries was a most suitable punishment for Franco; it could not be called harsh, for the post was ordinarily entrusted to a man of his rank, and his zealous attention to the problems of Mallorca had given him experience in problems of coastal defence which would be useful in the Canaries. On the other hand it effectively removed from his control any force which could threaten the government in Madrid, while making it much more difficult for him to conspire than if unemployed.

Doubtless Franco realised all this and bore it in mind when, before leaving Madrid, he made his official calls on the President and on the Prime Minister. He told Alcalá that Spain lacked men of backbone to stand up to the Revolution and that current military appointments were designed to open the way to it; but he received only the assurance that Communism would be averted even without his services. Nor did Azaña agree that Franco would better be able to serve the tranquillity of Spain in Madrid. Understandably, perhaps, the Prime Minister did not share Franco's doubts about his government's patriotism and political competence, and he simply used the cautionary example of the Sanjurjo fiasco to warn him against plotting.

The warning did not deter Franco from considering the contingency in which it might be necessary for him and his colleagues to step in to save Spain. At the beginning of March he attended a meeting of a dozen or so senior officers to discuss possible courses of action. Here it was agreed that, while an immediate rising in Madrid could not succeed, in certain circumstances rapid action would have to be taken whatever the risk. These circumstances would include any attempt to disband the forces of order, armed insurrection by the Left, or a premature coup by any garrison. This was virtually all that was definitely decided. Franco, at this stage, seems to have distrusted a highly organised conspiracy, probably because of the security risks it entailed. He had told Fanjul and Colonel Aranda at the end of February that martial law should be declared when necessary region by region and co-ordination arranged afterwards. He did agree, though, to keep in touch with the generals in Madrid, who would continue to meet at intervals. Shortly afterwards, on 8 March, Franco left the capital to take up his post.

It was a bitter journey. He was being forced to leave the centre of the stage when he felt that he had an important part to play, and as he travelled he found further evidence of Spain's tragedy. In Cádiz he found that religious buildings had been burned and that the military authorities had obeyed instructions by not intervening. In Tenerife he was greeted by a hostile demonstration of the Left, who did not forget his role in October 1934. The same day General López Ochoa, the field commander in Asturias whom Yagüe had almost shot because of his leniency, was arraigned for atrocities committed in the repression. Although Franco told the Press how he had always wanted to come to the Canaries, and set about the tasks of his new command with his customary energy, he longed to be back in Madrid.

Shortly a hope dawned. The elections in Cuenca province, which had been won by the Right in February, were on 1 April annulled by the Cortes because of irregularities, and shortly afterwards Franco was persuaded to ask the CEDA for a place on their list. Acción Popular (one of the constituent groups of the CEDA) had in 1933 offered him a seat in the Balearics, and even then he had not refused outright, but had reflected before finally deciding that his military career must come first. Now his military career was in the doldrums for as long as the Popular Front remained in office, and with a seat in the Cortes he could return to the Peninsula, with a platform from which to warn the country of its danger, and in a position to influence and advise his fellow generals. Unfortunately, although Gil Robles accepted his candidature, it immediately met with strong opposition from another member of the list, José Antonio Primo de Rivera.[12]

José Antonio, known always by his Christian name, was the Dictator's eldest son, and the leader of a small fascist group called FE de las JONS[13] or more usually Falange. His party was principally distinguished by the combativeness of its members in street encounters with Left-wing gangsters, but he himself had great charm and considerable personal standing. He also had a developed sense both of social justice and of national destiny, despising the straightforward reactionaries with whom he was willy-nilly associated. More than most he despised General Franco, to whom in October 1934 he had addressed an urgent appeal to save Spain by a military rising, receiving in reply only the advice 'to wait watchfully without losing faith in the Army'.[14] Now he had sent Gil Robles word from prison that if Franco's candidature were not withdrawn, he would refuse to run himself, so weakening the Rightist candidature as a whole. Meanwhile the Cortes ruled that only those who had taken part in the original elections might stand in the re-run, and Franco took the opportunity to withdraw his name.

Meanwhile the Army continued to seethe with plots and rumours of plots. Everywhere little groups discussed more or less far-fetched schemes to overthrow the government; everywhere there were more conspiracies which existed only in the imagination of the government's supporters. Most of the groups of officers, even of generals, were harmless, without any clear plans. Even a relatively serious undertaking like the revolt planned for 20 April aborted when its

[12] Gil Robles, op. cit., pp. 563–5.
[13] Short for Falange Española de las Juntas Ofensivas Nacional-Sindicalistas (Spanish Phalanx of National Syndicalist Fighting Committees).
[14] Salvador de Madariaga: *Spain* (London 1961) p. 459. Speech of Franco reported in *El Adelanto* (Salamanca), 19 July 1938.

leader, General Rodríguez del Barrio, fell ill. The following month another plot foundered on the unwillingness of Alcalá Zamora to resist the Cortes' deposition of him from the Presidency[15]. Stranded in Tenerife Franco could do no more than direct a stream of letters to his friend Lieutenant-Colonel Galarza in Madrid about the lines on which such a revolt should be planned.

Politicians like Azaña who prided themselves on a cool head became so used to false alarms that they underrated the real threats —such as the promising conspiratorial organisation that was being put together in Pamplona by Emilio Mola, the commander of the 12th Infantry Brigade. By May 1936 he had worked out a coherent strategy for a revolt, basing it on the four divisions based on Burgos, Valladolid, Zarogoza and Valencia. The garrison in Madrid would lock itself into barracks and await relief by these forces from the north and east. Mola had built a widespread and efficient network of junior officers, and already had several generals as adherents too. What he felt he lacked was the authority which the patronage of the Army's leading figures might give him. He wanted the blessing first and foremost of the exiled Sanjurjo, secondarily of Franco.

It is known that by the end of May Mola had received Sanjurjo's authority to act in his name, but it seems probable that, although he was in contact with General Franco through Galarza, he did not yet have any assurance of cooperation from him. Certainly Mola's associates were kept wondering. Franco's shyness to commit himself led them to dub him Miss Canary Islands 1936, while Sanjurjo exclaimed that 'with or without Franquito we shall save Spain'[16]. At first he may indeed have been dispensable, but as June progressed the optimism with which Mola had entered the month began to wane. In a secret circular he warned that 'enthusiasm for the Cause has not yet reached the pitch of excitement necessary for a complete victory'. He went on to say that 'an effort has been made to provoke two opposing political sectors into a state of violence which might form a basis for progress. But the

[15] S. G. Payne: *Politics and the Military in Modern Spain* (Stanford 1967), p. 320 (Testimony of Eduardo Pardo Reina).
[16] Payne: *Politics and the Military*, p. 332 (Testimony of José María Iribarren); Ansaldo, op. cit., p. 121.

85

fact is that, up to now, despite the assistance given by some political elements, this has not come about, because there are still stupid people who believe that it is possible to coexist with the representatives of the masses whose puppet is the Popular Front'[17]. Moreover he had heard that the government had wind of the plot and were taking preventive steps. During the third week in June he planned for the first time what to do if the *putsch* were unsuccessful. He also issued Directives for Morocco (dated 24 June but possibly drafted earlier), which incorporated the Army of Africa into his plans for the march on Madrid.

This was probably what Franco had been waiting for. He had never been eager to associate himself with failure, and he wanted to see how likely the conspiracy was to succeed before joining it; but he had to bear in mind the probability that if a serious rising took place without his participation he would suffer whatever its outcome. If it failed, the Left would surely take the opportunity to purge all Army officers not regarded as reliable, if not to disband the officer corps altogether. On the other hand Mola had warned that 'he who is not with us is against us, and will be treated as an enemy'.[18] So Franco could not afford to cheer on the rebellion from the sidelines.

He had in fact less room for manœuvre than might appear, and would probably have felt obliged in the end to support Mola under any circumstances. Nevertheless he did his best to ensure that his talents would not be wasted in a back-water, and was helped in this by Mola's growing recognition that the rising 'was going to cost much blood and many tears'.[19] The greatest possible strength would be required in the field and an important role—and a prestigious general—would have to be assigned to Spain's best fighting force, the Army of Africa. Since the generals stationed in Africa in 1936 were all considered staunch supporters of the Government the obvious choice to lead the rising there was Francisco Franco. Mola and the former head of the Aviation Ser-

[17] B. Félix Maíz: *Alzamiento en España. De un diario de la conspiración* (Pamplona 1952), p. 141.
[18] Maíz, op. cit., pp. 155–6.
[19] José María Iribarren: *Con el general Mola. Escenas y aspectos inéditos de la guerra civil* (Zaragoza 1937), p. 35.

vice, General Kindelán, discussed as early as 11 June means of transporting him from the Canary Islands to Morocco, and by the end of June an authoritative list of prospective leaders named him as commander in Africa.[20]

Franco was now committed to the Movement and convinced of its necessity. The passage of time after February elections had brought increasing evidence of the disintegration of Spain as he knew it. Not only did political excitement lead to incidental violence, but political bitterness was also engendering campaigns of planned murder. The government seemed to have lost all control of public order, to have abdicated from the defence of life and property. Franco had come across one example of church-burning at Cádiz on his way to Tenerife; Gil Robles claimed in the Cortes on 16 June that a total of 160 churches had been destroyed since the February elections. He went on to claim a figure of 269 violent deaths in the same period, a not unlikely figure, considering the currency of inflammatory language and the constant street battles. It is impossible to tell who drew first blood in these, but it is certain that there were always those ready to take justice into their own hands for want of confidence in the government's will to punish the guilty. Political organisations made it their policy to take reprisals for attacks on their members. All the same, gang warfare and arson were only elements in the threat to middle-class security. They stood as a symbol for the whole, but were not in themselves very important. The Left attacked churches: the Falange attacked *Casas del Pueblo*[21], if not so often, perhaps. The Falange acted in some sense as the Right's champion in the squalid tournament of political violence, and charming middle-class girls were proud to wear its yoke-and-arrows symbol as a favour. In the limited field of political hooliganism, the Right could give as good as it got; but in the wider field of national life it reeled before the progress of a piecemeal social revolution that roused the greater indignation because of its tenuous hold on legality.

[20] This list was written 'some days after' 23 June, according to Iribarren: op. cit. p. 17, 'at the end of June', according to Jorge Vigón: *General Mola (el conspirador)* (Barcelona 1957), p. 98.

[21] The *Casa del Pueblo* was the local social and administrative headquarters of the Socialist Party. It was frequently also a cultural centre.

In the country the advent of the Popular Front was the signal for an assault on the rights of property. The peasants of the south and west of Spain were not constitutionalists who would wait for the enactment of agrarian legislation in due form. A Communist writer estimated that a full land settlement under existing legislation would take a hundred years.[22] The peasants knew that the government programme promised them a settlement and that there was fallow land which they would be glad to till, so they made haste to expropriate it. During the two years of rule by the Right, the employers had held the whip hand in the countryside. Freed from government wage regulation and protected by the Civil Guard, employers had reduced wages by half in their efforts to sell at competitive prices in a time of agricultural overproduction. The countryside had then been quiet, even cowed, but the pendulum had now swung the other way.

The peasants were confident of strength, and landowners were forced to employ on the land all the men who demanded work and to pay them greatly increased wages. If they decided to cut their losses and not harvest the crops, their land was invaded and the crop stolen. In instances where the Civil Guard had intervened they had been resisted with bloody consequences, so it was generally official policy to let events take their course, to save lives rather than property. In Extremadura the government had simply ratified the occupation of large properties in order to preserve some façade of legality.

Labour unrest was as bad in industry as in agriculture. There was a vast strike wave. As in the countryside, employers had in 1933–5 tried to maintain profitability at a time of low demand by reducing the level of wages. They had also reduced their manpower, and frequently the politically active had been among the redundant. Here too the wheel had turned. The Popular Front had promised and soon decreed the reinstatement of workers dismissed for political reasons since 1933, and the unions did not allow firms to dismiss anybody to make room for those reinstated. Often higher pay-rates were claimed with effect from dates months in the past, and demands were even made for pay which workmen

[22] *International Press Correspondence*, quoted by B. H. Bolloten, *The Grand Camouflage* (London 1961), p. 21.

had lost through being in gaol. In the context of a stagnant economy the employers regarded this as ruinous.

Yet, even where they were prepared to agree to economic demands, they were often faced with purely political stoppages, part of the battle between Anarchist and Socialist unions. During the Madrid building strike which started at the beginning of June, the Anarchist strikers ate and drank free with tradesmen and restaurant owners not daring to challenge them. And the important factor differentiating this strike from others was only that it took place in the capital rather than in a small town, and was therefore better publicised. All the while the government maintained a position of neutrality. Even in the Canaries Franco experienced what seemed to him wilful disregard for public order. On the eve of May Day, at Puerto de la Luz, the Civil Governor had ordered the removal of troops which had been posted there as a precaution against trouble with demonstrators the following day. Protests had been in vain.[23] Indeed the government seemed in some ways to be actively encouraging the spread of disorder. Franco's associates in Tenerife claimed later to have frustrated three attempts on his life during the summer of 1936 and believed the civil authorities to be implicated in at least one of them. In Alcalá de Henares there was an ugly incident when a troop of cavalry, provoked by jeering, charged a left wing crowd. The government blamed the garrison and suspended its officers, so exposing the military to the ridicule of the mob. At the same time key officers throughout the Army were shuffled around, and as many troops as possible sent on leave. This impaired the potential of the Army as a prop for law and order just when the government might badly need it at any moment. Yet the Prime Minister felt that he must make the conspiracy, of which his government was well aware, more difficult to bring to fruition.

In this he had some success: for instance, the dismissal of Lt-Col. Heli Tella at the beginning of June removed an important conspirator. But the policy was only half-heartedly carried out: Yagüe, the key conspirator in Africa, was offered a post as Military

[23] *Claridad* 18 May 1936. This article is Document No. 64 in *Los Documentos de la Primavera Trágica*, edited by Ricardo de la Cierva (Madrid 1966).

Attaché, out of harm's way, but was permitted to stay in command of the 2nd Legion when he declined it. Left wing officers were as dismayed at the government's indifference to reactionary subversion as were right wing officers at its complaisance with creeping revolution. The Government was being ground between the upper millstone of the Army, which it feared to provoke to a *putsch*, and the nether millstone of the revolutionary Left, which it feared even more. Its problem was made more nightmarish by the near certainty that a *putsch* would provoke a social revolution and *vice versa*.

On 23 June Franco wrote to the Prime Minister and Minister of War, Casares Quiroga, to warn him against alienating the Army, which might otherwise be the government's friend.[24] He complained bitterly about the trend of recent appointments and in particular about the reinstatement of officers dismissed the service for their part in the Catalan revolt in 1934. He recalled that 'favouritism and arbitrariness' had caused the Junta movement in 1917, and warned: 'As an expert on discipline, to the preservation of which I devoted many years, I can assure you that the feeling for justice which reigns in our military cadres is such that any unjustified strong measures will be counter-productive in their effects on the mass of the Army as a whole, which feels itself at the mercy of anonymous actions and slanderous accusations'.[25] This letter has been presented by some as an honest attempt to influence the government's policy, to give it a last chance to save itself. Alternatively it has been called an attempt to help the planning of the rising by throwing Casares off the scent. Certainly it sought to allay Casares' suspicions of the Army. 'Those who present the Army as disaffected from the Republic are failing in truthfulness', he wrote. 'Those who make up plots to suit their wishful thinking are liars; those people serve the country ill who sully or impugn the dignity and patriotism of the officer corps by diagnosing in it conspiracy and disaffection.' Yet however unpatriotic it might be for

[24] Azaña had been elected to succeed Alcalá as President of the Republic on 10 May.
[25] The letter is printed in full in Arrarás: *Franco* (San Sebastián ed.), p. 240–44.

people to mention the fact, Franco knew quite well that at least one conspiracy against the government was far advanced. He may also have known that elements of the officer corps wanted to try as a traitor everyone who had served as a minister under the Republic, a policy which signified some hostility to that regime. Indeed Franco would have been naïve to suppose that the Popular Front would, or even could, heed his advice, and one is led to reject the idea that his letter was a genuine bid for peace.

There is little doubt that by the first days of July Franco was fully committed to the rising, which was scheduled to break out on 9 or 10 July while the Carlists were gathered for the festival of San Fermín[26] and the Army of Africa for manœuvres. But after a Falangist was arrested carrying part of the plan on 6 July, it was postponed until the 15th despite the impatience of many conspirators, including Franco. Then in the early hours of 13 July a group of Madrid riot police, incensed by the murder of one of their number by Falangists, revenged themselves by shooting the Rightist political leader, Calvo Sotelo. There was an immediate uproar all over Spain. It was the final demonstration of the Government's unworthiness that uniformed police could cold-bloodedly murder opposition leaders. Many who had previously been lukewarm to the idea of rising had now to be restrained from an immediate move.

After yet another postponement, the final date for the rising in Spain was set for the 18th, the Army of Africa being instructed to rise at 5 p.m. the day before. Franco would leave the Canaries as soon as he heard from Africa that the rising had started. On the 16th the final date was given him by a diplomat called Sangróniz. The same afternoon he heard that his aircraft had arrived in Grand Canary, and although the dangerous prevalence of cloud over Tenerife meant that it could come no farther, he was that evening providentially granted an innocent reason to leave Tenerife. His old African colleague, General Balmes, his subordinate commander on Grand Canary, had shot himself while at target practice, and Franco got permission from the War Ministry to attend his funeral

[26] The famous bull-fighting festival of San Fermín takes place annually at Pamplona, the capital of Carlist Navarre. It is described by Ernest Hemingway in his novel *Fiesta*.

at Las Palmas the following day. Leaving detailed instructions for the rising on Tenerife, he sailed that night on the overnight steamer for Puerto de la Luz on Grand Canary.

The day of the 17th he spent in attending Balmes' funeral, working out the details of the rising on the island of Grand Canary, and drafting his manifesto. He also arranged for his wife and daughter to sail to France in a German ship. Late that night he received a telegram forwarded from Tenerife announcing that the Army of Africa had risen and was in full control. A security leak in Melilla had made it necessary to strike a few hours early, but otherwise all had gone well. At five o'clock in the morning of the 18th, Franco declared martial law in the Canaries, and at a quarter past five he published his first manifesto. This drew attention to all the ills of the Republic which we have been examining: the violence, the industrial chaos, the attacks on 'your monuments and art treasures', (he forbore to say churches). The Constitution lay in ruins. Those who had violated it in October 1934 were glorified, while its defenders, the armed forces were slandered. The masses had been hoaxed by Soviet agents. 'Is it possible', he asked, 'to consent for a single day more to the shameful spectacle we are presenting to the world? ... No; that we cannot do! Let the traitors do that, but not we who have sworn to defend Spain.' He finished by making clear that his mission was not reaction but social reconciliation. He called for Liberty and Equality yes, but, first of all, for Fraternity.[27]

The population of Las Palmas did not all heed this call, and the Socialist UGT called a general strike; but when Franco left the island, the success of the rising there was assured. At ten o'clock Franco had heard from Tetuán that all resistance in Morocco was at an end, and at midday he flew out towards Agadir *en route* for Spanish Morocco. That night he spent in Casablanca, and he landed at Sania Ramel airfield near Tetuán at seven o'clock on the morning of Sunday the 19th to be greeted by Colonel Sáenz de Buruaga, the leader of the rising there.

News from the peninsula was hard to come by, but it was clear

[27] The Manifesto is printed in full in José Emilio Díez: *Colección de Proclamas y Arengas del Exemo. Sr. General D. Francisco Franco* (Seville 1937), pp. 27–30.

that the rising was not going to triumph without a struggle. The government was putting on a resolute face, although Casares had resigned and had been replaced by the more moderate Martínez Barrio. Risings had taken place in most large towns in Andalusia, but in none of them had the rebels fully subdued the Left, who had resisted stoutly everywhere. A number of troops had crossed the Straits of Gibraltar from Africa but had not as yet had a decisive effect. The passage of more troops was rendered problematic by the suspicious behaviour of naval vessels, which suggested that the fleet was not under rebel control. Franco had been counting on its adherence, since at a party when the naval squadron had visited Tenerife in May naval officers had showed themselves almost embarrassingly hostile to the government.

Even Morocco was not as quiet as it might have been; a nearby tribe seemed likely to prove hostile, and since Aviation Service officers loyal to the government had sabotaged their aircraft, it was not possible to bomb the dissidents into submission. Aircraft headed the list of urgent requirements, and Franco decided immediately to appeal for help abroad. On the morning of the 19th he dispatched Luis Bolín to Rome to ask for twelve bomber and three fighter aircraft together with bombs and bombing equipment. On 22 July he had one of his colonels, Juan Beigbeder, formerly military attaché in Berlin, make a request to Germany for ten transport planes with maximum seating capacity, and to back this request, Captain Arranz and two German residents of Morocco flew to Berlin on 24 July.

By this time the plight of the military rebellion was more serious still. The leader, General Sanjurjo, had been killed when the aircraft in which he was flying from Portugal crashed shortly after take-off on 20 July. The insurgents now controlled Morocco, Galicia, Northern Extremadura, Old Castile, Navarre, and Aragon as far as Huesca and Teruel. They also had a reasonable foothold in Western Andalusia, and isolated outposts in various other places, notably Córdoba, Granada, Oviedo and the Alcázar at Toledo. On the other hand they had failed in Madrid, Barcelona, Valencia, Bilbao and Málaga, five of Spain's six largest cities. They had had no success in Catalonia and the Basque country, the areas in which some rudimentary industry existed. They had little war material, and they were heavily outnumbered by the irregular militias who had sprung up for the defence of the Republic.

The Army of Africa was both numerous, well-trained and relatively well-armed, but it was in Africa. To keep it there the Republic had mustered a fleet of two cruisers, two destroyers, three gunboats and seven submarines, against which the insurgents had a single gunboat. Even though the Republican ships were without their officers, whom the crew had mostly murdered for their sympathy with the rising, they maintained naval command of the straits. The insurgents had superior airpower, even with only nine aircraft, but they could transport a maximum of 200 men a day to the peninsula and at that rate it would be months before the forces of Southern Spain could be decisively reinforced.

A week to ten days after the rising, the position looked almost hopeless. Although an expeditionary force had entered the province of Madrid from the north and captured the pass of Alto de León in the Guadarrama mountains, no further progress could be made while Mola had not even enough ammunition for each of his weapons to fire a single shot. He and other generals in the north began to contemplate means of escape. The world's press wrote the rising off as a failure; the Italian ambassador commiserated with an envoy of Mola's in Biarritz. The only achievements of the adventure seemed to be negative: a river of blood and the very social revolution it had been staged to prevent. Central authority had completely disintegrated. In parts of Republican Spain small towns and villages had even set up independent communes, expropriating large landowners and often abolishing money and private property altogether. Opponents of the Left were always imprisoned and frequently murdered. The Madrid government, now led by José Giral, was just one of many influences on these bodies, and frequently a less powerful one than the revolutionary left wing unions. This division was of course a source of weakness to the enemies of the rising, but the insurgents themselves were scarcely more coordinated, and Franco's slogan, 'Blind faith in victory', was an apt one. Everybody with his eyes open was giving long odds against his victory.

Then, on 28 July, came good news with the arrival in Tetuán of the first of the transport aircraft with which Hitler had decided to aid Nationalist Spain. Two days later the first Italian aid was sent: a squadron of Savoia-Marchetti bombers.[28] With the full cooperation also of Portugal, which Salazar had promised to Mola's representative on the 26th, the cause of the insurgents was now looking more promising. Franco was now able to telegraph Mola that 'we are the masters of the straits; we are in command of the situation', and to fly 600,000 rounds of ammunition to the Army of the North. On 5 August he decided to run the Republican blockade of the straits, embarking 3,000 men and successfully convoying them across, while his newly acquired aircraft drove off the ill-managed Republican ships towards Cartagena. Now that every day brought more aircraft, more foreign technicians and more effectives from Africa to the peninsula, the march towards Madrid, which had begun in a small way on 2 August could gather momentum.

On the other hand Mola's columns were halted by stiff resistance in the sierra north of Madrid. In consequence Franco became more and more the preeminent leader as attention was focused on the success of forces under his control. From the first moment he had acted as leader; his Las Palmas manifesto, for instance, did not mention General Sanjurjo as prospective head of state. The original proclamations of martial law in Africa were in the name of Franco, and the fact that he was one of the first to rise meant that he was regarded as the leader by the world's press. He did nothing to dispel this view, which he probably shared, and he never in his broadcasts mentioned the provisional government that Mola had set up in Burgos.

This was a military junta presided over by Major-General Miguel Cabanellas, a Radical (i.e. moderate) in politics and the only divisional commander to join the rising. Though he was formally appointed Commander-in-Chief of the Armies of Africa and the South of Spain, Franco was not named a member until 3 August, because, according to Cabanellas, 'it has not been possible to get into contact with him'.[29] This did not prevent Achille Benedetti of the *Corriere della Sera* from getting the impression a few days

[28] Unfortunately, three of these crashed in French territory, providing untimely proof of fascist intervention.

[29] *Corriere della Sera* (Milan), 26 July 1936.

95

later that Franco 'is in continuous contact with the military chiefs of the north and south of Spain and directs their movements by radio and also by telephone.'[30]

Nor did Franco himself hesitate to depreciate possible rivals. Queipo de Llano, a senior general to him, who had dramatically seized Seville and was winning world-wide fame for his blood-thirsty broadcasts, he dismissed as 'a mere peon of the movement'.[31] He was also able to impress his overall authority on the German Consul in Tetuán who reported categorically that 'the leader of the movement is General Franco'.[32] He was fortunate too that the head of German military intelligence, Admiral Canaris, who had a personal interest in Spain, preferred him to the other candidates for the leadership.

In fact, in the early stages of the war, 'Nationalist' Spain, as the territory under the insurgents came to be called, was under divided authority. Broadly speaking, Mola controlled the north and Franco the south, but various other leaders, notably Queipo, controlled more or less independent fiefs. Nominally the National Defence Junta was the supreme body, but in practice it had few staff and not much authority. No foreign powers recognised it, and for Franco at least it had little significance; by 1967 he had even forgotten when he became a member of it.[33]

After August 11, when the occupation of Mérida established a junction between the Nationalist Armies of North and South, Franco and Mola were in constant contact about the military situation. However, as each was in command of a separate theatre, disagreements inevitably arose about the allocation of resources, particularly as foreign suppliers dealt with individual commanders rather than with the Junta. By the end of August the desire was growing for a more realistic chain of command to be set up with a single leader at its apex, and in the middle of September General Kindelán, who as commander of the insurgent air forces was faced with the difficulty of deciding on priorities for aircraft allocation,

[30] *Corriere della Sera*, 30 July 1936.
[31] *Chicago Daily Tribune*, 31 July 1936.
[32] *Documents on German Foreign Policy* (hereafter cited as DGFP) series D, Vol III, No. 9.
[33] Brian Crozier: *Franco, a biographical history* (London 1967), p. 192.

advocated a meeting of generals at which the issue might be discussed. To this, after some consideration, Franco agreed, and went to Salamanca for the meeting on 21 September[34]

At the meeting were gathered Franco, Mola, Queipo de Llano, Kindelán, Cabanellas, four other generals, and the two colonels on the Burgos Junta. There was general agreement on the desirability of a unified military command, and Mola in particular insisted on it, while only Cabanellas, who stood to lose his leading position, opposed the principle. It was also unanimously decided that Franco would be the most suitable generalissimo, endowed as he was with great prestige both at home and abroad, but that the appointment would remain secret until it was formally announced by the Burgos Junta. With that the meeting broke up, and the generals returned to their respective commands. Nothing more happened for several days though the need for military coordination became more pressing as Franco's forces approached Madrid.

It seems that Franco himself was not eager to add the responsibilities of formal leadership to the substance of power already in his hands as commander of the principal Nationalist Army, but he had backers who were more impatient. General Kindelán and General Orgaz, who was acting as High Commissioner in Morocco, were both staunch monarchists, and they regarded the installation of Franco as supreme commander as the best step towards an eventual restoration. Not that Franco was one hundred per cent monarchist: he had told the Portuguese press on 9 August that 'Spain is Republican and will remain so. Neither the flag nor the regime will be changed'[34]. Less than a week later he was unfurling the red and gold flag of the monarchy amid emotional scenes in Seville with the words: 'Here it is, the glorious Spanish flag. Now it is yours.'[36] At any rate the monarchists felt him to be more promising than the frankly Republican Mola and Queipo de Llano, and they determined to get him made interim head of

[34] See Alfredo Kindelán y Duany: *Mis cuadernos de guerra* (Madrid 1945) pp. 49–53, and (for the date) José María Iribarren: *Mola: datos para una biografía y para la historia del Alzamiento Nacional* (Zaragoza 1938), p. 232.
[35] *The Times*, 11 August 1936.
[36] Dez, op. cit., p. 42.

state. In this they were encouraged by two prominent and influential ex-legionaries, Millán Astray and Yagüe, and by Franco's elder brother Nicolás.

On 27 September, under pressure from these friends and perhaps also from his wife, who had joined him in Cáceres on the 23rd, Franco agreed to another meeting on the following day. Yagüe promptly made it public that Franco would 'tomorrow be our generalissimo, the Chief of State'.[37] And indeed, when the gathering of the 21st reconvened in Salamanca the following morning, Kindelán presented a draft decree which would name Franco generalissimo and would also give him 'the function of Chief of State so long as the war may last'. This was not at first approved, but over lunch the generals met Yagüe who had not been present at the meeting and who strongly advocated the acceptance of the decree. His voice may have been decisive, because he was felt to be in touch with the opinion of the fighting men, and was by no means a monarchist. After lunch a decree was approved which named Franco 'Chief of the Government of the Spanish State', apparently for an indefinite term, and the meeting broke up.

When the decree was published the following day, it was found that the decree had been amended so as to grant Franco 'all powers of the new State'. Nicolás Franco and Lorenzo Martínez Fuset, who had been legal adviser to General Franco in the Canaries, seem to have been responsible for this *fait accompli*, which was consolidated when the first decree of the 'new State' referred to the Generalissimo not as Chief of the Government but as Chief of the State.[38]

The accession of Franco to the headship of state with unlimited powers was accepted without serious question. The original plans for the rising had after all envisaged a military dictatorship, and Franco himself had before the end of July announced that as his aim.[39] Not everybody might be happy about the choice of dic-

[37] *Extremadura* (Cáceres), 28 September 1936.

[38] For this rather obscure, though much discussed, episode, see in particular Kindelán, op. cit., pp. 51–6; *Boletín Oficial de la Junta de Defensa Nacional* (Burgos), 30 September 1936; Payne: *Politics and the Military*, pp. 371–2: Vigón, op. cit., p. 253.

[39] *News Chronicle*, 29 July 1936.

tator, but a representative gathering of Army leaders had agreed to Franco's exercising supreme military command, and in time of war the distinction was more apparent than real between this mandate and the full powers given him by the decree as published. Besides, the additional measure of prestige he had just won by the relief of the Alcázar of Toledo made it more difficult to speak against him.

The relief was a brilliant propaganda success. At the time of the rising, Colonel Moscardó, the Director of the Physical Training School, had been forced to shut himself into the Alcázar together with the other insurgent forces in Toledo, some of their families, and a number of hostages. There they waited for relief, able to withstand attempts to dislodge them partly because of the incompetence of their opponents and partly because of the massive solidity of the buildings. They were also surprisingly well provided with food and had almost unlimited ammunition, so their ability to withstand a siege of ten weeks is not surprising, if all the same commendable. Their heroism was quite outclassed by, for instance, the unsuccessful defenders of Gijón barracks, but there is something about the raising of a siege which lends itself to public joy, or 'mafficking'. This inherent propaganda advantage was enhanced by the false supposition that the Alcázar was full of Infantry Cadets,[40] and by the fact that the Republic had imprudently invited the press to witness its fall, with the final result that the 'epic of the Alcázar' is probably the second most famous episode of the civil war.[41] While it must be said that Toledo was a very important military objective apart from its propaganda value, its relief certainly occurred at a politically convenient moment for Franco.

Franco did not let the laurels wither on his brow. He knew that his power was far from secure. He had achieved it by grasping the opportunity 'to fix the main lines of the future government ... prior to the occupation of Madrid, since, now in the middle of the undecided fight, no resistance was to be expected.'[42] Yet if the end of the war came soon, as was expected, the generals might unmake

[40] It was in fact the vacation period, and only seven cadets were in residence.
[41] I should imagine the bombing of Guernica to be the most famous.
[42] DGFP, Series D, Vol. III, No. 96.

him as they had made him. The propaganda resources of the Nationalists were accordingly set to build up the person of Franco as the symbol of their cause. To this no objection could be made, since it was the logical consequence of the unified command that the prestige of the commander be used as a weapon in the propaganda battle. Other generals retained a share of power and glory, but it was Franco's portrait that was ubiquitous, Franco's public activities that were always headline news, Franco's name that was used as a rhythmic patriotic chant. His tasselled Foreign Legion cap, short stature and incipient middle-aged spread became grist to the mills of hostile cartoonists. Every day that passed consolidated his position, metaphorically (though not literally) head and shoulders above his colleagues. He became the 'Caudillo'[43], politically more and more the Spanish equivalent of Hitler and Mussolini.

[43] The word means chief or leader with a military rather than a political or tribal connotation. Garibaldi was the 'caudillo' par excellence. Franco himself had frequently been referred to in the Press as *a* 'caudillo' ever since his Legion days. Now he became *the* 'Caudillo'.

5 Caudillo

Posters of Franco at this time were captioned 'Caesars are victorious generals', but the general had to win his triumph before he could be sure of his apothesis. Certainly he had confidence and efficiency, talents which are supposed to help generals to be lucky. His army was superior in training and organisation; indeed in these respects, his command had from the first contrasted even with other Nationalist headquarters, for he alone had regular units which were both intact and at reasonable strength. By the beginning of September the Army of Africa was moving up the Tagus valley only a few miles from Talavera de la Reina. Its columns had moved rapidly indeed, thanks partly to their motor transport, and partly to lack of resistance. Often the Republican militias just melted before their advance, and even when they gave battle, their nerve and discipline tended to give way before the well directed fire of the Nationalists. They were then mown down by machine guns as they fled along the roads. Only at the battle of Badajoz on 14 August, when they had no easy line of retreat, did they show dangerous resistance, and here the Nationalist victory was only gained at a high cost in casualties.

But despite the heartening speed of their advance, there were many factors in the campaign which told against the Nationalists. Time was not on their side. They had always had many fewer effectives, and even though the Republicans lost far higher proportions of their forces as casualties or prisoners, and though nearly 14,000 Nationalist troops had been brought by air from Morocco by the end of October[1], the imbalance continued to grow. As the Nationalist columns approached Madrid, they had to assign more and more troops to guard their lines of communication, while conversely the Republican lines shortened. Throughout the advance the Republicans had maintained air superiority through their French and later Russian aircraft. The Nationalists therefore moved mostly under cover of night with fighting confined as far as possible to lightning attacks in the first hours of daylight. While resistance remained light this technique was sufficient to maintain a fairly rapid advance, but when resistance lasted long enough for the Republicans to bring up air support, Nationalist progress was severely restricted. The 245 miles to Talavera from Seville had taken their columns 38 days; the 17 miles on to Maqueda took them twelve. At Maqueda the road divides: they could fork left to Madrid, or right to Toledo.

Franco's decision to relieve Toledo rather than drive straight on to Madrid has often been criticised. Kindelán recalled that he had asked Franco whether he knew that it might cost him Madrid. Franco said that he was prepared to run that risk because he was publicly committed to the relief of the Alcázar. 'We must impress the enemy by putting in their mind the conviction that any task we set ourselves we can perform without their being able to prevent it,'[2] he said. It is too often assumed that the detour to Toledo was in fact responsible for Franco's failure to take Madrid in the first autumn of the war. Yet it is doubtful whether he could have taken it without securing the line of the Tagus as far as Toledo, which, even with the river almost dry, gave him some miles of defensible right flank, saving him manpower and denying to the Republicans a number of good roads and a railway line from which to menace his advance. Even as it was, the right flank was a source of anxiety to the Nationalists throughout October, and the following month they were unable to replace their losses in the battle for Madrid itself without weakening other parts of the line. Franco might tell the Germans as early as 6 October that he expected

[1] José Gomá: *La guerra en el aire: Vista, suerte y al toro* (Barcelona 1958), p. 82.
[2] Kindelán, op. cit., p. 23.

Madrid to fall 'in the near future', but he wisely refused to commit himself to a date.[3]

In fact his expectation was based on the assumption that Republican morale would collapse and permit a more or less unopposed breakthrough in the final stages. Although this still happened on a small scale quite frequently, Republican efficiency was increasing. A tremendous effort had been put into training, and, under the auspices principally of the Communists, constant propaganda had instilled into the militias a rudimentary sense of the importance of discipline. The fact that fighting was nearing Madrid was probably psychologically important too; after all, if a rural village was lost to the rebels, there were plenty more, but there was only one Madrid. About the middle of the month the Nationalists recognised that the advance must at all costs maintain its momentum, and on 16 October it was decided boldly to subordinate the tactical co-ordination of the larger fighting units to the occupation of ground. It was to be hoped that this would spread alarm on the other side, for by the 19th Nationalist intelligence was aware that their enemies were about to receive a fillip, both moral and material.[4]

Sure enough, on 29 October the Republicans launched a counter-attack of which newly-arrived Russian tanks formed the spearhead. They failed for lack of coordination with the infantry, but this did not wholly erase the beneficial effect on Republican morale. Nor did the continued Nationalist advance which reached the outskirts of Madrid on 5 November. The following day Largo Caballero, the Republican premier since 5 September, transferred the government to Valencia, but a Committee for the Defence of Madrid was appointed, and this was more rather than less resolute in its handling of the campaign. The Communists staked their prestige on the defence of Madrid, and Russian propaganda and technical advice were made available. General Varela's attack on the 7th, intended to penetrate the capital itself, was held by the militia in the great park to the west of the city, the Casa de Campo. On the 8th resistance was stiffened by the commitment of the first of the famous International Brigades.

[3] DGFP, Series D, Vol. III, No. 96.
[4] J. M. Martínez Bande: *La Marcha sobre Madrid* (Madrid 1967), pp. 95–6.

From the very first the war in Spain had been more than just a civil war. It was seen even in its first days as a paradigmatic struggle between those who regarded fascism as the deadly enemy and those who so regarded Communism. When the Republican Prime Minister Giral telegraphed the French government for aid, he did not invoke the 1935 commercial convention between the two countries: he made an emotional appeal from *Frente Popular* to *Front Populaire* signed 'Fraternally Yours'. And when Blum's decision to send aid, taken on 20 July, leaked out on the 24th, the Radicals in the Cabinet opposed support for the Republic on the grounds that it would be provocative to Germany and Italy, who were bound to support the insurgents. Yet Mussolini did not decide to intervene in Spain until the 25th, and Hitler not until the 26th.

All the countries which intervened in the war did so to a large extent because of ideological sympathy with one side and even more of ideological hostility to the other. France feared to see a fascist Spain, hostile to her Socialist-led government and sympathetic to Italian interests in the Mediterranean. Russia's policy of encouraging Popular Fronts against fascism would be discredited by its defeat in Spain. Germany and Italy feared the spread of Communism. With each of these attitudes strategic considerations were intermingled; Mexico, who acted openly throughout the war as a channel of arms to the Republic, was perhaps Spain's only helper in whom fraternity was unalloyed by other motives. Germany, in particular, cherished hopes of economic gain from an early stage.

Germany was at this time looking for secure sources of raw materials, especially for her growing armaments industry, so she insisted on instalment payments for her aid in such Spanish minerals as she could acquire in the Nationalist zone. These included the valuable copper and pyrites of the Huelva area, and the iron of the Rif. Much of the former belonged to British and French companies whose production was diverted from the democracies to Germany through an import–export organisation called Hisma–Rowak.[5] This

[5] These acronyms stand for Compañía Hispano-Marroquí de Transportes, which was based in Spain, and Rohstoffe-und-Waren-Einkaufsgesellschaft, the complementary German firm.

had a monopoly of Spanish–German trade and charged a commission of two per cent or more on the Spanish exports it handled. Its head was the shadowy figure of Johannes Bernhardt, who had carried to Hitler Franco's appeal for aid, and who did very well financially out of Nationalist Spain. His influence and that of Germans in general grew in proportion as they became more committed to the Nationalist cause.

By the end of October it was no secret to anybody that Germany was involved in the war in Spain; so she had considerable interest in preventing Franco from losing, and felt free to offer on military affairs advice which bordered on instruction. 'The following point of view is to be expressed most emphatically to General Franco', the German War Minister told Admiral Canaris on 30 October. 'In view of possible increased Russian help for Red Spain, the German Government does not consider the combat tactics hitherto employed by White Spain, in ground fighting as well as in aerial combat, promising of success. Continued adherence to this hesitant and routine procedure (failure to exploit the present favourable ground and air situation, scattered employment of the Air Force) is even endangering what has been gained so far'.[6] By this military back-seat driving Franco was not unduly dismayed, since it led to the formation of the Condor Legion, which increased German air and armoured support at a moment when he badly needed it.

The arrival of the first Italian ground forces was far less significant, for they were only infantrymen and not specialists. Not that the Germans were attempting to outdo the Italians. Indeed they were happy to yield Spain to Italy's sphere of influence so long as their economic needs were satisfied. The two countries agreed to keep in step diplomatically both in the Non-Intervention Committee in London, which had been set up to avert general war by keeping the Spanish war Spanish, at least superficially, and also in the matter of recognition of Franco. This they had intended to accord only after the fall of Madrid, but later they feared that an effective Republican blockade might choke off their aid to 'white Spain' unless they could protect their shipping with a semblance of legality. They therefore agreed on 18 November to establish

[6] DGFP, series D, Vol. III, No. 113 (Enclosure).

diplomatic relations with the Burgos Government. Even if this committed the dictators almost irrevocably to his defence, Franco must have found the resulting diplomatic missions a somewhat mixed blessing. The German head of mission, General von Faupel, particularly he found unsympathetic personally and too anxious to concern himself with the political structure of the regime.

The political organisation of the new state which had been set up in Burgos was, it is true, fairly rudimentary. A decree of 1 October provided for a State Technical Committee to deal with finance, commerce, labour, cultural affairs and so on, for the post of Governor-General which would be equivalent to the Ministry of the Interior, for a Secretary for Foreign Relations, and for a political secretariat to the Generalissimo. General Dávila, one of the key conspirators, was named Chairman of the Technical Committee, and a number of technical experts were called on to assist him, but Ambassador Serrat and General Fermoso the first Foreign Secretary and Governor-General, were neither well-known nor influential. The most important decisions were made not in Burgos at all but at Franco's headquarters in Salamanca, where Nicolás Franco was head of the political secretariat and Sangróniz was chief of the diplomatic staff. The government machine was designed purely for administrative convenience and not for any political purpose.

Franco regarded politicians as idle and selfish as a class, people who posed as leaders of men only to betray them and live at their expense. 'Only those who live off politics should fear our Movement', he had told Spaniards on 22 July.[7] 'Spaniards are tired of politics and of politicians', he told the American journalist Jay Allen on 28 July.[8] He did employ men with a political past: for example his commercial expert, Joaquín Bau, had been a Carlist deputy, but it was for his technical ability rather than his political opinions that he was employed. The Governor-General was instructed to employ on provincial or municipal councils 'people efficient in their work and not those prominent in politics, except, in the last resort, those whose inclinations are akin to the national

[7] *Cruzada*, Vol. III, p. 84.
[8] *Chicago Daily Tribune* 29 July 1936.

cause'.[9] Although not without policy in social and economic matters or in external relations, the Franco regime was in its early days without any political substructure.

This seemed to Nicolás Franco for one to be a source of weakness. Nicolás was rather the wheeler-dealer by temperament. Entering the Navy as an executive branch cadet, he had in 1915 transferred to the Corps of Naval Constructors, which was seriously undermanned and therefore promised rapid promotion. Indeed he became Lieutenant-Colonel[10] in 1921 at a younger age even than his brother Francisco, but in 1925 he left active service to work for a civilian shipbuilding organisation in which he made many business contacts. The outbreak of the military revolt found him in Madrid acting as an assessor for a naval constructors' examination, but he escaped to Lisbon where he acted as a liaison and intelligence-gatherer for his brother. Later he played, as we have seen, an important role in his brother's rise to Head of State, and that he played a key role thereafter is evidenced by the importance attached to him by the German and Italian representatives. His first wish was to strengthen the regime by building a political party based on personal loyalty to his brother. For this purpose he sounded out in the latter months of 1936 a number of Right-wing, and particularly CEDA politicians, but he seems to have limited success. The image his brother wished the regime to project combined social justice with 'making the trains run on time'. He had promised that 'confidence and creation of national wealth in a strongly organised state will permit us to make a substantial improvement in the workers' conditions of life'.[11] The conservatives and clericals, whom alone Nicolás could interest in a Franquista party, would take too unbendingly reactionary a line to accord with the Caudillo's aspirations.

The parties whose tone was most attuned to the Spain which Franco wanted were also those in Nationalist Spain which posed the greatest threat to him inasmuch as they had the greatest independent strength. These were the Traditionalist Communion and the Falange. The latter maintained the aims and traditions we have

[9] *Boletín Oficial del Estado* (Burgos), 6 October 1936.
[10] The Corps has Army ranks, like the Italian Genio Navale.
[11] *Cruzada*, Vol. III, p. 70.

referred to above, but had grown vastly as its ranks were joined by middle-class people looking for direct action in defence of Spain and by working-class people seeking to expiate their 'red' past, real or suspected. The Traditionalists, or Carlists, strongest in Navarre and Alava, were strongly Catholic and were anti-liberal. Their anti-liberalism stemmed from the eighteen-thirties when their movement was formed to prosecute the claim of the absolutist Don Carlos to the throne, but it had been theoretically updated to resemble clerical corporatism. They remained committed to the re-establishment of the 'traditional monarchy', and in December set up a Royal Military Academy to train their own officers. This alarmed Franco, who had not been consulted, and he summarily exiled the Carlist leader Fal Conde for what he chose to regard as a plot against himself.

The danger that loomed for Franco was the possibility of any element in Nationalist Spain escaping from the control of the Army. The Army itself was in a minority among the adherents of the rising, and if the mass parties, Falange and Carlist, could evolve their own leadership, they could present the Generalissimo with a serious challenge. Fortunately the Falange lacked a formidable leader; José Antonio had been shot by the Republicans in November, and his successor, Manuel Hedilla, despite the attempts of the German Ambassador to build him up, had neither the same formal powers nor the same moral authority. The Carlists, on the other hand, had several skilful leaders but were without the Falange's breadth of appeal. And, although the Falange had largely lost the strain of anticlericalism that had run through it originally, there remained a considerable gulf in temperament between the two movements. This appeared in unofficial talks held between Falangists and Carlists in February, when the growing rumours that a ministry was soon to be named in Nationalist Spain made politicians conscious of their lack of political leverage and of the need for alliances. The weaker they felt their own position to be, the greater was their enthusiasm for a single party. On 8 March 1937, the Alfonsine Monarchist party, which had virtually no mass organisation at all, dissolved itself altogether, and called for a patriotic front.

On 20 February another most important advocate of the unification of parties had arrived in Salamanca. He had just escaped from the Republican zone, and he was at once invited to stay in the Generalissimo's residence. He was Ramón Serrano Súñer, former leader of the CEDA youth movement, Deputy for Zaragoza, a friend of José Antonio, and one of the liaisons between Franco and the conspirators during the summer of 1936. He had all the advantages of close relations with the Generalissimo that Nicolás Franco had, and while Isabel Pascual del Pobil, Nicolás' wife, had apparently fallen out with Carmen Polo de Franco, Zita Polo de Serrano was her beloved younger sister. In addition, Serrano had the advantage over Nicolás in political talent, so he quickly took over as the most powerful civilian in Salamanca. He admired Fascist Italy, where he had studied law, and hoped to set up in Nationalist Spain a similar state, one which would have a real juridical structure, which would not depend solely on the person of one man. For this purpose a state party was required, and this could only be the Falange, since the Carlists suffered from 'a certain lack of modernity'.[12] The Falange would have, however, to absorb the Carlists, and neutralise the more sincere revolutionaries among its membership. Serrano found allies in a number of Falangists who were estranged from the current leadership, and persuaded Franco of the desirability of a unification, but did not plan any details about its execution.

Then on 12 April Franco told the Carlist Conde de Rodezno that a decree would soon be signed unifying the Carlists and the Falange. This precipitated events. Rodezno was clear that Franco would write his own terms and discouraged Carlists from trying to bargain. (The Count was already regarded as a renegade by true Carlists.) But the news of the impending decree seems to have galvanised the Falangist leader, Hedilla, into action. On 15 April he issued a summons for the National Council to meet on the 25th to elect a leader with full powers. Then the following morning a makeshift meeting of the Falange command purported to dismiss him, on the initiative of Sancho Dávila, who was bitterly hostile to Hedilla and not unsympathetic to a unification with the Carlists under Franco. That night, as Hedilla attempted to regain control by force, there was shooting and bloodshed in Salamanca, and the Army and Civil Guard intervened to arrest participants on both

[12] Ramón Serrano Súñer: *Enytre Hendaya y Gibraltar* (Madrid 1947), p. 32.

sides. Meanwhile, Hedilla had brought forward the date of the National Council meeting to the 18th. When this met he was elected to the vacant place of José Antonio, but it was now too late for the Falange to consolidate its strength.

Franco had remained closely in touch with the internal battles of the past few days, complimenting both sides on their actions, and now he decided to take the opportunity which presented itself. On the evening of 18 April[13] he broadcast an appeal for unification, not just 'a conglomeration of forces, not governmental coalitions, not more or less patriotic sacred unions, but an unification inward as well as outward'.[14] The following night, after consultation with Mola and Queipo de Llano, the Decree of Unification was published. The Falange and the Traditionalist Communion were amalgamated into a new organisation, the *Falange Española Tradicionalista y de las JONS*, with Franco as head both of the party and of its combined militia forces.

The decree was intended to subordinate politics to winning the war, and this found a ready echo among the men actually fighting, even when they were nominally party members of the Falange. Army commanders at the local level took the opportunity immediately after the Decree to annex the Falange to their sphere of command. Hedilla and his colleagues did not regard this as justified by the terms of the Unification Decree, which for want of norms for its implementation they regarded as not much more than a statement of intent. They quite openly telegraphed their subordinates at local level that the old command structure was to be respected ad interim, and hoped that Franco would leave the party substantially untouched. When the new Political Committee was announced Hedilla found that only one other prominent Falangist was included;[15] of the other eight members four were Carlists,

[13] Francisco Franco: *Palabras del Caudillo, 19 de abril 1937-7 de diciembre 1942* (Madrid 1943) p. 10. For the date, see H. R. Southworth *Antifalange* (Paris, 1967), p. 210.

[14] The words 'more or less patriotic or sacred unions' are a reference to the Unión Patriótica, which was General Primo de Rivera's lifeless political creation, and to the 'union sacrée' which French political parties formed to fight the war in 1914.

[15] That was Joaquín Miranda who was considered to have sold his soul to Queipo de Llano.

two were Army officers and the other two, while members of the Falange, were hardly prominent in it. On these grounds he refused the office of Secretary offered him and so spoiled the appearance of continuity with which Franco had hoped to appease those who really believed in the Falange.

Hedilla was imprisoned, and at his trial all that he had done to preserve the identity of the Falange was offered as evidence of high treason. He was sentenced to death, and Franco, who rather regretted having left Fal Conde alive after the 'Royal' Academy affair, would have confirmed the sentence had Serrano not pointed out how adversely this would affect relations with other Falangists. The commutation of Hedilla's sentence is symbolic of the fate of the Falange; it continued to have life of its own, but it owed it to the mercy of Franco, to the fact that he found it useful.

Meanwhile the military situation had been developing less satisfactorily than the political one. Nationalist troops tried for a little over a fortnight in November 1936 to take Madrid by direct assault, but, having crossed the river Manzanares and established a bridgehead in the university quarter of the city, they were unable to make any further progress. Franco denied that he would rather destroy the capital than leave it to the Reds, but the failure of the bombing of civilians to bring about the surrender in the Rif war ten years earlier had not wholly persuaded him of its uselessness, and Madrid became the first European city to suffer prolonged and heavy air raids. On 23 November a high-level meeting of generals took place under his chairmanship at Leganés, and it was decided to launch one more assault on the 25th, and if that failed, to abandon direct attack for the time being. Franco did not yet abandon his strategy, for he told the German Ambassador a week after the Leganés meeting that 'I will take Madrid, then all of Spain, including Catalonia, will fall into my hands more or less without a fight.'[16] But he decided that it would be necessary first to improve his lines of communication to the vital front.

The best way of implementing this new policy seemed to be to secure the main Corunna road, from the Guadarrama pass to the University City in the north-west of Madrid, where a short length

[16] DGFP, Series D, Vol. III, No. 148.

of the road was in Nationalist hands. To this end an attack was launched on 14 December, but after a sharp encounter with International Brigades at the village of Boadilla del Monte, the advance was called off, gaining no more than five miles. A further attempt was made just after the new year and on this occasion the Nationalists reached the coveted road but did not succeed in linking the University salient with Guadarrama. After twelve days of heavy fighting this offensive like its predecessor ran out of steam. The likelihood of Franco's breaking the stalemate appeared more and more remote. Worse still, his German and Italian allies seemed to be in ignorance of the extent of his needs. They were preparing to carry out their agreement with the other powers not to intervene any further in Spain. So desperately did Franco fear this that on 26 January he declared himself willing even to employ a joint German–Italian general staff in return for deliveries of material.

Fortunately the desire of his allies to extricate themselves from Spain was a transient one, and he was not taken up on the offer. Mussolini's mood was transformed by the Nationalists' Málaga offensive which reached its successful conclusion on 8 February. This important sea-port was the largest city to fall into Nationalist hands since the previous July, and all the world gave Italy the main credit for the victory. Mussolini's appetite for victories was whetted, and it would not be long before his troops were committed to the vital central front.

The emphasis in that theatre had shifted from the west to the east of Madrid. Instead of improving their own communications, the Nationalists intended now to cut off the Republicans from Valencia and Barcelona. The first offensive with this purpose was launched on 6 February before the Málaga campaign was over in the Jarama valley just north of Aranjuez and had as its target Arganda on the main road to Valencia. The Nationalists crossed the river and made about thirteen miles, but their advance was as keenly contested as in the Corunna road battle, and by the end of February they had lost up to 20,000 men without reaching Arganda or looking like doing so. Early March saw a new plan drawn up. One Nationalist force would advance southwards from the Sigüenza area aiming primarily at Guadalajara and secondarily at Alcalá de Henares, while another would renew the offensive on the

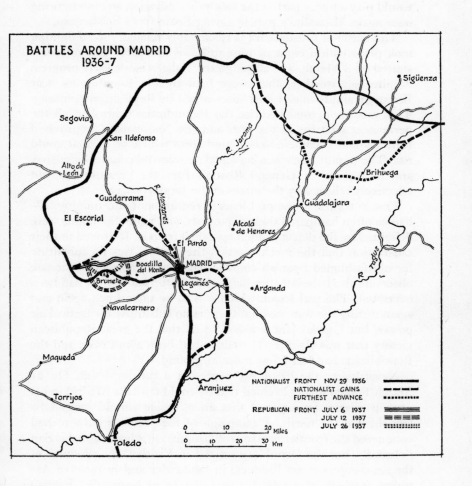

BATTLES AROUND MADRID
1936-7

Sigüenza

Segovia

San Ildefonso

R. Jarama

Alto de León

Brihuega

Guadarrama

R. Manzanes

Guadalajara

El Escorial

Alcalá de Henares

El Pardo

MADRID

Boadilla del Monte

R. Tajuña

Brunete

Leganés

Arganda

Navalcarnero

Maqueda

Torrijos

Aranjuez

NATIONALIST FRONT	NOV 29 1936	————
	NATIONALIST GAINS	————
	FURTHEST ADVANCE	....
REPUBLICAN FRONT	JULY 6 1937	≡≡≡
	JULY 12 1937	===
	JULY 26 1937	✕✕✕

0   10   20 Miles
0 10 20 30 Km

Toledo

Jarama front and hope to complete the encirclement of Madrid by meeting the main attack at Alcalá. An Italian motorised division would play a major part in the southward advance, so underscoring once again Mussolini's part in saving Spain from Bolshevism.

The battle of Guadalajara is remarkably named, for no fighting took place within eight or nine miles of that city. The offensive started on 8 March, and although the Italians made early progress despite bad weather, they were held by the Republicans near Brihuega, and then seriously discomfited by Republican bombing. This was unopposed because the Republicans controlled all the permanent airstrips in the area and the Nationalists' improvised runways had become a sea of mud from which no aircraft could rise. The Republicans then launched a successful counter-offensive, and to the Italian General Roatta's fury the pressure was not effectively relieved by the forces in the Jarama valley.

Franco turned to the problems of recruitment and training. Al-had so often hampered their opponents, and many Spaniards were delighted by the defeat of their so-called friends. It proved to their satisfaction that the mechanisation they lacked was no substitute for old-fashioned Spanish courage, and many more dispassionate observers also believed after battle that motorised warfare had been overrated. The real lesson which was to be underlined again and again during the war was that there is no substitute for tactical air power, but Guadalajara was not for all that the great Republican victory that was claimed. Casualties had been about even and the Republicans had lost a few miles of ground.

Nevertheless the battle did represent a turning-point. On 21 March Franco finally decided that he could not take Madrid in his present circumstances, and that an offensive should instead be launched in the north. A campaign of the previous autumn had conquered the frontier province of Guipúzcoa, whose capital is San Sebastián, but the Republic survived in Vizcaya, the province of the semi-autonomous Basques, in Santander and in most of Asturias. (Oviedo, the capital, was however in Nationalist hands.) This area contained much of the mineral wealth of Spain and most of the limited arms industry. Possession of these would give the Nationalists more independence of their foreign benefactors, and liquidation of the northern front would release forces for the central theatre. But meanwhile the recognition that the war was not yet nearing conclusion made it vital to take stock of the means to carry it on.

Franco turned to the problems of recruitment and training. Almost as much as on the Republican side, if less obviously, these had called for marvels of improvisation. Young men between 21 and 26 had already been mobilised, and some thousands of poverty-stricken Galician peasants had volunteered. Moroccan tribesmen had also come forward in large numbers with the encouragement of the native authorities. Quality was a greater problem than quantity. From the first officer training courses had been set up for educated young men, but there were never enough reinforcements. German assistance was provided on quite a large scale in the new year and this helped, but on 25 March a new office was set up to co-ordinate Mobilisation, Instruction and Recuperation. General Orgaz was placed in charge, and under his auspices most Spanish upper and middle class males born in the second decade of this century became 'temporary second lieutenants' in Franco's army. Their casualties were so disproportionately high that the saying went 'temporary second lieutenant, permanent corpse', but they were the backbone of the ultimately victorious Army, and it is possible that the foreign officers who helped train them made a more decisive intervention than any of the other 'armed tourists' in Spain's civil war.

Aid for Franco's cause was not forthcoming only from Germany and Italy, though they supplied the major part of his purely military equipment. Nationalist Spain continued to be involved in international trade with other countries. In December 1936 Britain signed an agreement with 'the insurgent authorities' without recognising even their *de facto* status as a government, by which trade would be legally resumed provided the Spaniards would import as much from Britain as they exported to her.[17] From the United States Franco received even commodities and articles that were embargoed, particularly oil from the Texas and Standard Oil Companies, and motor vehicles; Studebakers were favourites. These were in fact the most important imports of

[17] The text is in the Public Record Office. F. O. Series 371, Vol. 20519, W 17747/46/41.

Nationalist Spain after weapons, since food was not an immediate problem. The Nationalists controlled most of the principal grain-producing areas without having the largest cities to feed, so they could let the support price of wheat fall and stop importing phosphate fertilisers. Nevertheless, it was a shock when Johannes Bernhardt suggested that he might as well control all the Nationalists' foreign exchange, and the proposal was firmly rejected.[18]

A good deal of the Nationalists' needs were imported on credit for which some security had to be offered. But those lenders who had anything to lose in Spain were usually happy to spend money on Franco's cause, for if he were going to win his goodwill would be invaluable, and if he were not they expected in any case to be expropriated by the Communists. International business was also heartened to find that men like Juan March and Juan Ventosa had confidence in Franco. The former was a Majorcan multi-millionaire, a legend in his own time, after the style of Onassis but more of a politician; the latter was the leader of the Lliga, the party of Catalan businessmen attracted to regionalism by economic self-interest; both were active in the Nationalist interest.

Besides confidence, the Nationalists commanded a certain amount of money which they had been given, more or (sometimes) less voluntarily by individuals and commercial concerns. King Alfonso XIII was said by his aunt to have given two million pounds from his personal fortune.[19] J. & P. Coats were asked for £6,000 and feared reprisals on the Spanish directors of its subsidiary if the sum were not paid.[20] There was a great patriotic campaign for the conversion of foreign currency, foreign securities, and gold into paper pesetas, and in May 1937 the holding of foreign currency was made illegal. Foreign companies were obliged to retain the proceeds of their exports in Spain, receiving pesetas in return for hard currency. All those measures were parallel to those taken in 'red' Spain, but owing to lack of confidence and to lack of modera-

[18] D.G.F.P., Series D, Vol. III, No. 213.
[19] HRH Princess Eulalia to the London *Daily Express*, quoted Theo Aronson: *Royal Vendetta: The Crown of Spain 1829–1965* (Indianapolis 1966), p. 218.
[20] Index to the Foreign Office General Correspondence for 1936, Part IV, p. 146, in the Public Record Office, but the document to which it refers has apparently not been kept.

tion in the supply of money the value of their peseta fell far further on the free markets than that of Nationalist Spain's.

The support for which Franco looked abroad was not entirely financial. It was also extremely important to him that the world think well of his cause, both for the material importance of political support and for his patriotic *amour propre*. From the early days of the revolt Franco devoted a considerable amount of his valuable time to public relations. His first press interview was on 28 July 1936, and, even in those busy and anxious times, he was prepared to devote more than an hour to a journalist whose hostility must soon have become evident.[21] After his return from Italy Luis Bolín handled his press relations for some time, but once Franco became Head of State, more widespread propaganda services were organised culminating in the establishment in January 1937 of the Delegacy of Press and Propaganda. This was specifically directed 'to make known such news as may serve to counter the campaign of slander being carried on by "red" elements in the international field',[22] for the Nationalists never felt that they held the initiative in this matter, perhaps because they were, at least *prima facie*, rebels and therefore in the wrong.

An example of this tendency in the Nationalists' propaganda is to be found even in what became their most powerful and positive line of attack, the identification of their war effort with the defence of religion. This was not an aspect that was mentioned by Franco in his earliest speeches, and even when after a week or so he spoke of the war as a Crusade, this did not invest it with the clerical aura it later took on. (Eisenhower's memoirs of the Second World War are entitled 'Crusade in Europe' and he was scarcely a clerical.) But the fact was that the Republican *enragés* (or *exaltados* in Spanish) were particularly vicious to the property and personnel of the Catholic Church, that these people were in many cases transparently undeserving of their fate, and that many people who supported the insurgents for quite different reasons were infuriated particularly by the anticlerical outrages of their opponents.

In these circumstances Franco was assured of the support of the Church and he capitalised on it, being photographed as early as 15

[21] The interview was with Jay Allen and has been quoted above.
[22] *Boletín Oficial del Estado* (Burgos), 17 January 1937.

August 1936 with the Cardinal Archbishop of Seville at his side. He began to refer more and more frequently to God in speeches, to attend religious ceremonies and, encouraged by his wife, actually to become more religious. According to an anecdote which he has himself told more than once, his insistence on Mola's praying for new supplies of ammunition considerably irritated that worldly man, and it must have done so the more for seeming so out of character.[23] When he came to Salamanca he kept, besides a military and political staff, a small ecclesiastical household which did its best to persuade him of his providential role in Spanish history. Its most prominent member, the Jesuit Menéndez–Reigada, also wrote a pamphlet justifying the rising by the doctrine of the lesser evil.[24] But the Vatican was less straightforward in its encouragement.

The Pope hesitated to endorse the Nationalist war effort for the very reason that Franco was most anxious that he should. Not all the Catholics in Spain were on Franco's side; indeed, the deeply religious Basques were extremely hostile to him. Before and during the civil war the Basques had chosen alliance with the Left because of their desire for regional autonomy on the Catalan pattern, to which the Castilian Right were hostile but which the Popular Front was prepared to grant. This did not in any way imply enthusiasm for most of the left-wing programme. The politics of the Basque Nationalist Party were such as to win approval from British Conservatives like Anthony Eden. It was not therefore silly of the Holy See to hope that if Franco would guarantee them autonomy they would drop out of the war and save the Church the embarrassment of Catholics fighting one another.

It was all the same a vain hope, for Franco would make no political concessions. 'The Pope,' he told General von Faupel, 'was indeed recognised as the highest religious authority in Spain, but any interference by the Vatican in internal Spanish affairs had to be rejected'[25]—except of course a Papal condemnation of the

[23] Coles, op. cit., p. 48; Alejandro Vicuña: *Franco* (Santiago de Chile 1956), pp. 222–3.
[24] Ignacio González Menéndez-Reigada: *La guerra nacional española ante la moral y el derecho* (Salamanca 1937).
[25] DGFP, Series D, Vol. III, No. 264.

Basques. This Pius XI did not intend to give, partly because he deplored the action Franco was taking against Basque priests and partly because he was afraid that the Republicans might win. Consequently, Franco had to enter the Basque campaign without any more moral backing of the Vatican than a general exhortation to Catholics not to support Communism. Diplomatic recognition of Franco came finally shortly after the Basques had surrendered.

The northern campaign opened on 31 March with Mola in command. The plan was to make the main advance from the line between Villarreal and Mondragón over the mountains to Durango, whence a road, railway and river valley ran through Amorebieta to Bilbao, the financial and industrial centre of the region. The Nationalists had a heavy superiority in equipment, especially aircraft and artillery, with which they hoped to overcome the difficulties of terrain. The Basques were always waiting for aircraft reinforcements which never came, but even if they had, they would have been terribly vulnerable on the few short landing strips that existed in Basque territory. The Nationalists made full use of the clear skies to develop the techniques of air bombardment in preparation for infantry attacks. The German and Italian airmen not only bombed the trenches, they also bombed lines of communication, particularly with incendiary bombs which they regarded as both more destructive and more frightening than ordinary explosives.

It was in this context that on 26 April just as the Nationalists were breaking through on the northern part of the front that the German Condor Legion bombed the town of Guernica. An important centre of communications, standing at the head of a deep inlet, it was bombed for about three hours and almost destroyed. The bombardment certainly exceeded what was militarily justifiable except inasmuch as civilian morale is a factor in war, but the Nationalists were clearly unprepared for the international cry of horror that was raised. In the following days the Nationalist propaganda authorities issued a number of statements which demonstrated their own confusion. The central point of their story was that Guernica had been destroyed by the 'Reds' as Irún had been the previous summer, by petrol and dynamite. Few believed it. Germans in Spain admitted privately that bombardment had taken place, and attached no particular significance to the fact. After all, other towns had been bombed before on a smaller but comparable scale, Durango for instance on 31 March. Guernica was of course more important in what Franco would call the 'spiritual' sense, for there stood the oak tree symbolic of Basque liberty; but the tree itself was not destroyed. It is a tribute to the mystique of the

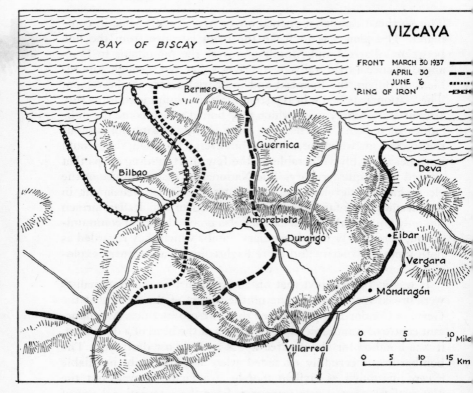

bomber at that time and to the power of propaganda that this raid, which had probably not had any special significance for those concerned in its planning, should have become the most famous episode of the Civil War. Franco, not being concerned with the details of the campaign, was very likely not even informed.

Painfully slowly the northern campaign continued. It was held up by bad weather and by unexpectedly tenacious resistance in places. Several days were lost as part of an Italian division had to be extricated from a trap which had been sprung for them at Bermeo. There was a change of command when Mola was killed in an air crash on 3 June.[26] But the outcome was never in doubt unless the Nationalist forces could be diverted by a Republican offensive.

On 31 May a force of International Brigades started to advance north from San Ildefonso towards Segovia, but were halted almost at once by Varela. Thereafter weeks passed in talk but without agreement as to the direction of an alternative offensive until, on 6 July, under the pressure of their Russian advisers, the Republic launched an attack to the south of El Escorial. Its aim was to cut Nationalist communications to the west of Madrid, securing the crossroads at Brunete and perhaps also at Navalcarnero. Despite the advantage of surprise little ground was gained before the Nationalists brought up reinforcements both of infantry and artillery. That this was possible within forty-eight hours of the attack was a tribute to Nationalist organisation, but it was also due in great part to the bad timing of the attack. The Nationalists were between campaigns. Bilbao fell on 19 June. The Vizcaya campaign had finished, while the next stage, the Santander campaign, had not started.

Brunete was a Republican failure, for it cost far heavier losses both in men and material to them than to the Nationalists without winning them any strategical advantage. Indeed, General Varela correctly divined a heavy fall in their morale, and was anxious to follow up with an assault on Madrid. Franco would not allow this. He did not have plans drawn up or forces disposed to that end, and he could not afford the effects on his prestige of a second failure to take Madrid. If the Russians had done so much to save the capital before they could and certainly would do so again, and their supplies seemed to be flooding into Republican territory as it was. The northern front must remain the first priority.

The Vizcaya campaign had been a source of displeasure to

[26] He was succeeded by General Dávila. Sabotage has been alleged without any evidence of it, but this is of course usual when important people have died in air crashes.

Franco. With the field command exercised by Mola, the campaign had developed with painful slowness and he had allowed long pauses for regrouping between each phase. After Mola's death Franco freely admitted that it was not difficult to replace him militarily, even though his political acumen might have come in useful. For the Santander campaign, the Generalissimo resolved to be nearer the front line, where he could watch it more closely. He moved his headquarters from Salamanca to Burgos. The province of Santander was occupied in less than a fortnight, the campaign marred only by the disagreeable circumstances of the Basque surrender.

The Basque forces had decided to collect at Santoña and give up the fight rather than continue the defence of the Republic from Asturias, and to this end they negotiated surrender with the Italian commander, from whom they correctly expected to obtain reasonable terms. Unfortunately the Italians had no authority to make the terms they did, which Franco countermanded and did not regard as binding. Basques who had surrendered on the understanding that their lives be spared were in many cases executed for rebellion. Franco for his part had Bastico, the offending Italian general, recalled, but the episode did nothing to expunge the memory of Guernica.

August and September brought a number of Republican offensives, most of them on Aragon front, but they followed the familiar pattern of making little ground at disproportionate cost. Fierce resistance on the mountainous borders of Asturias held up the Nationalists in the north for six weeks, but it could not turn the tide of the war. As was so frequently demonstrated, the Republicans were good at static defence, quite good at initial attack, but manœuvre was beyond them, either to maintain an orderly defence in retreat or to exploit a victory. Both sides lacked good officers at company level, and lacked them increasingly as the war went on, but the Nationalists were not prone to the lightning evaporations of morale that occurred in the Republican ranks. Once a Republican front was broken it caved in rapidly, and all was lost. From the breakthrough to the conclusion in Asturias took General Aranda a week, from 14 October to 21 October. On the latter day, Gijón fell, the war in the north was over, and with it a phase in the struggle in which the Nationalists continuously gained ground militarily and consequently also politically.

This was not without help from their allies. During the late summer of 1937 the Italian alliance was considerably more useful to Franco than was the Russian alliance to the Republic. Since Spain was not a great industrial power both sides depended for their supplies on imports from abroad. Most nations of the world were formally participants in the scheme of non-intervention in Spain, so there should theoretically have been very little fuel for the fires of war. Yet each party had friends who did not wish to see it lose, and were therefore prepared to circumvent the agreement.

The friends of the Nationalists were both more brazen and more powerful. The French government had closed the land frontier to arms traffic and had almost staunched the flow into Republican territory, whose only land frontier was with France. Supplies to the Republic by sea had to run the gauntlet of the Nationalist blockade. At the beginning of the war most of Spain's naval tonnage was in 'Red' hands, but the Nationalists had the advantage both of competent officers and of the discreet protective screening of German and Italian warships, and of course aircraft. When the extent of the Republic's equipment at Brunete suggested that the blockade was still not sufficient Franco sent his brother Nicolás to Rome to ask for more direct Italian assistance. This was granted. For six weeks Italian bombers and submarines attacked all shipping bound for 'Red' Spain, and a good deal that was not. It is not clear how much effect this actually had on the Republican war effort, but it seems to have pleased the Nationalists. The Spanish Ambassador in Rome felt that a few weeks more would have been decisive, but the Italians feared that British patience might finally be exhausted, and there was nothing they wanted less than a Mediterranean war.

The losers are often as much responsible for the course of a war as the victors, and perhaps the Republicans contributed as much as anybody to the Nationalists' successes in the summer and autumn of 1937. At the time when the Unification Decree was formalising cohesion and dedication to the war effort in Franco's Spain, the uneasy alliance of anti-fascists on the other side was coming close to dissolution. This weakening was largely caused by suspicions against the two parties most effective in the defence of the Republic, the Basque Nationalists and the Communists. The Basques were suspected of putting out feelers for a separate peace, and the Republican Government was therefore not as determined to send them aid as it might otherwise have been. The suspicion was in fact without foundation until the end of the Santander campaign.

The mistrust of the communists was much better founded. The Spanish Communist Party had been very small at the time of the February elections of 1936, but their size and influence had grown steadily thereafter. What they lacked in numbers they made up for in political skill. They were probably also helped by the tendency of the ill-informed (the Right, foreign diplomats and the like) to give all proletarian parties the portmanteau title of Communists. In April 1936 they had made what one might call a reverse take-over of the Socialist Youth, and they dominated the PSUC (United Socialist Party in Catalonia) from its formation at the beginning of the war. We have already seen how great a role they played in the defence of Madrid. Their Leninist lack of preoccupation with long-term objectives and concentration on the task at hand, in this case winning the war, meant that they came to represent the Right wing of the Republican coalition and won much support from apolitical moderates. They did not hesitate to use their reputation for common sense to entrench themselves in every department of government. In case of argument they played the trump card of their special relationship with the Republic's staunchest friend, the Soviet Union. Resistance to them could therefore all too easily be represented as unpatriotic, which in the short term perhaps it was, but their widening grasp made enemies, particularly of the Anarchists and of course the Trotskyite POUM.[27]

Finally, inter-party fighting flared up in Barcelona during the first week of May, a disturbance so helpful to the Nationalists at the height of their campaign in Vizcaya that Franco hastened to take the credit for it on behalf of his espionage agents. In mid-May the Communists forced Largo Caballero to resign the premiership to make way for Juan Negrín, whom they thought to be pliable. In June they arranged for the dissolution and destruc-

[27] Partido Obrero de Unificación Marxista (United Marxist Workers' Party).

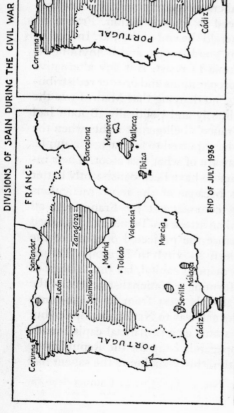

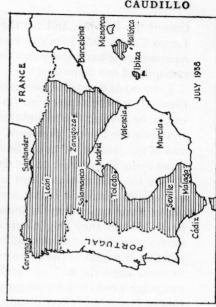

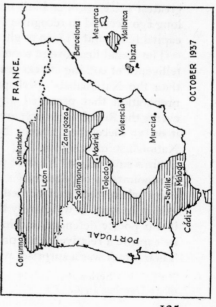

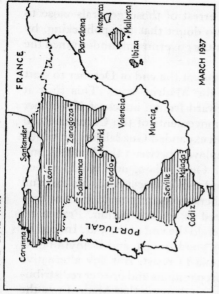

DIVISIONS OF SPAIN DURING THE CIVIL WAR

MARCH 1937

JULY 1938

END OF JULY 1936

OCTOBER 1937

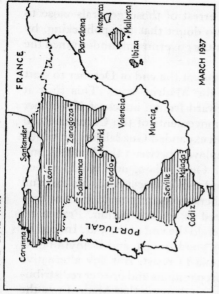

FRANCE

Santander
Corunna
León
Zaragoza
Salamanca
Madrid
Toledo
Valencia
Murcia
Seville
Málaga
Cádiz
Barcelona
Menorca
Mallorca
Ibiza
PORTUGAL

tion of the POUM, and for the arrest of those generals close to Largo Caballero. There can be no doubt that this politicking, by narrowing the basis of support for the government, undermined the strength of the Republic.

Franco felt himself strong enough at the end of October to start planning another campaign on the Madrid front. This time it would be neither the straightforward frontal attack of November 1936 nor the limited positional movements of the Corunna Road and of the Jarama. It would be an expanded Guadalajara, in which three army corps were to be deployed between the Henares and Tagus rivers north and east of Guadalajara, and would sweep through to Alcalá de Henares and the Valencia road, making full use of their superiority in numbers and equipment. Having isolated Madrid they might proceed to its occupation. Franco no longer believed that this would herald the end of the war. Indeed he felt that it would tie down many good troops, and if anything he overestimated the will of Catalonia to resist. But any alternative campaign would require longer preparations and greater redistribution of forces, and there could be no denying that Madrid was the greatest prize on offer both militarily and politically. Britain had long ago decided to recognise Franco's belligerent rights when the capital fell,[28] and France might be expected to follow her example.

The Republicans were soon aware of what was afoot. Their intelligence of coming attacks seems to have been consistently better than the Nationalists', perhaps because of the more meticulous preparation that preceded any commitment by Franco. At all events the Republicans prepared an attack on Teruel and launched it on 15 December, a week before the projected opening of the Nationalist offensive it had been so vital to forestall. Teruel, Spain's smallest and bleakest provincial capital, lay in the heart of the mountains of Maestrazgo, forming a Nationalist salient at the point where the front turned sharply west from its north-south axis in Aragon. It was hardly the gateway to Nationalist Spain, but it was poorly defended and its status as a provincial capital made its capture a relatively easy propaganda coup for the Republicans. Their attack was a surprise; within thirty-six hours the salient had

[28] PRO FO Series 371, Vol. 20544, No. W 14173/62/41 Cabinet decision of 21 October 1936.

been pinched off, and it remained only to reduce the moderate forces trapped within.

The Germans and Italians hoped that Franco would admit that Teruel was of no consequence, and refusing to let the Republicans choose their ground, proceed with his own planned offensive. They hoped in vain. Ciano, the Italian Foreign Minister, wrote in his diary on 20 December: 'The news from Spain is not good. The Guadalajara offensive is put off indefinitely because of the spiritual vacillations of Franco's commanders and the preventive offensive of the Reds at Teruel ... Franco has no idea of synthesis in war. His operations are those of a magnificent battalion commander. His objective is always ground, never the enemy'.[29] The army corps under Aranda and Varela which had been earmarked for the Guadalajara campaign were transferred to Teruel, and on 29 December the counter-attack began in earnest. Franco had subordinated technical military considerations to those of prestige. He had taken Teruel at the Republicans' valuation, and decided that he must deny them any victory, however inconclusive, lest their morale be raised. This presupposes a serious lack of confidence in his own forthcoming offensive, which is so difficult to explain that it is impossible not to sympathise with Ciano's remarks.

With the decision to meet the Republican challenge at Teruel Franco renounced the possibility of victory by the knockout blow and settled for a war of attrition. He bargained that he could maintain the higher level of armament and morale and so eventually win through the exhaustion of his enemies. He relied on Germany and Italy continuing to supply him more consistently than the Soviet Union supplied the Republic, yet this involved a political risk at least as great as many military risks he had refused to take, for the Germans were becoming disillusioned with him. 'The expectation ... that within a few months Franco would succeed by means of a large-scale offensive in bringing the war to a close, was unjustified', sighed the German Foreign Office on 28 January.[30] About the same time they decided that Germany's interests were satisfied so long as the Republic did not win, that a Franco victory was by no

[29] *Ciano's Diary 1937–1938*, tr. Andreas Mayor (London, 1952), p. 46.
[30] DGFP, Series D, Vol. III, No. 511.

means vital. While it is impossible to be sure, it seems likely that Franco's commitment at Teruel served to increase the bloodshed and prolong the war.

The battle of Teruel was particularly long and bloody. It was nearly the end of February when the Nationalists cleared out the last Republicans from the town, but the attrition policy did at least seem to work. The Nationalists followed up with an offensive on the Aragon front as early as 9 March. They were devastatingly effective, superior as they were in every kind of material and especially in aircraft. By the end of the month they had occupied the plain of Aragon up to the borders of Catalonia. In the succeeding three weeks their rapid progress was maintained. In the north they took the rest of Aragon as far as the French border and almost as far as Andorra, excepting only a small area in the Pyrenees. In the centre they took Lérida, their first major town in Catalonia. In the south they pressed eastwards to the sea. General Alonso Vega reached the seaport of Vinaroz on the Mediterranean on 15 April, Good Friday, cutting Republican Spain in two. In the next four days the Nationalists stabilised a front on the south bank of the Ebro. Meanwhile the Republic suffered a dangerous bout of defeatism, but its friends came to its aid. On 16 March France reopened the frontier and Russian equipment flooded in. In the course of the next month resistance became tougher and tougher. The Nationalists had made a great deal of ground that spring, but the cheering promise of victory proved to be delusive: they were hardly nearer the end of the war than before.

It was the realisation that the Republic was again gathering strength that caused Franco in mid-April to decide once more to avoid the obvious strategy. He did not attempt to advance into Catalonia towards Barcelona, which had been since October 1937 the seat of Republican government. He thought that the resistance would be too strong, and that, with the French frontier open, the enemy could in any event be reinforced more efficiently than he could. Accordingly he decided to push south towards Valencia, reckoning that the greater the wedge he could drive between the halves of Republican Spain, the weaker each of the halves would become. With good luck a great part of south-eastern Spain might drop into his lap. Besides, this was an operation he could mount immediately, for he already had Varela with a fresh Army corps in the Teruel area, whence he could strike south-eastwards through the southern Maestrazgo towards Valencia. Aranda and García Valiño would also push southwards nearer the sea. The operation began on 23 April, and Varela met with some initial success, but heavy rain then held him up, and from that moment on the whole campaign became slow, hard going.

Franco's decision was not vindicated by success, and the failure to make an immediate breakthrough probably doomed the campaign. The area had irregular terrain, few roads and inadequate maps, and Republican morale rose as that of the Nationalists declined. The Nationalist infantry, even the crack divisions, had lost their élan. The battalion commanders who had contributed so much in the earlier stages were now in command of brigades and divisions. Their replacements were not of the same calibre. The troops were weary with long months of fighting over difficult terrain, and the thwarted hope of an end to the war had lowered their morale further. Those who dared whispered that Franco's lack of imagination was responsible, that he should have invaded Catalonia. Others whispered—and the Germans prophesied—that a compromise peace would result.

While Franco's armies continued to battle against the Republican front in the Levante the Republic was mustering its forces for another major counter-offensive. On 25 July this was launched across the Ebro north of Tortosa where that great river bent eastwards to form a salient in the Nationalist line. It achieved a large measure of surprise and immediate success. For a while Franco seems not to have grasped the strength of the enemy, not to have believed that at the same time as contesting his every step towards Valencia the Republic had been able to mount so strong an attack. Fortunately the Republicans followed their usual pattern of failing to capitalise on their early success and by the early days of August they were doggedly resisting Nationalist counter-attacks.

The Ebro became a bigger and bloodier version of Teruel, fought in torrid instead of freezing conditions. Every small Nationalist advance was preceded by a massive bombardment by artillery and from the air. The Nationalists were prodigal of their ammunition, but resistance continued, and it took them until 16

November to regain what they had lost in a couple of days. Franco had in the latter stages moved his headquarters close to the front lines, waving aside the subordinates' protests at the danger to his life and demanding that they be bolder in their attacks. This is an indication that many of the criticisms of his plodding methods could be more fairly directed at subordinate commanders. Besides, his troops now lacked all zest. They were worn out and even their supplies of ammunition were running short. The only comfort was that, thanks to Nationalist superiority in aircraft and artillery, the Republicans were in even worse case.

A few days after the end of the battle of the Ebro, Franco paid the price for yet another re-equipment of his Army so that he might launch the campaign in Catalonia he had refused the previous spring. The Germans' principal object in helping Franco was by this time to secure the right to Spanish strategic minerals, in particular iron ore, and it was essential for them actually to own the mines, for they had not the foreign currency to compete on the open market with Britain and France. It was their intention to buy mineral rights with arms supplies, and from early in 1937 Bernhardt had been looking for suitable concessions. Throughout 1937 and most of 1938 Franco had managed to hold out against any firm commitment to make over Spanish mineral rights. He was as hostile to German economic colonialism as he was to any other, and he regarded the extent of foreign investment in Spain as excessive already.

After the battle of the Ebro he could however hold out no longer. On 19 November his government agreed to allow the Germans complete freedom to acquire mines in Spanish Morocco and a special right to acquire a majority interest in a handful of concessions in the peninsula. In return for this Germany would give him the wherewithal to win the war, for Hitler seems to have felt after Munich that nothing he might do in Spain would lead to any complication with the democracies. Conversely, Stalin had decided that collective security was an unattainable ideal and that no further sacrifices on Spain's behalf would be worthwhile.

The campaign in Catalonia began, after two postponements, two days before Christmas. It was completely one-sided. The Republicans were without equipment and largely without enthusiasm. They were suffering from a serious food shortage, which the Nationalists brought home to their civilian population by dropping loaves of bread from aeroplanes. Tarragona fell on 14 January, Barcelona on the 26th. A diversionary offensive in the province of Córdoba, which began on 4 January, was contained. Instead of putting up the desperate resistance which had been expected of them in 1938, the Catalans fled in their tens of thousands into France. Franco let them go, preventing the Germans from attacking them from the air. Victory was now at hand so there was no purpose in terrorism. The last Republican forces in Catalonia withdrew into France on 10 February, and Franco began to prepare the final campaign against the south-eastern third of Spain which remained in Republican hands. He continued to demand what was in effect unconditional surrender, but more and more Republicans wished to end the war at any price.

On 8 March an armed uprising took place against Negrín and the Communists who wished to pursue the war *à l'outrance*, and after some days of fighting it triumphed. Its leader, Colonel Casado, believed that an anti-communist professional officer would be able to win better terms than would be available to the Communists. He was, however, proved wrong, and when Franco promised over the radio on 26 March that 'all who are not criminals and have been deceived into fighting' would be pardoned, the Republican armies just melted away, and went home. On 31 March Franco heard that his armies had achieved their final objectives. He received the news with the Olympian calm that befitted his station, thanking the messenger, it is said, without even looking up from his desk.[31] Perhaps he was more concerned with the cold with which he was at the time afflicted.

[31] José Díaz de Villegas: *La Guerra de Liberación* (Barcelona 1957), p. 384.

6 The New Spain

In the closing stages of the war the advancing Nationalists had been greeted with more and more extravagant rapture. There was little spirit in the Republican population once it became clear that resistance meant no more than a prolongation of the war, that their victory was only a remote possibility. The Nationalists brought with them much-needed food, but, most important, they brought the peace which the people now desired at any price. Franco's patience had been repaid. He had always regarded complete victory as essential, and he had made as many sacrifices as were required to attain it. Now it was his, but Spain had had to pay for her salvation from the chaos of the Popular Front. A 'new Spain' was to arise from the ashes of the Civil War. Would it be a phoenix or merely a pale ghost?

The economic situation of Nationalist Spain had been reasonably good *vis-à-vis* Republican Spain, but at the end of the war the economy of the country overall was in a very poor state. In the battle areas there was direct devastation, and virtually all the 173 localities scheduled for the purposes of state aid in reconstruction as 75 per cent destroyed had either been for a long period on the front line or the site of a major battle.[1] Most of them were very small villages, though the list included some larger towns whose claim to be three-quarters destroyed must have been debatable. Progress in reconstruction was very slow. This was in part because

[1] *La Reconstrucción de España. Resumen de 2 años de labor* (Madrid 1942).

132

of technical difficulties like Spain's low capacity for cement manu-facturing, and in part because only a few showpiece projects received a high priority.

Perhaps this was right, for dwelling houses and public buildings suffered far more than Spain's vital industrial installations. Most of these remained intact, having fallen into Nationalist hands either initially or in one of the great breakthroughs. Air-raid damage was, with a few spectacular exceptions, notable for its lightness, especi-ally in comparison with subsequent experience in Europe and Japan. It was striking in 1937 how quickly the mining and metallur-gical industries of the North achieved pre-war production figures after their capture by Nationalists. Only in the Levante was serious damage done, to the orange trees and their irrigation system, but even this did not greatly impair production. During the Second World War fruit production did not fall much below 80 per cent of pre-1936 levels,[2] and some of the fall can be accounted for by demand factors. All in all it was not in actual destruction of fixed installations that Spain suffered most, but in barriers to the full utilisation of her productive capacity.

Even without war geographical factors make it difficult for Spain to develop her resources. She is a large country: of European countries only Russia and France are larger.[3] Moreover, her many mountains create obstacles to communications, while, apart from Madrid, the main centres of population and of production are on the coasts, and at a great distance one from another. The needs of internal distribution therefore make a heavy demand on her rail-ways and coastal shipping. Both suffered losses during the war, and lacked spare capacity to absorb them, for the pre-war period had seen a low level of capital investment in Spain. Spain lost about 10 per cent of her shipping altogether.[4] The figure appeared to be far worse at first, but during the summer of 1939 many ships, transferred to other flags during the war, re-registered in Spain.

[2] See Statistical table in H. París Eguilaz: *Diez años de Política económica en España 1939–1949* (Madrid 1949), p. 44.
[3] Between 1938 and 1945 Germany was also larger, thanks to the Anschluss with Austria.
[4] *Lloyd's Register Book*, July 1936, quoted in *Whitaker's Almanack 1937*, p. 687. *Frankfurter Zeitung*, 12 January 1940.

The railways suffered more severely: their war losses in rolling stock were reported in 1942 as 34·5 per cent as of locomotives, 60·2 per cent of passenger coaches and 39·7 per cent of wagons.[5] This apart, the track was everywhere in poor repair and sometimes destroyed. Speeds fell and coal consumption rose; the efficiency of the railways declined and their costs increased, while neither ships nor roads could offer a viable alternative.

Transportation was hampered at a moment when the swift distribution of goods was particularly desirable. The division of Spain into two, and the dislocation caused by the war even within each zone, had considerably distorted the economic situation in the country. Spain had lost as much by the diversion of her efforts into war as she had by the destructiveness of the war itself. She was economically exhausted, her stocks run down. While in normal times, most concerns keep, with or without official insistence, stockpiles in goods to tide over shortages in production or delays in delivery, the conditions of the war militated against this. Both Franco and the Republic established priorities for imports, and of course armament and allied strategic goods came first. Catalonia, for instance, was to a large extent starved of raw cotton for her textile industry, and was able to maintain sufficient production for the Republican zone only by running down stocks. By 1939 the mills were in no position to meet the heavy demand that the Nationalist zone, with only a minuscule textile industry, made for clothes.

A similar exhaustion of stocks had occurred in most consumer goods, but it was most serious in the case of food. Livestock had been so recklessly slaughtered for meat that in 1949 there were still fewer livestock than there had been in 1936. In both zones of Spain, a good deal of land went out of cultivation. This was due in part to the enlistment of peasants in one or other Army, or the flight of some country people from the Nationalists to the large cities, where they caused a serious refugee problem. It was also due in part to the serious fall in the use of fertilisers. Phosphates are rare in Spain, and, since they have a high ratio of weight to value, particularly in comparison with munitions, neither side was keen to

[5] U.K. Naval Intelligence Division: *Spain and Portugal*, Vol. III, p. 475 (hereafter cited as UKNID).

import them. So land, which might have previously given an annual crop or a crop two years in three, now needed an extra fallow year in the cycle. Even in Nationalist Spain, the National Wheat Service, set up by Franco in 1937, did not manage, despite its wide powers, to prevent a fall in production, though it ensured that there was always plenty to eat in its own zone. Only after the end of the war was rationing imposed.

Spain had also suffered enormous human losses, 'a million dead' according to the set phrase. This figure is recognised today as an exaggeration, but it was perpetuated because it enabled both sides to boast of the price Spain had paid. The Right used it to enhance the value of Spain's sacrifice to save Europe from communism. The Left used it to point up the bloodstained criminality of the victors. How many people actually died as a result of the war will never be determined at all accurately, for the combatants lacked the clerical organisation to keep full records, a task that would in any case have been intolerably complicated by the semi-private nature of recruiting. So estimates of overall numbers vary widely. The evidence available favours an estimate of some 70,000 Nationalist deaths with a figure roughly equal on the other side, a total of about 140,000, of whom probably 20,000 or more were not Spanish.[6]

Spain suffered even more from the mass emigration which followed the fall of Catalonia. About half a million people fled into France. Some of these moved on to Latin America, a few to England; a good many stayed in France. Perhaps as many as 250,000 returned to Spain, either because they had fled in groundless panic, or because after the outbreak of the Second World War they were prepared to risk Franco's justice sooner that conscription into the French Army. But 250,000 émigrés were lost to Spain for ever, they and their children.

Then there were civilian deaths, or deaths away from the battle line but attributable to the war. There were those killed in air raids (10,000 would be a generous figure), those shot as fascists, those shot as Communists, those shot for neither of these reasons but for

[6] For other estimates see Payne: *Politics and the Military*, pp. 458–61, Thomas, op. cit., pp. 631–3: Gabriel Jackson: *The Spanish Republic and the Civil War, 1931–1939*, pp. 526–40.

others which seemed cogent at the time. The Nationalists, having started with an estimate four or five times as high, now claim that 85,940 people died violently behind the Republican lines. There is reason, however, to suppose that this is still four times the figure which would be just. The Nationalists certainly shot more people than their opponents, if only because they had many more identifiable enemies. Yet we may agree with Professor Thomas that the figure is unlikely to have exceeded 40,000 during the war although many would regard that as a gross understatement. Of course the execution of Republicans did not end with the war. The Spanish Government has itself conceded a figure of 40,000 post-war executions, while in 1944 an official gave an American correspondent a figure off the record of 192,684 for the same period.[7] The former figure is certainly not too high, and the latter may not be an exaggeration, but it is probable that the civil war and its aftermath were responsible for a little over 200,000 violent deaths away from the battlefield.

The emigration and the civilian deaths were closely interconnected, for all those who fled did so because they were afraid of what the Nationalists might do to them. Some may themselves have had bloody deeds on their conscience, others may have been seized by blind panic and others again deceived by misleading propaganda, but the reputation of the Nationalists for wholesale butchery was well founded. The killings were characteristically different from those of the Republicans but they were just as real, and if they are less meticulously documented, that is only because the Republicans lost the war and therefore had fewer facilities for this morbid research. There is a tendency for the casual observer, if he refrains from excusing one hecatomb while condemning another, to duck the subject by attributing the killings to the unfathomable workings of the Spanish character. But to understand the course of events it is necessary to examine the nature and purpose of the carnage, and to form a judgement of Franco one must assess the nature of his responsibility for it.

From the very outset of the military conspiracy it had been

[7] Brian Crozier: Letter to *New Statesman*, published 26 January 1968; Charles Foltz: *The Masquerade in Spain* (Boston 1948), p. 97.

planned to use terror as a weapon. In Mola's preliminary instructions drawn up on 20 April 1936, he writes: 'It will be borne in mind that the action must be extremely violent in order to reduce the enemy, who is strong and well organised, as soon as possible. Of course all the leaders of political parties, associations or trade unions not joining the movement will be imprisoned and exemplary punishments meted out to strangle rebellious movements or strikes.'[8] It was regarded as absolutely natural that since the officers in the conspiracy were a tightly knit and determined few, facing large but initially inchoate forces, they could by a swift and savage blow at their opponents' leaders inhibit the growth of effective opposition. Assuming the rapid success of the coup this need not have cost more than a handful of lives.

But the success of the coup was not rapid, it was long drawn out, and the odds against the military were lengthened by the Left's improvised resistance. The importance of terror as a weapon grew greater and so did the scale necessary for its effectiveness. It was perhaps used the most in the areas where the rising was least secure, such as Granada, and Galicia. But everywhere Leftists were shot and hostages taken for the good behaviour of others still at large. And the terror was not concealed but broadcast, most notoriously by General Queipo de Llano, who boasted on Radio Seville of the rapes and murders the *Regulares* would commit on the 'marxist rabble'.

The effectiveness of this as a weapon was frequently demonstrated in the advance of Franco's forces towards Madrid. Frequently the fear of being cut off and so falling into the hands of the Legion and of the Moors led militiamen to abandon positions which were in fact still quite sound. Later, in the Basque campaign, the cry 'We are cut off' was enough to dislodge whole brigades from excellent defensive positions. Of course, the converse of this was that, when a Republican unit was cornered, it did not surrender, and even if it was disarmed, its continued hostility had to be allowed for.

With so few effectives available for any purpose there were

[8] Joaquín Pérez Madrigal: *Augurios, estallido y episodios de la Guerra Civil* (Avila, 3rd ed., 1936), p. 137.

certainly none for manning prison camps. Therefore men captured in arms were often shot. Where there were many prisoners, hundreds might be shot, as at Badajoz. 'What do you expect? ...' Yagüe asked a journalist. 'Was I supposed to turn them loose in my rear and let them make Badajoz red again?'[9] Even those who had not been obviously fighting might make a place 'red' again, so in village after village a more or less imposing example would be made of supporters of the Left. The military commanders could consult local landowners or bourgeois on the identity of such men, but their decision was often far from judicial and even the numbers condemned might depend on entirely personal factors. For instance the massacre of villagers at Palma del Rio in Córdoba province in August 1936 was in large part a private act of vengeance by a local landowner for the slaughter of his fighting bulls. The leading socialists of the village had escaped.[10]

It was perhaps difficult to prevent these acts of private vengeance and to curb the amused sadism of certain officers. Franco issued orders that no bodies were to be mutilated and that rape was to be a capital offence. But he did not discontinue the shootings, for he clearly considered them a military necessity. They were early clothed in the respectability of legal executions but the trials which preceded them were, even in their official designation, 'very summary'. And these orders from Franco's headquarters as to the treatment of prisoners were certainly not always carried out. Franco may perhaps have been unaware of the extent to which they were disregarded. When an SS intelligence officer, who was also special correspondent for the official Nazi press, protested that his harshness was stiffening Republican resistance, he replied: 'Why, this sort of thing can't be true—you have got the facts wrong, Captain Strunk.'[11]

Later, after the mass executions at Málaga in February 1937, he admitted to the Italian Ambassador that there were cases in which

[9] John T. Whitaker: 'Prelude to War: A Witness from Spain' in *Foreign Affairs* (New York), Vol. XXI, No. 1 (October 1942), p. 106.
[10] Larry Collins and Dominique Lapierre: *Or I'll dress you in Mourning* (London 1968), pp. 74–89.
[11] John T. Whittaker, loc. cit.

it was impossible to exercise control at the local level.[12] In fact he did not try particularly hard to do so. Certain officers might be a little over-zealous, but the rights of Reds were not so important to him that he felt it necessary to be meticulously inquisitive about their treatment.

He shared the general sense of outrage at the atrocities committed in Republican territory at the beginning of the Civil War. He knew that the respectable classes of any village were ordinarily shot as his armies approached it. He therefore regarded those active on the Republican side as *prima facie* murderers besides being evident traitors. His regime regarded itself as the legitimate power in all Spain from the moment when the rising took place. A man who had subsequently served the Republic was therefore a rebel against the constituted government and liable to punishment accordingly. It was a hard doctrine, and one often carried to its logical conclusion.

Yet, if Franco made harsh rules, he did make some effort to abide by them. He spent some of every day looking at death sentences, either confirming or commuting them, and deciding whether an execution was to be published in the press or not. A detailed examination of the merits of every case would, however, have taxed the entire legal profession. In a situation where the accused faced partisan judges, usually ignorant of the law, without any facilities for his defence, only the most glaring injustices can have come to light under the hurried scrutiny of Franco and his legal advisers. Quite apart from the illegal and spontaneous killings, there were doubtless many innocent men whose death sentences were confirmed and executed impeccably within the judicial framework of Franco's law. In their struggle to regain the rule of law, both contending governments claimed the exclusive right to confirm capital sentences in their territory, but, while the Republican government confirmed virtually no sentences, the rule of law in Franco's Spain exacted the death penalty over and over again.

When Franco constructed his first orthodox cabinet to succeed the State Technical Committee in January 1938, he created a special

[12] Roberto Cantalupo: *Fu la Spagna: Ambasciata presso Franco, Febbraio-Aprile 1937* (Verona 1948), p. 133.

ministry separate from the Ministry of the Interior to deal with 'public order'. His choice of minister confirmed the impression that an uncompromising policy would be pursued against political offenders. Lieutenant-General Martínez Anido's name for 'public order' had been made in Barcelona, where as Military (and later Civil) Governor, he had displayed violent hostility towards left-wing labour unions. He died at the end of 1938, and his ministry was merged again with the Interior under Serrano Súñer, but this foreshadowed no change in policy. Serrano had lost his two brothers in 1936, murdered in Republican prisons, and he was as strong a believer as any in the need to excise malignant tissue from the Spanish people.

The surgical metaphor is an apt one, for Franco and his supporters often thought of Spain's troubles in those terms. Spain had been attacked by a 'red' cancer of which she must be cured. And it was as infectious as it was malignant. Naturally, those with an open mind would perceive the superiority of Catholic and Spanish virtues over Communism, but once infected by Communism people closed their minds and would not listen to priests and good moral teachers. In order to restore Spain as a whole to moral health, the sources of infection would have to be isolated until they were ideologically sound; the incurables would have to be eliminated.

Of course many would be indictable for crimes under the ordinary law or at any rate under martial law, and could be punished accordingly. But even if they had not offended the letter of the law, their political views made them a danger to society as long as they held them. Franco was fighting for a Spain in which left-wing opinions would not be expressed, and ultimately would not exist. His feelings towards Communism were analogous to those of the Second World War Allies towards fascism. The Civil War would be the ideological war to end war only if the 'reds' surrendered unconditionally. If their ideas were allowed any chance of resurgence, the dead martyred for Spain would have died in vain. Franco did not believe the freedom of Spain from left-wing ideas to be a chimera, for he considered such ideas to be un-Spanish, wholly imported phenomena. He acknowledged the task of uprooting them to be a great one, but he attached to it the same importance that the Allies attached to denazification in Germany after 1945.

The Law of Political Responsibilities decreed on 9 February 1939 was far-reaching in its definition of political offences. In general, all those who contributed to the deterioration of Spain's political situation between 1934 and 1936, or who opposed the Nationalists thereafter, were guilty of an offence. All parties who had any part in the Government after February 1936 were black-listed, and all their members guilty of an offence, except rank-and-file trade union affiliates who had taken no active part whatever in politics. In addition, anybody was guilty who had given the slightest support to the Popular Front government, or who had looked on at the conflict from abroad as a neutral. All freemasons were guilty; and to have been of the eighteenth degree or higher was an aggravating circumstance. Signal services to the Nationalists subsequent to the offence might extenuate and, in extreme circumstances, expiate the crime. All punishments would include a fine which might be equivalent to confiscation of all goods and assets, and conviction by a court martial for opposition to the Movement was made another offence in itself, in order that fines might be levied on this category of offenders, or on their surviving relatives. A political offender might, in addition to a fine, be sentenced to a term of imprisonment not less than six months nor more than fifteen years, or he might be exiled to a remote area of Spain, or he might simply be disqualified from holding any form of public office, or any office in any firm dealing with any official or semi-official organisation.

Anybody engaged in commerce would of course be ruined by any of these punishments, and nobody could afford to laugh them off. But the preamble of the law made it clear that it did not, in Franco's view, err on the side of harshness. 'The international magnitude and the material consequences of the crimes perpetrated against Spain are such that they prevent punishment and reparation reaching any proportionate scale, since this would be repugnant to the deep feelings of our National Revolution, which wishes neither to punish cruelly, nor to bring misery into homes.'[13] At least the law did not prescribe a death penalty for the purely

[13] *Boletín Oficial del Estado,* 13 February 1939.

political offence. Only those accused under other laws could be shot.

But as a result of the Civil War there were well over half a million people less to share the burden of Spain's recovery,[14] and among those remaining there were thousands of mutilated soldiers and more thousands of prisoners lying unconstructively in gaol. In theory, prisoners had the option of earning remission for themselves by work. Franco took a personal interest in fostering this idea of 'redemption', under which a man was paid a wage which went to support his family, and received a day's remission of sentence for every day worked. The idea was that a man should be given the opportunity to see the folly of his past ways without losing his self-respect. A newspaper called *Redención* published the true confessions of prisoners who had renounced their former subversive doctrines. The Church was involved in the work at every level, but for all the good intentions with which the system had been instituted it did not much help the majority of prisoners. In 1941 the prison population was 233,373, but of those only eight per cent whose 'moral conduct' was satisfactory were redeeming themselves through work.[15] The fact was that, for all Spain's tragic losses of manpower, her social and economic state after the war was such that she could not absorb even what she had left.

This is not to say that all those in prison would have been unemployed outside it. Sadly for Spain, many skilled men had quite unacceptable political records. Admiral Canaris was alarmed to find in July 1939 that qualified engineers were being shot as 'reds'.[16] Education had come almost to a halt, so unreliable were schoolmasters as a class; there were sixty of them in a single prison in Barcelona.[17] Franco was not unaware of the problem. 'On the one hand,' he told a journalist, 'I have a lively interest in saving the life and redeeming the spirit of all Spaniards who may be capable ... of

[14] The population in 1930 had been 23½ million.
[15] *Anuario Estadístico de España*, 1943-4, p. 885, P. Martín; Torrent García: *¿Qué me dice usted de los presos? Contestaciones* (Alcalá de Henares, 1942), pp. 104–14.
[16] Robert H. Whealey: *German-Spanish Relations, January–August 1939* (Ph.D. Dissertation, University of Michigan, 1963), p. 262.
[17] Torrent, op. cit., p. 34.

adding their grain of sand to the common effort,' but on the other hand the protection of Spain from moral and political contagion was paramount.[18]

It was also important that those who had served Spain well should be rewarded. On 25 August 1939, it was decreed that eighty per cent of the posts in the lower échelons of the Civil Service should be reserved for those who had made sacrifices for the Nationalist cause, officers, disabled veterans, former prisoners in Republican gaols and relatives of those executed by the Republic. Another decree of the same day demanded that directors of all important companies be approved by the Government. Both decrees gave the regime opportunities, which it took, to pension off its supporters in relative sinecures. The net result was not to oil the wheels of the administrative machine at a time when its smooth running was of great importance.

From its inception the Nationalist State had suffered from administrative problems. If the Spanish civil service before the war had not been always a model of efficiency it did at least have a pattern of procedure, and a staff familiar with that pattern and concentrated in Madrid. The outbreak of war swept all this away. The Nationalists in particular had to construct a new bureaucratic machine out of such makeshift materials as were to hand. They did not lack competent administrators and negotiators. For example, Andrés Amado, the first Minister of Finance, had created the Government petrol monopoly under the Dictator. Demetrio Carceller and José Pan y Soraluce, who were used in economic negotiations, were in former times respectively Juan March's right hand and the Governor of the Bank of Spain.

Where the Nationalists were less strong was in the lower rungs. The clerks, who were masters of the routines, remained in Madrid, and so did all the records. This meant that until the Government moved back there at the end of the summer of 1939 many administrative decisions and some important political ones had to be deferred. In the cities of the Nationalist heartland there was insufficient space even for such civil service as Franco had, with the result that ministries and agencies were spread throughout North

[18] Interview with Manuel Aznar. Franco: *Palabras*, p. 97.

Central Spain to the detriment of efficient administration. The official seat of government was in Burgos but several ministries were situated in Salamanca, while the Ministry of Education was in Vitoria and Martínez Anido's Ministry of Public Order was in Valladolid. To add further to the confusion many of the foreign diplomats in contact with the Nationalists lived either in San Sebastián or across the frontier on the French Côte Basque.

This geographical dispersion gave rise to severe delays. The problem of convening an interdepartmental committee was almost insoluble, with the result that problems which could have been resolved by mutual discussion had simply to be referred to higher authority. Higher authority of course meant the Caudillo, and his headquarters was not organised for the rapid dispatch of civil problems. During the war he was frequently at a mobile head-quarters near the front called the 'Terminus', and since he busied himself primarily with military matters, decisions on civil problems were kept waiting. He was unwilling either rapidly to dispatch them or to delegate their solution to others. He would rather postpone action until he had time to master the complexities of a situation himself than trust somebody else who had the necessary technical knowledge, but who might commit him to a political line of which he disapproved. And this entailed delays even after the war was over, for in the first two months of peace he toured the country as on a royal progress, congratulating the people on their victory and urging them to build from it a prosperous and a powerful Spain.

It was abundantly obvious that in 1939 Spain was neither prosperous nor powerful, and, despite her great losses of manpower, it was also clear that her primary need was for capital. Spain needed raw cotton to put the Catalan textile industry in work again. She had a continuing need for petroleum products. For all this she had to pay. Before the war her balance of payments was already in deficit, for her mineral exports had been affected in the early thirties by the industrial stagnation of her customer countries, while the market for her oranges in Britain had been seriously damaged by the competitive advantage given to Palestine by British imperial preference. Up to 1936 one of the largest gold reserves in the world enabled Spain to view her trade imbalance without serious alarm, but the war changed all that. In October 1936 the Republic sent the bulk of its monetary gold (sixty-three million pounds worth) to the Soviet Union to prevent its falling into Franco's hands should he take Madrid and to provide payment for Russian war material. Franco regards the gold as having been stolen by the Russians, while they claim that it did not meet more than three-quarters of the cost of supplying the Republic.

Since there is no fixed market value for armaments the argument is fruitless—the important fact is that at the end of the war only a negligible amount of Spain's 1936 reserves remained. The French courts in July 1936 ordered the release to the Bank of Spain of 1500 million francs deposited in Paris in 1936, but this amounted to only nine per cent of the pre-war volume of reserves. Spain would have either to guarantee her own resources for recovery, slowly and painfully, or to rely on overseas credit.

Spain would find it difficult to raise her own capital. She already had a large public debt, even without taking into consideration the debt to Germany and Italy for arms and the claims of various countries for war damage compensation. And she did not have a sophisticated internal capital market on which to float a loan, though the Government was in fact able to relieve its financial pressures by a debt conversion in October 1939. Her internal financial position was further confused by the existence of two separate pesetas, Nationalist and Republican, of widely differing values. The country was still more agricultural than industrial, and many landowners felt a prejudice against stock exchange investment and even against banks. Even the Spanish industrialist was usually more interested in retaining management in his own hands than in maximising his money income.

The Government could of course invest the proceeds of taxation in the creation of capital, but this was not without its own difficulties. There was the administrative difficulty of collecting taxes. As a British official publication commented sardonically in 1943: 'The collection of taxes has not reached the same degree of infallibility in Spain as in many other European countries.'[19] Indirect taxes were the easiest to collect, but to increase the burden of taxation that was not progressive in its incidence was to reduce the level of

[19] UKNID, p. 302.

F

145

demand in the economy and, in human terms, to face the working class with the starkest poverty.

It was not altogether surprising that peace should have proved so much more difficult to finance than war. During the war Franco had chosen a strategy which made him heavily dependent on foreign assistance, and his opponents had persistently predicted that an unacceptable price would be extracted for this. But he had bargained that the interest his friends had in sustaining him would enable him to keep their price within moderate bounds. The moment when this seemed to have been a miscalculation was one of the blackest of the war for him. As the constant hope of Negrín was that a European war would involve Britain and France willy-nilly in the defence of the Republic, so the Czech crisis in the late summer of 1938 was a nightmare for Franco. In September Britain and France conveyed to him through various channels that they would remain neutral in Spain if he would remain neutral in Europe: this would of course mean his dispensing with the aid of his friends in the event of war, and without it he feared he might have to withdraw to a mountain redoubt. Yet the war would anyway cut his communications with other countries, so he had no choice but to declare his neutrality, particularly since his allies kept him completely in the dark. It was from his own Press Office that he heard the immensely relieving news of the Munich Agreement.

His public dissociation of himself from Hitler and Mussolini had nevertheless left a poor impression on them, and certainly strengthened the growing desire of the Germans to extract as much as they could from Spain. But it was a surprise for Franco's foreign critics to find at the end of the Civil War that he was able to keep his word and that Spain would preserve her integrity and independence. The postponement of the 'volunteers' departure until the end of May 1939 caused some anxiety, but not an inch of Spanish soil was given up either to foreign possession or to foreign military occupation. Even Mallorca was evacuated after having been virtually an Italian colony during the war, from which Italian bombing raids on Barcelona had taken place against Franco's wishes. But by now Italy was more interested in the Balkans. She had in March reached a financial settlement with Spain whereby the war credits she had extended would be repaid at an annual rate of 250 million lire, but

Franco later got payment of the first instalment postponed. Spain's adherence to the Anti-Comintern Pact was announced on 27 March 1939, but to the annoyance of Germany it had been long delayed and committed Spain only to a defensive alliance. The Germans had extorted concessions on mining rights in November 1938, yet in this too their victory was one of principle rather than of substance. Their special privileges included no rights in any mines in current operation and no concessions in the principal iron producing province, Vizcaya. In the short term, at least, their advantage was very slight. Franco's regime faced ideologically in the direction of Germany and Italy, but he could boast of an independent foreign policy characterised by 'nimble prudence'.

All the same Franco Spain might be expected to turn to her friends in Germany for help in reconstruction, and in fact in March 1939 Juan Antonio Suanzes, Franco's Minister of Industry and Commerce, and the son of his schoolmaster at the Naval Preparatory Academy, asked for immediate consultations on debts, trade and credits. But Germany was not a nation rich in capital for foreign investment. It was her Government's policy to concentrate on industry and import substitution schemes. If she loaned Spain money it would only be in order to keep the influence of the democratic nations at bay.

The democratic powers were aware of the shortage of German capital, and possessed also the advantage of having already widespread investments, licensing agreements and tariff concessions in Spain, whereas German investment in Spain remained comparatively insignificant even in 1939. The French, and to a lesser degree the British, were unpopular in Spain for their governments' equivocal attitude to the Nationalists during the war, and they were aware of this. Marshal Pétain, whom the French had sent as Ambassador to Franco, could hardly overlook the fact that people turned away and spat in the street as he passed.[20] Still, Neville Chamberlain thought in February 1939 that 'we ought to be able to establish relations with Franco who seems well disposed to us'.[21] Optimism about statesmen's dispositions was of course characteristic of Chamberlain, but it was true that feelers were

[20] Georges Blond: *Pétain, 1856–1951* (Paris 1966), p. 171.
[21] Keith Feiling: *The Life of Neville Chamberlain* (London 1946), p. 394.

being put out for credit all over Western Europe and in the United States in the spring of 1939.

On 18 May the Spanish Ambassador in Washington called on the Secretary of State to ask for a credit for the purchase of 300,000 bales of cotton. This was eventually granted, but the United States held out a while for certain political concessions. They wanted Spain to drop a lawsuit against the US Treasury and to give the International Telegraph and Telephone Company freedom to run its Spanish subsidiary without hindrance. (The subsidiary held a monopoly of Spanish telephones.)[22] If the Americans named a price for their aid, it was a small one compared with what the Western Europeans felt able to ask. During May the French persuaded M. van Zeeland, the former Prime Minister of Belgium, to sponsor a loan from an international banking consortium. But those concerned seem to have overestimated Franco's hunger for capital very seriously. The terms they offered were not such as a proud country like Spain would be likely to accept. Spain was not only to produce for the bankers all the documents they considered relevant. She was also to commit herself not to promise Germany or Italy that she would set up a totalitarian political or economic structure, and not in fact to set one up.[23]

It was small wonder that Franco told the National Council of the Falange meeting at Burgos on 5 June that Spain could expect no constructive help from Britain or France, and announced a policy of self-sufficiency or autarky on the German model (though not explicitly so). 'Our victory,' he said, 'constitutes the triumph of certain economic principles in conflict with the old liberal theories, under the shelter of whose mythology many sovereign states were subjected to colonialism. It is undoubtedly this characteristic of our Revolution which awakens the most suspicion.'[24] The doctrine of self-sufficiency was indeed an old theme of the Falange. Its currency had not prevented Spain's practical politicians from seeking loans abroad, but it had meant that the terms of any loan would

[22] Herbert Feis: *The Spanish Story: Franco and the Nations at War* (New York, 1948), pp. 10–15.
[23] Whealey, op. cit., pp. 167–8, quoting dispatch from U.S. Ambassador in Paris, 15 May 1939.
[24] Franco: *Palabras*, pp. 135–45.

be scrutinised with suspicion in Burgos, not least by Franco himself. The Germans had had constantly to be reminded that Franco Spain did not wish to exchange British economic hegemony for German. Now the Zeeland plan underlined Franco's belief that Spain should make her own way. He was confident that eventually she could, and in the speech quoted above he pointed out those undesirable features of the economic scene which were alterable.

For a start Spain should make herself self-sufficient in agricultural products. There was no important food-stuff which would not grow on Spanish soil,[25] and yet scarce foreign exchange was being expended on food imports. In addition, Spanish investments overseas should be repatriated, and the Spanish merchant fleet should be expanded so that all Spanish trade could be carried in native bottoms. Importation of foreign films was another quite unnecessary extravagance. These were the negative gains, the savings that could be made. On the positive side the country's motto must be: 'Produce, produce, produce!' In sum, 'the first and most urgent problem which faces our economy is to get the balance of payments into equilibrium',[26] for there must always be ample cash available for the purchase of petroleum products and other strategic goods which Spain could not herself produce. If Franco was over-optimistic about the country's chances of achieving sustained economic growth by its own efforts, he was doubtless led on by his hopes for the future of Spain.

When in 1928 the Barón de Mora had asked him: 'What is your greatest ambition?' he had replied: 'That Spain become as great again as she was of old.'[27] In 1939 he felt in a position soon to bring about the achievement of his ambition. He found that the Falangist rhetoric about Empire struck a chord in him, as indeed did their emphasis on the austerity and self-sacrifice which would be necessary to attain it. 'Only by tenacity and work shall we make the Empire and fulfil the mandate of our dead,' he told Sevillians shortly after the Civil War.[28] Where exactly this Empire was to be

[25] Tea is not important in the context of Spain, and coffee is grown in Equatorial Guinea, then a Spanish colony.
[26] Franco: *Palabras*, loc. cit.
[27] *Estampa* 29 May 1928.
[28] Speech of 17 April 1939. Franco: *Palabras*, p. 97.

was not at this stage clear, though 1940 was to afford some elucidation. It was hardly going to be wholly cultural though, for
Franco spoke of 'the nation in arms' and warned the Air Force that
peace would probably not last long.[29] He was confident that Spain
had almost completed the creation of the industrial base necessary
for an independent war effort, and he believed that the more
developed nations of Europe owed their advantages over Spain to
the cheap labour of their colonies. It followed that Spain would pursue a policy of territorial expansion as soon as she had recovered
her economic health and strength.

Of a piece with his imperialist aspirations went his enthusiasm for
things youthful. Youth was the theme of the new regime. Its vigour
and boldness was contrasted with the decadence of age. Franco
recognised that it was young men, particularly bourgeois, who had
made the most sacrifices in his cause during the war. It was they
who in their thousands had died for it, and it was from among the
survivors that were drawn the most committed of his supporters,
those who were too young to look back nostalgically on the
Monarchy but old enough to want none of the Republic. Dionisio
Ridruejo, one of the leading young Falangists of the time, has
written that the keynote of the war was Hope.[30] In youth Franco
sought the idealism to justify that hope, to build the new Spain
which was so earnestly desired. On 16 August 1939 he welcomed
with tears in his eyes the plans of the young Enrique Sotomayor
to build a strong, independent Falangist youth movement.[31]

Then during the next three days he realised that a youth
movement was liable to formulate unreasonable demands, to
question authority and generally to disturb the good order of his
state. The structure of the SEU (Spanish University Syndicate)
was altered so as to bring it under hierarchical control. This was
typical of the period. The brightly coloured vision gave place
to the drab reality, just as later the dream of empire was to fade before the waking nightmare of the economic crisis we have seen

[29] Franco: Palabras, p. 111. Speech at Barajas, 12 May 1939.
[30] Dionisio Ridruejo: Escrito en España (Buenos Aires 1962) p. 12.
[31] S. G. Payne: Falange: A History of Spanish Fascism (Stanford 1962)
p. 109.

150

portended. The ultimate goals were not relinquished, and their attainment continued to be prophesied in all the media of communication, which were controlled largely by Falangist intellectuals. But for the time being it was business as usual, and the substance of the *ancien régime* was retained and, where necessary, restored. Disillusionment inevitably set in, and it gave rise to a riddle which asked 'How do you find the new Spain?' and was answered: 'When I find it, I shall tell you'.[32]

The Church was restored to a position of privilege. Civil marriage and divorce were of course abolished, and the severest restrictions placed on Protestantism. Couples who had had civil marriages in the Republican zone during the Civil War were obliged to be remarried in church before they were legally regarded as man and wife. Church attendances rose sharply partly as a result of indirect official pressure. The Church gained the right to censor literature. It held a key position in the prison service, and in education, where the clergy was represented at every level. Even the Falange, which had originally been hostile to the temporal pretensions of the Church, and had valued it chiefly for its national character, now become Catholicised. Blue Falange shirts and perpendicular right arms were to be seen in Church on every occasion which offered an excuse for ceremonial. The Church also came close to acquiring a new saint and martyr in José Antonio Primo de Rivera. His cult had been officially established on the second anniversary of his execution by the Republicans on 20 November 1936, and occasionally reached an extravagance which blasphemed the Christian faith. This disgusted many ecclesiastics, but in general they were content with the situation, which gave them a greater role than they had played for centuries.

Conversely the regions of Spain played a smaller role than ever before. The whole country was ruthlessly Castilianised, the use of the Catalan or Basque language being proscribed as far as possible. Words and phrases of foreign origin were also officially purged from the Spanish language. The administrative privileges of Catalonia, both political and judicial, were cancelled, and Barcelona was placed on a level with any other provincial capital. The special status of the Basques had been granted by the Republic after July

[32] DGFP, series D, Vol III, No. 740.

1936 and had therefore never been recognised by the Nationalists. But far from the cultural separateness of the Catalans and of the Basques being extinguished, the arrogance of the attempt aroused resentment in classes of people who might otherwise have been supporters of the regime. It was no coincidence that monarchism was particularly strong in Catalonia even before decentralisation was written into its programme.

Gradually the dangers of their alienation were recognised and a distinction drawn between permitted cultural expressions of regional consciousness and impermissible political manifestations. Publication of poetry and novels in Catalan, and to a lesser extent in the Basque language, was resumed after the Second World War. Yet the only official language and the only language of instruction remains Castilian, and the use of Catalan and Basque at public gatherings, even in church, is regarded with suspicion. A considerable crisis occurred in 1960 after Luis de Galinsoga, the Castilian editor of the Barcelona newspaper, *La Vanguardia Española*, scandalised the congregation at a Catalan-language service by shouting out: 'All Catalans are shit.' Public disorders and a boycott of the newspaper followed, and Galinsoga was eventually forced to resign. But this was only the most extreme of the numerous examples of intolerance or insensitivity which have wounded the considerable pride of Catalans and Basques. Regionalism is an aspiration to which Franco's government has not accorded the slightest political recognition.

Problems of class relationship for which the Falange had more constructive plans were given more attention. A grandiloquent Labour Charter was issued as early as March 1938, promising paid holidays, a land settlement and a variety of other benefits. The political system of the new state was 'National Syndicalism' in analogy with German National Socialism. Vertical syndicates were set up by incorporating employers and workers in a single trade union. They were supposed to do away with industrial strife and to watch also over the public interest.

By 1939 little had been achieved, but in 1940 the syndical organisation was entrusted to Gerardo Salvador Merino. In common with other 'old shirts'—that is Falangists who had been members of the party prior to the Civil War—he attached little importance to the employer branches of syndicates. The syndicates envisaged by him would be an organised political mass not greatly differing from the old left-wing labour unions except that they would have a chauvinist rather than internationalist outlook. Rather naturally this aroused hostility both among employers and in the Army. Led by General Varela they worked steadfastly for Salvador Merino's fall, which they secured in May 1941. It was discovered that he had once had masonic affiliations, and he was banished to the Balearics.

The outlook for an authentic labour movement in Franco's Spain was always bleaker even than that for an independent student movement. However genuine might be the enthusiasm of Falangist ideologues for giving the workers a better deal, bankers and industrialists regarded any such move as unjustified either by the merits of the workers or by the economic condition of the country. These were the men who remained masters of the economy's commanding heights, and Franco was hardly the man to court chaos by a massive redistribution of property or economic power. The only significant alteration of property rights which was made by the 'new Spain' was to undo what little agrarian reform the Republic had achieved. Observers might be forgiven for finding less significance in the Labour Charter than in such measures as the removal of the nationalisation of credit institutions from the programme of the Falange, and the enactment of severe penalties for the vague crime of 'misdeeds committed at work and, in particular, for the deliberate reduction of the output due'.[33] Franco might speak against the evils of capitalism and of exploitation of the worker, but in April 1938 he placed first on his list of those who were undermining the war effort 'those who wish to cause alarm to capital with the spectre of certain demagogic reforms'.[34]

By the end of the war, however, few had the energy to call for 'demagogic reforms'. They felt that they had earned a rest from self-sacrifice, and hoped to reap rewards for their endeavours. This was granted to them in the decrees on recruitment to the public service. To those Falangists who wanted not just employment but also power, those who had some political consciousness, the regime

[33] *Boletín oficial del Estado* 13 January 1939.
[34] Franco: *Palabras*, p. 59.

distributed posts in provincial and municipal government. Genuine Falangists were perhaps better represented at these levels than at the centre of power where, apart from Serrano Súñer, the leading members of the administration were mostly service officers. On the other hand, outsiders, who saw blue-shirted men emerge from large cars, were often mistaken in believing that this betokened a predominance of the Falange in any sense that José Antonio would have understood. All service officers and government officials above a certain rank were *ex officio* members of the Falange, so the *jefe local* was frequently simply the village boss (*cacique*) in a new guise.

Meanwhile Franco had removed the only man in Spain who could remotely have challenged his position, General Queipo de Llano. In fact the independence of Queipo's Andalusian fief had already been eroded, and while he seems to have resented Franco he had apparently no plans to supplant him. He simply felt, as he had felt in 1931 after his long service to the Republicans, that he had been ungratefully treated, and on 18 July 1939 he was unwise enough to say as much. Franco summoned him to Madrid to explain this indiscretion and, while he was in transit had him relieved. There was no trouble, and Franco's power was more solid than ever. Unencumbered now by the onerous tasks of a wartime Generalissimo, he could devote his whole attention to the government of Spain. If perhaps he did not attach the urgency to post-war problems that he had to the critical moments of the war, it was because increasingly he permitted himself to raise his eyes from the details of Spain's present to the grandeur of her future, and to savour a little the glory of being the ordained architect of a new epoch. 'Lord God' he prayed in a public service in Madrid on 20 May, 'in whose hands are all right and all power, lend me Thine assistance to lead this people to the full glory of Empire, to Thy glory and the glory of Thy Church.'[35]

[35] Galinsoga, op. cit., pp. 334-5.

7 Neutrality

The summer of 1939 did not bring rapid strides towards the recovery of Spain. Spain was in confusion both politically and administratively, and the great Powers who might have interested themselves in the reconstruction of Spain were more concerned with the gathering stormclouds of war. Mussolini had decided that it was time to open the map of Europe at a different page, had in April seized Albania and was concentrating his gaze on the Balkans. Hitler was hastily trying to assemble a coalition against Britain and France which could deter or defeat their intervention in his forthcoming conflict with Poland. What he principally required from Spain was a menacing attitude towards France to ease the pressure on his western frontier by an Army Corps or so. This he was unable to achieve, for on 19 June the London *Daily Express* published an interview in which General Aranda unofficially announced Spanish neutrality, and the following day official Spanish assurances to the French government were leaked to the world's press. The following month Franco underlined the point by telling a Portuguese diplomat for the record that his foreign policy was 'geographical' rather than ideological![1]

It was no surprise therefore when on 5 September Franco decreed the strictest neutrality of all Spaniards in the European conflict. In fact he made it the policy of the Government not to

[1] Interview with Dr Augusto Castro published in *Diário de Notícias* (Lisbon) 14 July 1939.

allow the export of any goods to belligerent countries which could not freely go to every country in the world. This meant that, because the Allies classed iron ore and pyrites, for instance, as strategic goods and forbade their delivery to Germany, Spain would not export these commodities to the Allies either. Since in the year prior to the outbreak of war about half Spain's foreign trade was with Germany, and since a large proportion of the other half was in strategic goods, this strict interpretation of neutrality was potentially disastrous to Spanish commerce. Fortunately the decision of the United States to set aside the provisions of the Neutrality Act and supply arms to the Allies gave Franco an excuse in November to relax the constrictions of his economic neutrality. But politically he remained staunchly peaceful, if sympathetic to Germany. He refused a French offer to conclude a non-aggression pact, and rejected the ingenuous suggestion from Lord Lloyd of a Latin Union with France, Italy and Portugal against Hitler and Stalin. In October 1939 after the fall of Poland he, like Mussolini, appealed to the belligerents for peace.

Nobody in Spain welcomed the war, though once it had broken out most Spaniards had their sympathies engaged on one side or the other. For the conservative businessman or landowner, the ideal configuration of the international scene was a rapprochement between Britain and Germany and a firm watch on Soviet ambition. While they might not necessarily renounce Spanish colonial expansion if it could be achieved, they tended to be admirers of the liberal economic system of which Britain was the champion, and they took as a very ill omen the pact signed between the Nazis and the Soviet Union on the eve of the war. Moreover, in spite of the Spanish censors' ban on the publication of the anti-Nazi encyclical *Mit Brennender Sorge* they were deeply concerned by the persecution of the German Church. Their view was privately expressed by the Spanish Ambassador in Berlin, an old admiral and former member of the Primo de Rivera's Directory, the Marqués de Magaz, who saw nothing surprising in the Hitler–Stalin pact since 'Soviet Communism is the nearest thing to German National Socialism.'[2]

[2] Ramón Garriga: *Las relaciones secretas entre Franco y Hitler* (Buenos Aires, 1965), p. 72.

Those who were of such an opinion tended naturally to be more or less sympathetic to the Allies, at any rate up to June 1941. They included many powerful Nationalists from General Varela, the Minister of War, to Juan March, who volunteered in 1939 to work for British naval intelligence.[3] Besides, all those in Spain who still hoped for a Republican government, with the exception in the first years of the war of the Communists, were pro-Allies, so one must be cautious of overemphasising the leanings of Spain towards Germany and Italy during the Second World War.

Nevertheless the Allies had reason to regard Spain as a country whose neutrality might in certain circumstances change into belligerent hostility. As soon as it was organised, the British Ministry of Economic Warfare began to watch Spain carefully lest she re-export to Germany goods which she had been permitted to import through the British blockade. Similarly, the British Secret Intelligence Service deployed a large organisation in Spain to combat the German spying against Allied shipping which was organised from Madrid. In the black market Spain of the early forties both contestants found sufficient corruptibility in Spanish life on which to thrive. Yet Germany's position was indubitably superior, and was founded not on superior financial strength, but on genuine enthusiasm for her cause in certain important official quarters, and on the personal contacts which she had had good opportunity to build up during the Civil War years.

Both these factors were operative from the outset of the war and before, and are not to be explained as gestures to appease the Germans after their conquest of most of Europe. Already in the summer of 1939, Lazar, the German press attaché, was able to place German-written articles in the Spanish press. In September 1939, German nationals were able to tap the telephone conversations of the British Embassy in San Sebastián.[4] Franco himself had agreed in advance that the Germans might carry out secret naval repairs and replenishment in wartime so long as the British did not find out. Particularly in the police and in the media of communica-

[3] Donald McLachlan: *Room 39: Naval Intelligence in Action* (London 1968), pp. 203–4.
[4] Whealey, op. cit., p. 279. Sir Maurice Peterson: *Both sides of the Curtain* (London 1950.), p. 192.

tion, branches of the government under the overall control of Ramón Serrano Súñer, Germany could be sure of widespread collaboration.

Serrano himself knew little of Germany, but he knew that he hated Britain and France. He regarded them as the appeasers if not the willing tools of Communism, and he blamed them for not saving the lives of his brothers, who were murdered in 'red' Madrid. Germany he saw as a bulwark for Europe against the Bolshevist expansion, and what he greatly regretted about the Second World War was that it seemed to have come too soon for Spain to be able to take part and to win her share of the spoils. He believed in Spain's imperial mission, and he feared that, because of Spain's temporary weakness owing to the Civil War, the new 'world order' might be constructed without reference to his country's aspirations. At least Spain should proclaim by word, and as far as practicable by deed, her solidarity with the crusade against the 'pluto-democracies'.

Serrano remained Minister of the Interior and was also Chairman of the Political Committee of the Falange, and since all newspapers and journalists were subordinate to the National Press Delegacy of the Ministry or to the Press Under-Secretary of the Falange, he had wide freedom of action in press matters. He was able to appoint such journalists as had views in concord with his own and to suppress the appearance of such news as did not suit him. After all it was not too difficult to find literate Falangists and other educated men who were hostile to the decadent democracies and who were sincerely happy to follow the rising star of the totalitarian order in international affairs. Nor did Serrano encounter difficulties in staffing the other branches of his personal empire, notably the police, with adherents of his pro-German line.

Extensive as was Serrano's influence, however, he was not in the early months of the war able to influence Spanish foreign policy in a pro-German sense. The Spanish diplomatic corps were, almost to a man, conservative and monarchist, and the Minister of Foreign Affairs, Colonel Beigbeder, was a military man, though also experienced in diplomacy. Before becoming Minister in the cabinet reshuffle of August 1939 he had been a successful High Commissioner in Morocco, and earlier in his career he had served as Military Attaché in Berlin. He was far from a Germanophile though; indeed, persistent rumours linked him with British intelligence. Beigbeder's policy and that of his department was one of firm neutrality, and, while Franco permitted the press to take an independent and strongly anti-Allied tone under the guidance of his brother-in-law, he took a much more personal interest in the development of foreign affairs.

Spanish diplomacy was in fact being forced by economic exigencies to move towards closer accommodation with the Allies. The harvest of 1939 had been very poor, and, though this fact was for a while denied or even unappreciated, shortly after the Government's return to Madrid Serrano said in a broadcast that it would be foolish to hide the fact that they were facing difficult times, and that foodstuffs would have to be imported.[5]

Spain had before the war been virtually self-sufficient in foodstuffs so the need for her now to import them in large quantities meant that she must conclude new economic agreements. In the 1930s world trade was conducted largely on a bilateral basis, and narrow limits on quantity and price were negotiated for individual commodities every two or three years. Naturally, between 1936 and 1939 most of Spain's economic agreements had run out and her international trade was by the beginning of the World War running on a precarious series of ad hoc arrangements, all the more complicated because of the broad change which had taken place in the pattern of trade.

If Spain now needed grain in quantities she had never before required, she also faced a grave problem in disposing of her wine and oranges, non-strategic goods of low value per cubic metre, for which her traditional customers could no longer afford the transport. She must renegotiate her trade and payments agreements to take account of her changed circumstances holding out for high prices for the strategic raw materials with which she was well endowed, and avoiding being used as a dumping ground for surplus and non-essential manufactures. An agreement was signed with France in January 1940 which enabled Spain to import phosphate fertilisers, besides rice and wheat in exchange for minerals, in particular pyrites. In March an agreement was signed with Britain

5 *New York Times* 2 November 1939.

which was similar in its trading provisions and also incorporated sterling credit facilities. Belgium, Switzerland and Portugal also signed economic agreements with Spain during the winter, but with Germany no progress was made, for it became clear in negotiations with a German mission in November and December that Germany could deliver virtually nothing.

By May 1940 Spain's rapprochement with the capitalist world was virtually complete. A Spanish Air Force mission to Berlin was told by Ribbentrop, the German Foreign Minister, that 'the reconstruction of an economy must take place without outside credits and must spring from the country's own strength if it is to be effective and if national independence is to be maintained'.[6] But there was the growing recognition in the cabinet that Germany's enthusiasm for Spanish self-sufficiency stemmed from Germany's lack of available capital and that in fact Spain must of necessity look for overseas financial aid. Franco's conversion to this point of view probably occurred about the middle of April, for it was then that the negotiations with the United States over the rights of IT&T in Spain, which had been intractably deadlocked, began to make rapid progress. An agreement was finally initialled on 15 May and on the same day the Spanish Ambassador in Washington began to take soundings about a loan of up to £200 million. On 24 May, while the American Ambassador to Spain was on leave, Larraz, the Finance Minister, put the formal request for a loan.

The State Department cabled on 27 May that they would send their Ambassador back by air with the answer. But events in Europe had outstripped them. The Allied front in Flanders was in irretrievable confusion. On 28 May the King of the Belgians offered Hitler his unconditional surrender. The British Army fell back on Dunkirk, and although many thousands of their number were rescued by sea before the town was finally captured on 4 June they lost virtually all their equipment. On 5 June the Germans launched four successful thrusts through the French line, crossing the Somme and passing Verdun.

Poland, Denmark, Norway might have demonstrated the efficiency of German staff work, but none of these countries were

[6] DGFP, series D Vol. IX, No. 230.

first-class military powers. France on the other hand had been considered the greatest military power in Europe. It was her experience in the First World War that Franco and his colleagues had studied and her prowess in North African colonial warfare that they had grudgingly admired. Now they watched amazed as France seemed likely to endure no longer than Poland under the onslaught of Germany's aircraft and armour. It was hardly the moment to strengthen economic relations with so declared an enemy of the apparent victor as President Roosevelt. Franco did not hurry to receive the American Ambassador.

On 3 June Franco wrote to Hitler to express his regret that he had been unable to be more than neutral in the war. He pointed out the vulnerability of the Canaries and Balearic Islands and the exhaustion of his country after the civil war, but he told the Führer that 'I do not need to assure you how great is my desire not to remain aloof from your cares and how great is my satisfaction in rendering to you at all times those services which you regard as most valuable'.[7] He did not immediately send the letter, for, while, such a timely reminder of his common ground with the victor might help Spain diplomatically, he was acutely aware of the hazards of war and was not anxious to cast away his neutrality. He feared that Italian intervention would involve Spain willy nilly, and had told Mussolini at the end of April that 'I regard as very wise anything you may do to postpone the moment of Italian intervention'.[8] When the news of Italy's war broke on the world, it was no surprise to Spain, but Beigbeder called it 'madness'.[9] Nevertheless, Franco sent Mussolini 'my best wishes for the success of your arms'[10] and judged the moment opportune for General Juan Vigón, his Chief of Higher General Staff, to deliver his letter to Hitler.

On 11 June Spanish forces occupied the International Zone of

[7] DGFP, Series D, Vol. IX, No. 378.
[8] *Documenti Diplomatici Italiani*, 9th Series (Rome 1954) Vol. IV, No 260 (herafter cited as DDI).
[9] To the American Ambassador. See *Foreign Relations of the United States, Diplomatic Papers, 1940* (Washington 1957), Vol. II, p. 796 (hereafter cited as FRUS).
[10] DDI, 9th series, Vol. IV, No. 847.

Tangier, and Spain took over responsibility for the administration. To the diplomatic corps she explained that since two of her partners in the zone's administration (Britain and France) were now at war with the third (Italy) she felt obliged to assume control in order to preserve its neutrality. But her press saluted the takeover as the harbinger of Spanish imperial expansion and called for the return of Gibraltar to Spain. This old irredentist claim had bubbled to the surface in a number of press articles and in a number of semi-spontaneous public demonstrations since the end of the civil war, but had been somewhat discouraged by Franco. He had told the cabinet that, while Gibraltar was Spanish by right such demonstrations only caused trouble. 'We shall put forward our demands at the appropriate time,' he promised.[11]

On 13 June Spain cast off neutrality for 'non-belligerency', the status which Mussolini had invented for Italy in the previous September. It was, Franco was to tell the American Ambassador, 'a form of national sympathy with the Axis'.[12] On 14 June Paris fell to the Germans. The war appeared to be almost over. The 'appropriate time' had arrived for Spain to consider what demands she would make of the defeated democracies.

On 19 June the Spanish Ambassador was asked by Marshal Pétain's new French government to arrange an armistice with the Germans. On the same day Spain delivered to the Germans a memorandum on her territorial claims. 'Since the Spanish government considers the further existence of the French empire in North Africa, which was partly created by the efforts of Spanish workers, to be impossible, it demands the territory of Oran, the unification of Morocco under a Spanish protectorate, the extension of Spanish territory in the Sahara to the 20th parallel, and the extension of Spain's coastal territories situated in the area on the coast between the mouth of the Niger and Cape López. Should England continue the war after France has ceased fighting, Spain would be willing to enter the war after a short period of preparing

[11] According to a reliable informant of the German Ambassador, report of 6 May 1940. Donald S. Detwiler: *Hitler, Franco and Gibraltar: Die Frage des spanischen Eintritts in den zweiten Weltkrieg* (Wiesbaden 1962) p. 18, quoting German Foreign Ministry Document 4091/E069336–7.
[12] FRUS, 1940, Vol. II, p. 888.

the public. In this case she would need some support from Germany in the form of war materials, heavy artillery, aircraft for the attack on Gibraltar, and perhaps the co-operation of German submarines in the defence of the Canary Islands. Also supplies of some foodstuffs, ammunition, motor fuels and equipment, which will certainly be available from the French war stocks.'[13]

As early as 3 June Beigbeder had in conversation with Stohrer, the German Ambassador, envisaged a similar programme of Spanish expansion. What changed in the ensuing two weeks was not Spain's aspirations but her confidence. On 13 June Beigbeder assured Stohrer that Spain's economic situation was improving. The memorandum of the 19th implied confidence that Spain would soon have all the wherewithal to enter the war. The caution of early June had apparently been shed, and replaced by haste to vindicate Spain's rights before the war was over and it was too late. And it would then be too late, for Franco constantly reiterated that Spain could not accept Gibraltar as a gift from anybody.

In any case Spain did not fully trust the Germans to support her imperial ambitions, and indeed their reply to the Spanish memorandum of 19 June was non-committal when it came. Franco in the meanwhile decided that pressure might profitably be put on the French. Attempts were made to stir up the Moroccans against their French-protected Sultan. On 21 June, the day before the conclusion of the Franco-German armistice, Beigbeder told the French Ambassador: 'Spain has reason to think that the question of Morocco will arise in the armistice negotiations … The French Government …, being led to make concession in any case, would do well to agree to make some of them to Spain. That would be that much which would not fall to the Germans and Italians.'[14]

Would France cede the territory of the Beni Zerual and of the Beni Snassen in Morocco? In the end the fear of losing such prestige with the natives in Morocco as remained to her after her defeat in Europe weighed more heavily with the French than the fear of driving Spain into the arms of the Germans. They stalled, and Spain lost the chance of winning further spoils without

[13] DGFP Series D, Vol IX, No. 488.
[14] F. Charles-Roux: *Cinq mois tragiques aux affaires étrangères (21 mai — 1er novembre 1940)*, (Paris 1949), pp. 224–225.

fighting. She now had no alternative but to weigh up her potential gains against the risks of war itself.

The Spanish Government was as usual deeply divided on the desirability of entry into the war. Beigbeder was as keen as ever to preserve Spain's neutrality, and hoped to do so by linking pro-Axis Spain with pro-Allied Portugal. The two countries had signed a Treaty of Friendship in March 1939, and during July Beigbeder negotiated an additional protocol providing that either party might call for consultations if Iberian peace seemed to be endangered. Meanwhile, Serrano Súñer did his best to undermine relations with Portugal. Franco, undecided between the contending factions, did nothing to prevent either the negotiations or the attempt to sabotage them. A press campaign was launched which hinted broadly at Spanish imperialistic designs on Portugal. Despite the official policy of friendship, war against Portugal was a very popular programme among the Falange rank and file. But the Portuguese were not to be alarmed by such stage thunder and, although Serrano managed to delay signature by a few days, the protocol was concluded on 29 July. On the same day Beigbeder told the American Ambassador that Spain had not thought of war unless attacked.[15]

During the first half of July, when the case for intervention had been strongest from Spain's point of view, she had received little encouragement from Germany to enter the war at her side. All the signs that the war was about to end, which might encourage the Spanish to involve themselves, were for Germany indications that she did not need further allies. Although Hoare, the new British Ambassador in Madrid, might speak of continuing the war from Canada, the British Minister in Bern was in touch with the Germans, and the Spanish government must have known this, for a meeting had taken place in the Spanish Legation itself.[16] Indeed there really seemed little for the British to fight for, and it was comforting to believe that only Churchill's Dutch courage was prolonging the struggle for a month or two. All the same the Germans decided to draw up plans for a joint operation against Gibraltar, and sent Admiral Canaris to Spain to investigate Spanish military

[15] Feis, op. cit., p. 47.
[16] Sir David Kelly: *The Ruling Few* (London 1952), p. 272.

capability. While Canaris was in Spain, General Vigón met the former commander of the Condor Legion, General von Richthofen, in Biarritz on 28 July and told him that Franco particularly wanted him to be the commander of the German expeditionary force in Spain.

But by this time Franco's enthusiasm for war had evaporated. Indeed, it was probably never very great, for he was always conscious of the uncertainty of war. 'You know how a thing will start, but not how it will end', he later told a French journalist in this connection.[17] And if confirmation were needed of this attitude, it is afforded by the caution with which he approached the rising of 1936, and by the care he took to plan for unexpected developments in his campaigns. It is characteristic of a man who believes in the inevitability of uncertainty to leave as little as possible to chance.

Not that entry into the war in July 1940 was without disadvantages clear at a glance. The theatre in which Spain would have to operate would be against Gibraltar and in North Africa. To take so strong a fortress as Gibraltar Spain would require either new equipment or expert German troops, and Franco was nervous of allowing German troops on his soil. Worse still was the outlook in North Africa, for before the final collapse of France General Weygand had allowed some seven hundred French aircraft to be transferred there.[18] From the moment it became clear that the terms of the Franco–German armistice signed on 22 June did not require the surrender of these machines, a Spanish campaign in Africa became a perilous proposition, because, although many of them were without spare parts and of slight use against modern machines, they would still give the French overwhelming superiority. This would entail Spain's calling on German aid, and Franco wanted German forces in Morocco even less than he wanted them in Spain, for German agents there had been busy intriguing with nationalists against both the protectorate powers, Spain as much as France. (Islamic movements everywhere had Nazi sympathy on account of their hostility to the Jews in Palestine.)

Furthermore, economic circumstances no longer appeared so

[17] Interview with Serge Groussard in *Figaro* (Paris), 12 June 1958.
[18] Article by Weygand in *Le Monde* (Paris) 10 March 1955.

favourable as they did in the previous month. In early June Franco had made light of his economic difficulties. He had even told Hoare that Spain would derive all the imports she needed from North Africa.[19] By the beginning of August it was obvious that the high hopes which had been entertained of the 1940 harvest had not been fulfilled, and that Spain would be as dependent as ever on imports. At the beginning of August the United States began to curtail supplies of petroleum products to Spain, and by this time the war looked like lasting much longer than Spain could survive on her reserves of food and fuel. In Madrid as at Berchtesgaden it had doubtless been noted that 'something has happened in London. The English were entirely "down"; now they are up again'.[20] Moreover, the chances of American intervention were rated high in Madrid, particularly once Roosevelt had been renominated on 19 July. It was time for Spain to back-pedal on her eagerness to enter the war.

On 8 August the Minister of Commerce and Industry, Colonel Alarcón de la Lastra, told German embassy officials at length of Spain's need for imports: 200,000 tons of grain at the very least, tin, jute, rubber, above all petroleum. Meanwhile, she could not export her oranges, and her ores lay in huge stockpiles for want of transport. In response to the German request for figures, the Ministry produced some on 16 August, though they confessed that they were drawn up in haste and reserved the right to change them. Their needs apparently included 700,000 tons of petroleum products, up to 600,000 tons of wheat, 20,000 tons of coal, 525,000 tons of nitrates, 100,000 tons of cotton, 125,000 tons of raw rubber, and so on. Huge though these figures were, they were by no means a ridiculous estimate of Spain's needs, but deliveries on this scale were considered out of the question by the Germans, and it is quite possible that the Spaniards knew that they would be.

Franco wrote to Mussolini on 15 August to tell him that he expected soon to enter the war, that he had approached the

[19] Viscount Templewood: *Ambassador on Special Mission* (London 1946), pp. 47–8.
[20] Colonel General Halder: *Kriegstagebuch*, (Stuttgart 1962–4), Vol. II, p. 49 (31. vii. 40).

Germans for what he needed, that he would be grateful to the Duce for his support of Spanish imperial aspirations.[21] Beigbeder on 20 August thought it 'almost certain' Spain would enter the war and was 'strangely unworried' about her economic circumstances.[22] This new eagerness and show of confidence can surely only have stemmed from the realisation that the Germans were now becoming seriously interested in Spanish belligerence, and that it would be prudent to appease them. On the other hand, Franco decided that he must have massive deliveries before he could commit himself, and that he would not be satisfied with promises whose fulfilment might be prevented by circumstances. Spain was too weak to be able to afford being left in the lurch.

There were plenty of Germans who saw well that Spain was too wise to enter a war in which she would be too weak to make any net contribution to her allies' strength. But their views were not listened to in Germany with sufficient attention. Stohrer did not like to be discouraging in his official reports, but when Schellenberg, a high official of the Security Service (SD), came to Madrid at the end of July the Ambassador asked him privately to dampen Ribbentrop's optimism.[23] In a memorandum of 8 August Stohrer himself dwelt on the dangers attendant on a Spanish entry into the war: the probable loss of the Canaries and the Spanish colonies would damage the internal position of the regime, the French in Morocco would make common cause with the British, vital supplies to Spain would be delayed by the difference in the rail gauge south of the Pyrenees, and so on. Canaris' report the following day was bleak in its assessment of Spain's military strength. There were few adequate coastal defences or frontier fortifications. There were also deficiencies in qualified manpower, in ammunition and in morale. 'Although in many groups and especially in the leadership pro-German sentiments prevail and there is a will for a complete break with England and to extend Spanish rule, a feeling of weakness and of present military impotence still predominates.' Spain

[21] DGFP, series D, Vol. X, No. 346.
[22] ibid., No. 369.
[23] Walter Schellenberg, *The Schellenberg Memoirs* (London 1956), pp. 134–5.

would only take the offensive if she could do so with certainty of success.[24]

This wave of pessimism did not prevent cooperation with Spain from taking its place in Hitler's strategic plan for the winter of 1939–1940, and once it was there incorporated, it was difficult to dislodge it. On 31 July it seems that the plans for Spain were envisaged as no more than a blind for preparations against Russia, but on 9 August the High Command's Staff War Diary noted that an operation against Gibraltar would be undertaken if the invasion of England had to be deferred from the autumn of 1940. Though the German commander was to be technically responsible to Franco, it was to be ensured that 'the leadership of the operation remains in practice in German hands'. A draft of the plan was complete by the 20th, and Hitler accepted it on the 24th, though General Halder continued to regard Spain's entry into the war as a 'pipedream', and though Canaris considered that 'Franco's policy from the start was not to come in until Britain was defeated'. It was arranged that Serrano should come to Germany to discuss details of Spain's prospective entry into the war. For instance, the Germans were not prepared to countenance the Spaniards' request to be allowed to make a protest against a German airborne assault on Gibraltar before they finally joined in.[25]

When Serrano arrived in Berlin, on 15 September, he was flattered by his gala reception, but within the kid glove of German hospitality lay hidden the mailed fist of Ribbentrop. In his first meeting with Serrano he began by impugning Spain's estimates of her needs, and went on to call for an agreement to settle her civil war claims and for investment opportunities in the Spanish economy. All this Serrano regarded as negotiable, but then the German Foreign Minister went on to say that Germany would require naval bases on the Atlantic coast of Morocco, and that she would like Spain to cede her one of the Canary Islands. Serrano was dumbfounded. Up to this moment he had hoped that, even though he had not been given full powers, he could arrange terms on which Spain could safely and honourably enter the war. But

[24] DGFP, Series D, Vol. X, No. 326.
[25] See Detwiler, op. cit., pp. 35–36. Halder: *Kriegstagebuch,* II, 79 (27 vii. 40).

terms involving the cession to Germany of an integral part of Spain were insupportable, and he told Ribbentrop so. 'From then on,' he wrote later, 'it was clear to me that we could not have any illusions but must refuse to budge from the shelter of our claims.'[26]

Accordingly, the following day he put forward an addition to the extensive claims made in the memorandum of 19 June. He now claimed the area he called French Catalonia and various rectifications of the Pyrenean frontier, and declined to give any ground on the cession of a Canary Island. Altogether the talks were spread over a fortnight with a gap in the middle, during which Hitler saw Ciano and complained bitterly of the price Spain was trying to exact for her aid, and Serrano was given a conducted tour of German dispositions in northern France. But Serrano made no concessions—he was not empowered to do so—and Hitler could only hope that he would gain more from the summit meeting with Franco which he had proposed for the near future.

The growing spate of conversations with the Axis had not prevented the process of economic accommodation with Britain and the United States, which had begun again about the beginning of August, as soon as the high tide of German triumph had ebbed a little. On 6 August the agreement with the Americans on the telephone system was reinstated. British officials were allowed to inspect the books of the Spanish petrol monopoly, CAMPSA, in order to establish how great the country's need was, and what might be allowed through the blockade to meet it. British policy was becoming increasingly favourable to Spain as Hoare's conviction that a well-fed Spain would remain neutral gained ground over the suspicions of the Socialist Minister of Economic Warfare, Hugh Dalton, that anything supplied to Spain would be either stockpiled for use in war against Britain or re-exported to the Axis. 'There can be no possible fear that a single grain of imported wheat will be exported,' wrote Hoare on 3 September, estimating the harvest shortfall at a million tons.[27] When Alarcón asked the Americans on 7 September for a loan of 100 million dollars to purchase American wheat, cotton and gasoline, the British wanted the request to be

[26] Serrano Súñer, op. cit., p. 170.
[27] W. N. Medlicott: *The Economic Blockade.* (London 1952–9), Vol. I, p. 540.

granted, and it was the liberal policy-makers in the American State Department who were hostile.

The British were beset with difficulties, for, in the words of their official history of the war, 'it was becoming clearer and clearer that if Spain was to be kept out of the war it was necessary not merely to fix quotas, but to guarantee the supplies to fill the quotas'.[28] Spanish officials were not always very helpful, and the British tended to attribute this to stupidity or to a perverse insistence on looking a gift horse in the mouth. 'Dense and slow-moving as horned cattle' was how one British official later described them.[29] But this was not very fair, for suspicion of the British was by no means always unjustified. In February 1941, for instance, Hoare got a British shipment of wheat publicised as a gift for the relief of a natural disaster at Santander, only to reveal later that it was not a gift after all.[30] Again, there was more than national pride involved in the reluctance of the Spanish government to agree to the administrative procedures which the British imposed for the easier running of their blockade (the navicert system). They feared the reaction of Germany to their openly coming to terms with Britain, all the more so after the Germans' hard words to Serrano on his visit to Berlin.

Beigbeder told the American Ambassador on 26 September that Serrano's trip had been a publicity stunt and that it would lead to no change in policy. While this was to some extent true, the statement contained an element of wishful thinking. Certainly Serrano had been chosen over Beigbeder for the September mission largely because his strong sympathy for the Axis leaders made him the man they wanted to deal with. The meetings would, it was hoped, be cordial, while without full powers Serrano could give nothing vital away. Yet Beigbeder's personal position had suddenly become extremely unsure. Franco now feared that Germany might actually invade Spain or seek to use force to bring Spain into the war. Ribbentrop had voiced an indirect threat to that effect, and in the same breath he had accused Beigbeder of working for the English.[31]

[28] Medlicott, loc. cit.
[29] Sir John Lomax: *The Diplomatic Smuggler* (London 1965), p. 70.
[30] ibid., pp. 87–9.
[31] Serrano Súñer, op. cit., p. 171.

(There is no doubt that he had recklessly paraded his friendship with the British Ambassador.) The dismissal of his Foreign Minister began to appear to Franco a necessary propitiation for German dissatisfaction with his foreign policy. And certain other considerations made the sacrifice seem relatively inexpensive.

Months earlier, the ambitious Serrano had decided that the Ministry of Foreign Affairs had become the key post in the government, and since then he had not ceased to intrigue for Beigbeder's removal and his own appointment. Now that Serrano's enthusiasm for the Axis cause had cooled a little, and he favoured 'the policy of friendship with Germany because I do not believe we have any alternative',[32] Franco faced making him Foreign Minister with substantially less apprehension. On 15 October Beigbeder met Franco and assured himself of the Caudillo's continued approval of his policy, which was directed towards remaining aloof from the war rather than towards removing obstacles to her entry into it. But on 17 October he read in the press that he had been replaced in office by Ramón Serrano Súñer.[33]

The first major occasion which Serrano attended in his new post was the meeting between Hitler and Franco at Hendaye, the French border town where rail travellers from Madrid to Paris change trains.[34] Franco, Serrano and their party spent the night of 22 October in San Sebastián, only fifteen miles from the rendezvous, but they nevertheless arrived half an hour or more late the following afternoon, leaving the Führer in the meanwhile to pace up and down the platform. Franco hoped by this ploy to throw his opposite number out of his stride, but it seems that the Führer overcame his irritation and greeted the Caudillo cordially enough. When their talks started, Hitler's remarks followed the usual pattern of his diplomatic discussions in that he immediately outlined his quite detailed plans for the future of German–Spanish relations in a manner that implied that Franco's agreement was a pure formality.

[32] José Ma. Doussinague: *España tenía razón (1939–1945)* (Madrid 1949), p. 46.
[33] Templewood, op. cit., p. 71.
[34] On the Hendaye meeting, see DGFP, Series D, Vol. XI, Nos. 220–22 & 224; ibid., Editors' Note on pp. 466–7; Erich Kordt: *Wahn und Wirklichkeit* (Stuttgart 1948), pp. 266–9; Paul Schmidt: *Hitler's Interpreter* (London 1951), pp. 194–1.

He proposed an immediate treaty providing for Spain's entry into the war in January 1941. Gibraltar, he said, would be taken on the 10th of that month by the same specialist paratroops who, by the skilful use of dead ground had taken the key Belgian fortress of Eben Emael near Liège. But the smooth course of events was disturbed for Hitler by the refusal of Franco to agree. The Caudillo's demands in fact were more exorbitant even than Serrano's in Berlin, for they included the immediate delivery of 200,000 tons of grain, belonging to Switzerland, and artillery of various kinds. Coastal and anti-aircraft batteries would be required for defence against the British navy and air force, heavy artillery for the assault on Gibraltar, for Franco refused to have Hitler's vaunted specialists present the Rock to him on a plate. How, he then asked, would Spain be compensated for the seizure of the Canary Islands by Britain, an eventuality he regarded as certain for all Hitler's submarines? All this was in itself extremely irritating for the Führer, but it was made a thousand times worse by Franco's cold, almost insultingly remote manner.

It was Hitler's wont in his conversations, even at the highest level, to demonstrate the breadth of his genius by taking the world as his canvas and sketching its situation in the present and in the future as he saw it. Those who met him often regarded his words either with awe or with discreet amusement, but they did not feel it either necessary or useful to enter into an argument with him on what was not as a rule the subject under discussion. Ciano a year later advised Serrano 'not to get too worked up about the Führer's little speeches, because he always makes fantastic statements which don't in the end turn out to be true'.[35] But nobody had given Franco this sage advice, and he saw no reason why he should not dispute with Hitler. He was quite clear that he knew a great deal more about the conduct of wars than Hitler did; after all, he was a professional, and Hitler was an amateur.

He flatly contradicted Hitler's statement that Britain was beaten and that his aircraft and submarines would shortly force her to admit it. He said that even if the home island were lost, the British would continue the struggle from Canada. He knew as well as the Germans did that no invasion of England could now take

[35] Garriga, op. cit., p. 297.

place before the spring, and his Ambassador in London had reported that everyone there believed the war would continue for a long time. Again, Franco poured scorn on Hitler's boasting of how his armoured divisions would conquer all Africa. He pointed out that he knew something of African warfare from personal experience, and begged leave to doubt whether the Panzers could operate beyond the fringes of the great desert. Hitler was furious. On at least one occasion he rose from the table and made as if to break up the meeting, but decided against it, steeling himself to listen some more to the assured, monotonous, high-pitched tones of the Caudillo's voice, which reminded the interpreter of a muezzin calling the faithful to prayer. When the leaders finally adjourned, the Foreign Ministers were left with the difficult task of drafting an agreement when their chiefs had not in fact reached one.

Once the conversations between Ribbentrop and Serrano started the distance between the two sides widened even further. If, as the Ciano Diaries record, Serrano had been briefed on Hitler's talk with Mussolini earlier in the month,[36] it can have come as little surprise, but Ribbentrop now made it clear that Germany was prepared to make even fewer territorial concessions to Spain than she had offered the month before in Berlin. The Führer was now keen to enlist the active support of the Vichy government in the fight against Britain. He was to see Pétain at Montoire-sur-Loir on the 24th, and he did not intend to prejudice his negotiations with him by allotting France's most cherished colonial possessions to Spain. The furthest that Germany was prepared to go in satisfying Spanish ambitions was to promise such portions of the French empire as France might be compensated for out of British possessions. This proposal gave the Spaniards practically no security, and they were not prepared to accept any protocol in which it was embodied. After dinner Hitler and Franco had a second meeting which was no more productive than the first. They continued to talk 'to or rather at one another'[37] until two o'clock in the morning, when Franco

[36] Hugh Gibson (ed.): *The Ciano Diaries, 1939–1943* (Garden City 1946), p. 299; M. Muggeridge (ed.) *Ciano's Diplomatic Papers* (London 1948), p. 396–7.

[37] Detwiler, op. cit., p. 59. Testimony of Paul Schmidt.

declared that it was 'physically impossible' to continue and went back to San Sebastián.

Hitler could not stay to pursue the negotiations without being late for Marshal Pétain, and he did not in any event relish another meeting with Franco. He subsequently told Mussolini that he would rather have three or four teeth out than go through the ordeal again.[38] He did leave Ribbentrop behind, but the Foreign Minister could not wait beyond eight o'clock in the morning, and demanded that the text of a protocol be agreed before then. Serrano went back to San Sebastián to work on the problem, and the following morning sent General Espinosa de los Monteros, the Ambassador to Germany, a staff officer who like Beigbeder had had previous diplomatic experience, to Hendaye with a text. It was unacceptable, for it contained the assertion that the French zone of Morocco 'is later to belong to Spain', and because it laid specific obligations on Germany with regard to deliveries to Spain. Ribbentrop concocted another draft, which Espinosa promised to commend to Franco, and then left in a rage. Under protest, Franco allowed Espinosa to sign. He could after all comfort himself that he had succeeded admirably in committing himself to nothing concrete, while making the Germans appear tight-fisted. All the protocol bound him to do was 'to accede to the Tripartite Pact[39] on a date to be agreed by the four powers'.

The Germans envisaged a date in the near future, for they were anxious to maintain the timetable by which Gibraltar would be taken on 10 January. The closure of the straits had assumed the greater importance for them now that Italian embroilment in the Balkans made the imminent closure of the Suez Canal unlikely. They stepped up the pressure on Spain to enter the war. On 12 November Serrano was invited to come to Berchtesgaden for discussions on the 18th. It looked seriously as if the scene was being set for an ultimatum of the kind delivered to Chancellor Schuschnigg of Austria and to President Hacha of Czecho-Slovakia. On the 14th Franco called a meeting of Serrano and his service ministers, General Vigón, who had in June become Minister of Air as well as Chief of Staff, General Varela and

[38] *Ciano's Diplomatic Papers*, p. 402.
[39] The Tripartite Pact between Germany, Italy and Japan.

Admiral Moreno, both anglophiles. They all agreed that Spain must at all costs stay out of the war, and, with that clear, Serrano was allowed to go to Germany.

Once he was there Hitler did not take long to come to the point. When could Spain enter the war, he asked? 186 out of 230 German divisions were at the moment idle and could be deployed anywhere, and 'I have decided to attack Gibraltar, and my operation is minutely prepared. It remains only to undertake it ...'[40] Serrano complained once again of the problems of food and equipment of the uncertain compensation provided for in the Hendaye protocol. All this was brushed aside. Spain had only to enter the war and everything she needed would be provided. Serrano managed to leave without committing himself to anything definite, but Franco had to agree on the 28th to expedite his entry into the war. He asked that economic and military experts be sent to assess his needs.

He was fortunate in that the military expert who was sent and who arrived on 7 December was his old friend Admiral Canaris, for Canaris had always been opposed to bringing Spain in, and he several times warned Franco that strong as Germany's position might appear she was in fact likely to lose the war.[41] Franco told him bluntly that he could not enter the war at the time the Führer wanted, and Canaris was able to write so pessimistic a report that the planned Gibraltar operation was cancelled on 10 December. Hitler seemed to have recognised that Spain's price was not worth paying, but the following month he again tried hard to bring Spain in, with Ribbentrop accusing Franco of ingratitude and demanding 'a final, clear answer'. Mussolini also tried to persuade Franco when the Caudillo went to Bordighera to meet him on 12 February, but Franco simply repeated with more corroborative detail, that his state of economic and military preparation was wholly inadequate, adding that he was not being offered a very attractive political price. It was a nightmare for him trying to convince the Germans of what seemed obvious to him, that the entry of Spain into the war could not bring any advantage to Germany, let alone Spain.

．　　　．　　　．

[40] Serrano Súñer, op. cit., p. 238. DGFP, series D, vol. XI. No. 352.
[41] Harold C. Deutsch: *The Conspiracy against Hitler in the Twilight War* (Minneapolis 1968), p. 355, n.

Franco took the threat which Hitler's idle divisions posed very seriously. He was not to know that Hitler had his eye on a Russian campaign the following summer, and that he would not therefore risk a debilitating war in Spain. When he met Marshal Pétain at Montpellier on his way back from Bordighera, he asked him to give him diplomatic support to avoid the passage of German troops through Spain, but the Marshal refused. He did not reciprocate Franco's admiration for him. 'He really shouldn't think he's the cousin of the Virgin Mary,' he told his secretary.[42] The Duce at least had been more sympathetic, and had told a subordinate that he could not blame Franco for his attitude, since Spain was in the same situation as Italy had been in September 1939.[43] But Italy herself needed Spanish intervention in the war, and he could not therefore lend Franco any support. In his isolation, apprehension about German intentions led Franco on occasion to show warmth even to the Americans.

Spanish relations with the United States and with Great Britain turned as usual on the questions of supplies for Spain. The democracies were demanding varying degrees of political concession in return for assistance in dealing with the increasingly desperate economic situation. The Spaniards were torn between fear of starvation and chaos if they refused the terms, and fear of German reprisals if they were seen to come to terms with the enemy. Some did all they could to persuade both the British and Americans that they were merely fobbing off the Germans with words. Demetrio Carceller, who had succeeded Alarcón as Minister of Commerce in October, was the most notable of these. He was an expert on petroleum and a strong critic of the bureaucratic strangulation of Spain. When he was talking to Hoare or Weddell (the American Ambassador) he was also a strong critic of Serrano Súñer, who refused to deny his sympathy for the Axis, while swearing that no question had ever arisen of Spain's entering the war.

Franco, as so often, did not make a firm choice between his ministers, but his pride made him reluctant to come to terms with

[42] Henry Du Moulin de Labarthète: *Le Temps des Illusions* (Geneva 1946), pp. 237–8.
[43] Filippo Anfuso: *Roma, Berlino, Salò, 1936–1945* (Milan 1950), p. 182.

countries who constantly emphasised his dependence on them. So Serrano Súñer was able to defer the conclusion of a harmless loan agreement and of a *modus vivendi* over Tangier which Spain had annexed to her zone of Morocco in November, although this delayed clearance for all Spain's seaborne imports. The American terms for aid during the winter of 1940–41 were so steep that they were scarcely considered. Franco was asked 'to make it publicly known that the policy of the Spanish Government does not envisage any change in the present neutral position of Spain',[44] and the State Department was not softened by any amount of private assurance or by Carceller's explanation that with Hitler at the Pyrenees such a declaration was impossibly dangerous.

Spain's anxieties were not at an end even when by the end of February 1941 new trade agreements had been signed with Britain and Argentina, and the Germans had ceased to exert pressure on her to fight at her side. On 28 February the Italians published an unofficial estimate of Spain's civil war debt just to remind her of her troubles. And as spring advanced so also did rumours of invasions: a British invasion of the Canaries to forestall the seizure of Gibraltar, a German invasion to forestall a British landing. The British were apparently the first to make any plans for a violation of Spanish territory. A plan to seize the Canaries if Gibraltar was put out of action was approved by the Cabinet on 9 April. That they feared for Gibraltar may be a tribute to the success of Germany's cover for the invasion of Russia, but apprehension about British moves soon caused Hitler to allocate eight divisions to help Spain in the event of invasion. This was the beginning of May, and Franco let the Germans know that he was worried that they might invade as a preventive measure, and that if they did Spain would resist. But the alarming rumours continued. The hostility of the American press to Spain, the increasing southward range of German submarine patrols in the Atlantic, the extension of the American naval patrol area as far east as the Azores, all seemed to bring the Spanish people closer to the war.

At the same time Spain's neutrality was being eroded by small violations. The British during the spring pirated an Italian liner

[44] FRUS, 1940. vol. II, p. 828.

from its refuge in the territorial waters of Fernando Póo.[45] As their U-Boat operations moved south, the Germans were invoking more frequently the agreed right of their ships to secret replenishment in Spanish ports. The espionage war in Iberia grew in intensity. At this stage the British were largely concerned with counter-espionage, but later in the war the Americans built a large network of political intelligence in Spain, using for the purpose the officials who oversaw Spanish oil consumption, and they also gave judicious moral and material support to 'red' groups in the country.[46] On the other side, the SD and Gestapo made good use of the opportunities which they were given by the Spanish invitation to Himmler to send advisers on police organisation. Nazi Party elements in the German Embassy were in touch with dissident Falangists, and indeed other dissatisfied Spanish Nationalists of every political hue made contact with the Germans, though without receiving much encouragement.

The government too remained loyal supporters of the Axis, on the whole. There was certainly no doubt that most of its members hoped for an Axis victory. Franco was doubtful whether his regime could survive its defeat, and he shared Serrano's opinions that 'in such a case Europe would be an impoverished congerie of peoples too weak to resist the Red attack'.[47] He was cheered by the success of the Germans in the Balkans, but he continued to advance economic arguments for not becoming involved. Then came the invasion of Russia. Although he had not been shocked by the *Realpolitik* of the Russo–German pact in 1939, he had not ceased to regard the Soviet Union as the real, long term enemy of Europe. Britain and France were his opponents largely because Spain had irredentist claims on them. The Soviet Union on the other hand was not hostile only to Franco's Spain, it was the sworn enemy of all Christian civilisation. Franco had publicly condemned the Russians' invasion of Finland and discreetly supplied arms to the Finns. Now he enthusiastically supported the Germans' attack on

[45] Bickham Sweet-Escott: *Baker Street Irregular* (London 1965), p. 59.
[46] Feis, op. cit., p. 162; Emmet J. Hughes: *Report from Spain* (New York 1947) pp. 191 ff.
[47] Expressed to the American Colonel Donovan, later head of OSS, on 28 February 1941. FRUS 1941, Vol. II, p. 882.

178

Russia. It was, he told the National Council of the Falange on 17 July; 'the battle which Europe and Christianity have for so many years awaited'.[48]

Within three days of the Germans crossing the Russian border, Franco had agreed with a Falangist proposal that a volunteer division be sent to fight with Germany on the Russian front. It would not be a very expensive gesture. At the post-war settlement it would give him grounds to claim recognition for Spain's colonial claims, and in the shorter term it would not, he calculated, harm Britain sufficiently for her to take any drastic action against Spain. He therefore let recruiting go ahead, dividing responsibility for it between the Falange and the Army, but ensuring that all the officers were real officers and not Falangist big-wigs. He also made sure that a large proportion of the volunteers had military experience. He did not wish the division—the Blue Division it was to be called, for dark blue is the Falange colour—to disgrace Spanish arms.

As a further assistance to the Axis cause it was agreed in August that Spanish workmen should be sent to work in German factories. The number which the leader of the Falange syndicates had promised was 100,000 but by 6 November not a single worker had left for Germany. Workers were suspicious of such an emigration, and there were struggles between employers unwilling to lose good workers and Falangists keen to send nothing but the best to the German ally. In the end, not more than 15,000 workers went, compared with 10,000 who worked regularly for the British in Gibraltar. Even these proved very undisciplined, so no more were sent. Instead Spanish consulates helped to round up 'red' expatriates in France to the number of some 40,000 who won golden opinions with the Germans. In one of his recurrent anti-Franco moods Hitler even dreamed of converting them to Nazism and using them as the shock troops of a new Spanish revolution![49]

In the summer of 1941, however, Hitler had no cause to chide

[48] *Pueblo* (Madrid) 18 July 1941.
[49] H. R. Trevor-Roper (ed.): *Hitler's Table Talk, 1941–1944* (London 1953), p. 568.

Franco. Spain was nearer to war than she had been since the summer before. Churchill was considering whether to wait for Spain to enter the war before seizing the Canary Islands. Eden, the British Foreign Secretary, told the House of Commons that Franco's speech to the Falange Council 'makes it appear that he does not require further economic assistance from this country'. (He had, after all, stated bluntly that Britain had lost the war.) 'Further policy,' continued Eden 'will depend on the actions and attitude of the Spanish Government.'[50] Spain was also in trouble with the United States, largely because of a personal quarrel between Serrano and Weddell.

Towards the end of July Spain believed that the American Government was in negotiation with Republican generals in exile, and that an attack on the Azores was imminent. On the 29th Serrano intimated in a press interview that 'Spain could not remain indifferent to an attack on the Portuguese possessions',[51] but at their meeting the following month Churchill and Roosevelt did not rule out the seizure of either Grand Canary or the Portuguese islands. Fortunately the collision never took place and the British shelved their invasion plans, primarily because the Russian campaign seemed to rule out any German move in the west, but partly also because the Spanish Government had responded to British demands to prevent German use of the islands. Franco, for all his public contempt for the democracies, was in private attempting to explain his fiery words away.

He was less prepared than ever to face the hazards of war, and for once neither the Germans nor the Italians were putting any pressure on him to do so. When in November Serrano went to Germany to renew Spain's adherence to the Anti-Comintern Pact, Hitler asked for no more than an undertaking to defend the Azores against attack. For the third year, Spain faced a hard winter following disastrous harvests in many parts of the country. Torrential rains during the spring had caused floods, destroying thousands of acres of crops altogether in the Guadalquivir valley, and harming many thousands more. In the drier areas agriculture had suffered more than in previous years from lack of fertilisers,

[50] Quoted in Templewood, op. cit., p. 113.
[51] *Il Messaggero* (Rome), 30 July 1941.

because in the autumn of 1940 the Government made a number of nitrate fertiliser factories turn over to the manufacture of high explosives and because the import of phosphates had fallen yet again. Distribution was also breaking down as the growing shortages pushed more and more goods into the black market. From 1 November 1941 serious black market offences were punishable by death, but no perceptible change took place in the situation except that black market prices increased.

There was all the same a glimmer of hope on the previously dark horizon. An advantage, which Spain had not previously enjoyed, stemmed from her proximity to the nations at war. As German submarine strength grew, Britain was prepared to pay substantially above world prices for her raw materials in order to economise on shipping costs, which had been vastly inflated by war risks and the slowness of convoys. She was also prepared to take more of Spanish commodities like iron ore, mercury and pyrites than heretofore. Germany too was requiring Spanish goods she had not previously imported. She needed whatever woollens she could lay hands on, since artificial fibre uniforms were inadequate for the Russian winter. She needed wolfram and other metals in which Spanish reserves were small, but which were now important to Germany owing to the loss of her trans-Siberian communications with the Far East.

These new export outlets were doubly valuable for Spain, since the Allies were prepared to expend considerable sums to raise the cost of German purchases or even to prevent them altogether. In order to gain the *entrée* to this unusual auction, the State Department was eventually prepared even to overlook the infuriatingly pro-Japanese tone of Spanish newspaper reports, and to come to a medium term agreement on petroleum supply, which after further delays came into force in the spring of 1942. It was very shakily based, because on more than one occasion the Americans decided that Spain was receiving dangerously large quantities of petroleum, with the result that Spain stopped export permits in reprisal for the interruption of the oil flow. But Franco was at least converted from the pursuit of autarky. He did not dissent from the new American Ambassador's opinion that 'no country . . . is capable of becoming self-sufficient without disastrously lowering the living standards of its people'.[52] Even Serrano had by the summer of 1942 become concerned to see that nothing offensive appeared in the Press 'that might cost us a navicert'.[53]

During the course of 1942, therefore, Spain became much less outspoken in her hostility to the Allies, while remaining cordial towards the Axis. In February Franco and the Portuguese Prime Minister Salazar met in Seville at Franco's request. Formally, his reason was continued fear of an American attack on the Azores, but the meeting served to demonstrate that Iberia would defend herself against any attack no matter whence it came. Perhaps it marked a first step on the long path towards Spanish impartial neutrality, but if so Franco immediately compensated for it by a fiery speech in which he promised that if the road to Berlin lay open to the Russians it would be defended not just by a Spanish division but by a million Spaniards in arms.

There was, however, no vilification of the western Allies, and this was in keeping with the new policy which Franco, now in even closer control of foreign policy than previously, was evolving of good relations with the United States. He divided the war into two separate conflicts. In the Japanese–American war in the Pacific he was an unconcerned neutral; but in the war on the Russian front he was decidedly not neutral. This viewpoint he expressed to Hayes when he presented his letters of credence on 9 June, and again to Roosevelt's special envoy Myron Taylor on 30 September. An Axis victory might be a disagreeable prospect, he said, but a Russian one would surely be a thousand times worse.[54] The public remarks of many American politicians about the prospect of aid to Stalin, and the tenor of some of his ambassador's reports from London may have convinced him that there was some sympathy for his position in Britain and the United States.[55]

As the summer advanced, fears of invasion grew again. On 29 May

---

[52] Carlton J. H. Hayes: *Wartime Mission in Spain, 1942–1945* (New York 1945), pp. 28–9.
[53] Garriga, op. cit., p. 336.
[54] FRUS 1942, Vol. III, p. 290. Hayes, op. cit., p. 71.
[55] See the Ambassador's Reports Nos. 326 & 616, quoted by Crozier, op. cit., p. 355.

Hitler issued a directive that 'we must reckon on possible enemy attempts to seize the Iberian peninsula which will call for immediate countermeasures on our part'.[56] Although any discussion with the Spaniards of plans for this contingency was forbidden, Franco's intelligence came to hear of it and Spain decided to improve her frontier fortifications. Later in the summer it was the Allies' turn to arouse Spanish suspicion, as a large armada built up in and around the harbour of Gibraltar. The Spanish intelligence appreciation was that the landings projected would be in French North Africa; in fact, the Allied planners had rejected the possibility of Iberian landings. Leaving aside political considerations, the lack of good harbours and the abundance of mountains would have made it impossible to bring their superior strength quickly and effectively to bear. But when in the very early hours of 8 November Hayes demanded an immediate audience with the Caudillo, the Foreign Minister—now no longer Serrano but Jordana—was extremely alarmed. In fact, Hayes's communication was a letter from Roosevelt assuring him that Spain's neutrality would be scrupulously respected by the troops who were at that moment landing in North Africa. Jordana was visibly relieved.[57]

For Spain passively to allow the Allies to take over the French colonies in North Africa would mean the renunciation of any immediate extension of her colonial empire, yet there were few voices raised in favour of a fight with the invaders. On the contrary, after 'Operation Torch' relations with the Western Allies improved rather than the reverse. The change of Foreign Minister from the pro-Axis Serrano Súñer to the pro-Allies General Gómez Jordana was so important a factor in this that Franco's desire for a new departure in foreign policy has often been regarded as the reason for the change.

In fact, Serrano's fall on 3 September is to be explained mainly in internal political terms, even in personal ones. It arose out of a shooting affray in Bilbao on 15 August which was alleged to be a Falangist attack on the Carlist War Minister, General Varela.

[56] H. R. Trevor-Roper (ed.): *Hitler's War Directives* (London 1964), pp. 121–3.
[57] Hayes, op. cit., p. 91.

Varela attempted to use the incident to gather support for a drastic attack on the power of the Falange in general, and of Serrano in particular, but his activities were thought by Franco to amount to an attempt to dictate to him, and he was dismissed. And to still the anger of conservatives Franco balanced the dismissal with that of Serrano, whose going few lamented.[58] His power in the Falange had been greatly reduced by the promotion of José Luis Arrese to the vacant Secretary-Generalship in May 1941 and by his consequent loss of control over the press. Worst of all, Franco himself was offended with him. Serrano 'talked of him (Franco) as one speaks of a moronic servant',[59] and doubtless the Caudillo heard of it through the private spy service which he operated through his military household. And the Caudillo does not regard the derogation of his dignity as a light offence.

What particularly heartened the Allies about the change was the emphasis which the Spanish Government began to place on its relations with Portugal. And in his first major speech after taking up office, on 20 September 1942, General Jordana referred to the importance of Spain's links with Latin America. It did not escape notice that almost all the countries of that continent had broken off relations with the Axis in accordance with the resolutions of the Rio de Janeiro conference of the previous January. In December 1942, Jordana went to Portugal for talks, and, on the 20th unveiled the new 'Iberian Bloc' at a banquet in Sintra. There was, he said, an urgent need for closer co-operation in the face of the uncertainties of the world situation; and after the end of the war a united peninsula could play a large part on the European scene. Behind these words lay a shrewd policy. Franco and Salazar were able to interpret the motive of their co-operation as fear of the Allies or as fear of the Axis—depending on which they were talking to. Not that this was particularly deceitful, for they had much to fear from the post-war period, whoever won. The combatants seemed likely to exhaust one another in a colossal but equal struggle, and the post-war period would as a result be one of chaos, the likely beneficiary of which would, as in 1917, be Communism, unless the forces of civilisation were watchful and forearmed.

[58] See Payne: *Falange* pp. 234–6.
[59] *The Ciano Diaries*, p. 520.

It was with this, as much as the immediate future, in mind that Spain approached Germany for military aid in November 1942. On 13 December Hitler promised the commander of the Blue Division, General Muñoz Grandes, that arms would be forthcoming, and on 17 December an agreement was signed, but the implementation of this was subject to long delays, as despite Spanish undertakings the Germans were not satisfied that the arms would be put to the right purpose or paid for at the right price. In June 1943, when Hitler feared an Allied landing near Barcelona, the Spanish refused to hold staff talks on the grounds that no such threat existed. In the end the Germans did deliver a little material, but the Americans, who were approached in June 1943, refused to supply any, and Franco had to forgo his ideal of strong neutrality, and rely on trimming his sails diplomatically to the prevailing wind.

This was made somewhat more difficult by the progress of the war in the last months of 1942. With the benefit of hindsight one may see Alamein, the success of the North Africa landings, and the relief of Stalingrad as military turning points of the war, but at that time they did not portend more than the indefinite prolongation of the war, the final shattering of hopes for a quick Axis victory. For Spain the consciousness of Axis power actually increased, as the German occupation in November of the formerly unoccupied zone of France gave her a much longer frontier with German-held territory. Nevertheless not only Jordana, but also Varela's rather pro-Axis successor as Minister, General Asensio Cabanillas, quickly agreed not to repatriate any of the thousands of Frenchmen who flooded into Spain, without papers or visas, to escape German occupation. Indeed, any refugee who could find somebody to take a personal interest in him was swiftly on his way to join the Free French in North Africa. Otherwise he had a somewhat unpleasant stay of up to a year in the concentration camp at Medina del Campo, while his case was pending. The conditions in this camp were bad, and later got so much publicity that it was often overlooked that Spain could quite properly have repatriated most of its inmates and was often under pressure from the Germans to do so. Besides, Asensio had warned the French Ambassador in advance that the Government unfortunately had only this one unsatisfactory camp in which it could intern refugees of military age.[60]

Their behaviour towards these refugees shows Franco and his ministers at their most neutral, and receiving hard words from both sides. During 1943 Franco evolved the 'two wars' theory he had broached to Hayes the previous June into a new 'three wars' theory. He did not abate his hostility to Communism or his solidarity with Hitler in his war against Soviet Russia, but during the summer of 1943 he gradually adopted a genuinely neutral stance as between the Axis and the western Allies. 'Non-belligerency' was publicly exchanged for neutrality on 3 October. Meanwhile, he had associated himself with Portugal in attempts to bring about peace talks between the Axis and the West so that a common fight on behalf of Christianity might result. Cautiously, he emphasised that he was following the lead of the Pope both in a public speech at Almería on 9 May and in the instructions he had sent to his brother Nicolás, who was his Ambassador in Lisbon, on 11 May.[61]

Like so many peacemakers, particularly those with an interest in the outcome, Franco met with little success. The Germans were embarrassed lest Franco might be considered their mouthpiece. The Allies simply referred him to the doctrine of unconditional surrender which Roosevelt and Churchill had pronounced at Casablanca in January. For his stance in the third of his 'three wars' he won similarly little applause. He moved from the neutrality in the Pacific War he had implied in 1942 to a position in April 1945, after the fall of Manila to the Americans, where he might have entered the war had he been given any encouragement. Unfortunately, while all his horror at Japanese treatment of Spaniards in the Philippines was forgotten, the Americans continued to feel slighted by a cordial telegram he had sent to Laurel in October 1943.[62]

Indeed although the position of the Allies in Spain improved steadily in 1943 in relation to the Axis, Allied goodwill towards

---

[60] François Piétri: *Mes Années d'Espagne 1940–1948* (Paris 1954) p. 194.
[61] See Richard Pattee: *Portugal and the Portuguese World* (Milwaukee 1957), p. 308.
[62] Laurel was the Japanese puppet President of the Philippines, which at that time remained *de jure* under U.S. sovereignty.

Spain did not increase greatly. The more concessions were made to their increasing strength, naturally the more concessions were demanded. In July 1943 Hoare presented what he called his 'grand remonstrance', complaining about the activities of German espionage, violations of neutrality by German ships and aircraft, the greater freedom accorded to Axis propaganda, and above all the retention of the Blue Division in Russia.[63] Hayes had also laid complaints about the Blue Division in Russia, and at the beginning of October the Führer's Headquarters was finally requested to pull the division out of the line. Then, on 6 November 1943, Hayes was instructed to make a number of further demands, prominent among which was one for complete embargo on the export of wolfram to Germany. These demands the United States were prepared to back up with the halting in February of petroleum shipments, whilst in the background the Allied press and broadcasting networks manifested their bitter hostility towards Franco's regime. The amount of wolfram at issue seemed to the Spanish too small to be the real reason for the Allied diplomatic onslaught. Franco later claimed to have documentary evidence of an Anglo-American plan to invade Iberia at this time, which was only shelved because Stalin realized that it was a bid to postpone the opening of a second front in France.[64] But in any case he determined not to give in to the Allies on the embargo issue, correctly believing that the British were less determined in their demands than the Americans, and that in the end they would force the Americans to compromise.

At all events by the end of the following summer a wolfram embargo was of only academic importance, for the Germans had withdrawn from the Pyrenean border areas to face the Anglo-American invaders farther north, abandoning their land communications with Spain. As soon as agreement was reached on the wolfram issue, in May 1944, a large number of other concessions followed the same month: the closure of the German Consulate in Tangier; the granting of overflying rights to anti-submarine patrol aircraft; permission for the Allies to evacuate casualties from France through Barcelona if necessary. Franco had finally decided

[63] Templewood, op. cit., pp. 197–204.
[64] See Francisco Franco: *Textos de Doctrina Política. Palabras y escritos de 1945 a 1950* (Madrid 1951), pp. 167–8.

that an Allied victory was inevitable and from then on he set out to ensure the survival of order in Spain surrounded by an unsympathetic world. As late as December 1943 he had agreed with the German Ambassador that he could never survive the defeat of the Axis.[65] Now he was going to try to prove himself wrong.

[65] US Department of State: *The Spanish Government and the Axis. Documents* (Washington 1945), No. 15.

8 Ostracism

Of the Allied leaders Churchill seemed the most likely to view Franco's presence on the international scene without hostility. He had sympathised with the Nationalists during the Civil War, though he had desired a Republican victory in the interests of Great Britain. On several occasions during the World War he had expressed himself warmly about Spain's neutrality both in private and in public. On 24 May 1944 he reminded the House of Commons how valuable it had been at crucial stages in the war. In October 1944 Franco decided to capitalise on this apparent goodwill. In order not to appear a suppliant he began by making a series of complaints about British behaviour towards Spain, which were almost a mirror image of British complaints: hostility of the Press, violations of neutrality and so forth. Then he suggested a post-war Europe led by a London–Madrid axis: 'But, once Germany is destroyed, England will have only one country left in Europe towards which she can turn her eyes—Spain. The French and Italian defeats, and the internal decomposition of those countries, will probably not allow anything solid to be built upon them for many years to come'.[1] The purpose of the proposed alliance would of course be defence against Soviet expansion.

Churchill's reply was long in coming and dampening when it came. Whatever Churchill's fears of Russian imperialism, he was

[1] This letter and Churchill's reply are printed in full as Appendix A to Templewood, op. cit., pp. 300–306.

not in a position to snub Stalin, least of all by embracing Franco, and he probably did not share Franco's confidence in the ability of Spain to play a greater role in Europe than France and Italy. Any hope which Franco may have placed in American goodwill was similarly destroyed when on 12 April the new American Ambassador, Norman Armour, read Lequerica his instructions from the President. Roosevelt made it clear that, in spite of being Franco's 'sincere friend' (as he had signed himself in November 1942), he felt unable to give any sign of friendship to Spain 'when American sentiment is so profoundly opposed to the present regime in power'.[2] Roosevelt's death the following week made no difference, for Truman had placed strong anti-Franco views on record as a Senator, and in August 1945 he assured a press conference that 'none of us like Franco or his government'.[3] After these demonstrations of dislike from impeccable non-Communists, the hostility of the Soviet Union and of France, where the Liberation movement had given great strength to the left, was taken for granted.

Franco was also quick to discern the sinister hand behind the surge of world opinion against his regime which was expressed in a mounting wave of international gestures. At the end of the San Francisco Conference on International Organisation in June the participants put it on record that they did not favour membership of any world organisation for such states as had been set up by Axis military force. Many delegates put it on record that they meant Spain, and after the Three-Power Conference at Potsdam the leaders stated in their communiqué 'that they would not favour any application for membership put forward by the present Spanish government'.[4] In March 1946 the Foreign Ministers of Britain, France and the United States made a joint appeal to Spain to change its government. And throughout this period a high level of abuse was poured on Franco by the press not only of socialist but also of liberal persuasion. The Spanish Government took every opportunity to point to central Communist direction for the various specific campaigns against them, unmasking as Communist front organisations like the World Federation of Trade Unions,

[2] FRUS 1945, Vol. V., pp. 667–8, 675.
[3] *New York Times*, 24 August 1945
[4] FRUS 1945, Vol. II, p. 1499. *The Times*, 3 August 1945

which many still supposed to be independent entities. Franco and his ministers enjoyed boasting in later years of their prescience with regard to the Communist threat. Less is now heard of Franco's second diagnosis of Spain's ills, the undermining of the regime by 'the masonic super-state, which lays down its laws for its members, to whom it sends its orders and its watchwords'.[5]

For all the bad faith and ulterior motives that Franco saw, in many cases correctly, behind the criticisms of his regime, he nevertheless took some steps to bring his government into greater conformity with the norms of the western world. From the earliest days it had been a goal of Serrano's to provide the new Spain with a juridical framework which would enable it to survive without Franco and independently of the Army. (An ambition to supplant his brother-in-law may have contributed to such an aspiration.) In 1941, as President of the Falange's Political Committee, he was already studying projects for a charter of citizens' rights and for limitations on the government's power within the framework of the corporative state.[6] The constitution of the Cortes in 1942 owed something to his influence, though it had been drawn up in detail by José Luis Arrese who had by that time supplanted him in the Falange. The Cortes which began work in 1943 was of course purely consultative, and the principles of its selection were basically corporative rather than democratic. Franco here accepted, as José Antonio had, the view that the true, organic subdivisions of the state were municipality, syndicate and family, and that it was these rather than parasitic and divisive political parties that should be represented in any legislative body. In fact this principle was not wholly adhered to, for the Cortes also included the Cabinet, some eighty members of the Falange National Council and fifty others nominated directly by the Caudillo.

Besides these, the members representing syndicates and municipalities were indirectly appointees of the Head of State. Indeed the syndicates had proved a disappointment to many. After the fall of Salvador Merino the principal function of the syndicates, apart

---

[5] Franco: *Textos*, p. 335. Speech to the Chaplains of the Falange's *Sección Femenina*, 11 September 1945.

[6] See André Corthis (pseud.): *L'Espagne de la Victoire* (Paris 1941), pp. 66-8.

from serving as a pork barrel from which to distribute jobs to the Falange, became to act in industry as an arm of the government. As such they were cordially loathed both by the workers and by the employers. The former regarded them as a sham under which their labour was exploited for unreasonably low wages. The latter disliked them as the inquisitors through whom the government manifested their interest in the details of industry and commerce. They were forever demanding statistics and they frequently prevented industrialists from running their businesses as they thought fit by prohibiting certain imports, fixing prices and sometimes dictating what they should produce.

The policy of government intervention which had alienated big business from the Dictator had come again, and on a larger scale. Although many employers had thought that the Nationalists were fighting for the freedom of the employing classes from the tyranny of the workers, they were as subject to regulation of wages and labour relations as under the Republic. They found themselves obliged to pay increasing social security contributions and to carry on their payrolls large numbers of workers for whom they had no work, for although such wage and price indices as there are for the forties show a falling standard of living for the industrial worker, he did have greater security than before both in employment and in sickness and old age. Great stress was laid on this in the propaganda for the 1947 referendum, but nobody could believe that the Falange syndicates were any more 'organic' than the old Socialist and Anarchist labour unions had been.

The municipalities were reformed by a law of 17 July 1945. Previously their corporations had been simply nominated by the Civil Governor of the province or in the case of the larger cities by the Ministry of the Interior. The new law provided for their election by the indirect suffrage of heads of families, and the first elections were promised for the autumn of 1945. This democratisation of the municipalities was one of the steps which was intended to convince the world that Franco was gradually liberalising his regime, and that he therefore merited support. Another such step was the promulgation of the Spaniards' Charter (*Fuero de los Españoles*), which occurred on the same day. This guaranteed all the democratic rights of assembly, free speech and so on, but outsiders were quick to note the proviso in Article 12 'that they do not oppose the basic principles of the State' and the right of the government to suspend the guarantees in an emergency.

Of course, most countries have similar saving clauses in their constitutions, but the Spanish government was in the dock, and the prosecutors, not believing in their sincerity, looked always for the holes in their arguments. Many of them were in the frame of mind where they would believe the most arrant nonsense provided that it was derogatory to Franco's Spain; for example, that Spain was planning to invade France in the early months of 1946, or that she was manufacturing atomic bombs at Ocaña, thirty-eight miles from Madrid.

It had been widely foreseen on all sides that public opinion in the Allied countries would be implacably hostile to Franco and throughout Spain the approach of Allied victory raised the hopes of the regime's opponents and the fears of its adherents. The end of Franco's rule was in 1944 and 1945 often taken for granted by people of every political colour and in every country. 'Which country will lose least from the war?', it was asked, the answer to the riddle being: 'Spain, which will lose only one Franco'.[7] (*Franco* is Spanish—and Portuguese and Italian—for franc.) The militant Republican opposition began to gird up its loins for the 'second round'. Some of them foresaw with a certain grim satisfaction a conflict at least as bloody as the first round in 1936. Others imagined that the political and economic dissatisfaction within Spain was such that the whole edifice of Franco's regime would collapse if they could only give it a firm push.

With this over-optimism a small force of perhaps some two thousand Republicans crossed the Pyrenean frontier in October 1944 hoping that their example, broadcast by Toulouse Radio, would bring about a general insurrection. Experienced in the Civil War, and subsequently in the French Resistance, they were good soldiers, but they were driven off by overwhelming force, having gained very little popular support. In spite of their secret lines of communication into Spain, they had wholly misjudged the mood in the country. Twenty years later the Communist General

[7] Abel Plenn: *Wind in the Olive Trees: Spain from the Inside* (New York 1946), p. 229.

Líster drew the moral that 'in organising a guerrilla movement one should never confuse popular sympathy with popular support'.[8]

This setback in conventional warfare did not affect guerrillas in Spain who had operated continuously from the end of the civil war, but who in 1944 and 1945 were able to step up their activities. It was much easier now to receive supplies from France, and new leaders trained in guerrilla techniques could also join their struggle. Having said that, one must add that this guerrilla warfare was largely indistinguishable from brigandage, and that political out-lawry and economic convenience were frequently conjoined motives for taking up arms. Even Cristino García, to save whom from exe-cution a world-wide propaganda campaign was sponsored by the Communists, and who had a distinguished record in the French Resistance, was convicted of several bank robberies. Such figures were, however, more a nuisance than a danger. In previous years regular formations in battalion, even brigade strength, were used against their bands without success. By 1945 much smaller num-bers of Civil Guards were employed to stalk and ambush them and, though this method achieved greater success, the number of guerrilla actions mounted, reaching its peak in 1947. Yet there was no chance of these political bandits taking over the country unless the government abdicated and left them a political vacuum into which to move.

All the same, men of position and property were alarmed by the coming of the Allied victory. Some who had been notoriously pro-German turned with the tide of war towards the Allies; but old-style conservatives, who had not really desired a new order in Europe, were even more alarmed at the uncertainties of the post-war world. They feared a 'red' revolution in the wake of Allied victory. 'If the Germans win,' they said to one another, 'I stand to lose all my money. If the Allies win, I stand to lose my head'.[9] While some favoured concessions to their workmen and acts of charity as an insurance, others thought that change could be pre-vented by greater firmness by the government and the police.[10] The

[8] Enrique Líster: 'Lessons of the Spanish Guerrilla War' in *World Marx-ist Review*, Vol. 8, No. 2, February 1965, p. 37.

[9] Doussinague, op. cit., p. 274.

[10] See Plenn, op. cit., p. 282.

political solution favoured by many of these frightened men was the restoration of the monarchy, accompanied by a modicum of liberal window-dressing for the benefit of the Allies. That this would at least ensure British support they had been firmly encouraged to believe by Sir Samuel Hoare while he was British Ambassador, and besides they had never ceased to look to the monarchy as the ideal form of Government. If these difficult times brought risks, they also promised the possibility of removing Franco, whom Kindelán the kingmaker and other Monarchist generals regarded as a traitor to their cause.

The Pretender to the throne was Juan, the second surviving son of Alfonso XIII, who had abdicated in his favour in January 1941, and died shortly afterwards.[11] Juan had served in the British Navy in the early thirties and was anglophile in outlook, but he also had contacts in Germany. It was not until just after the Allied landings in North Africa in November 1942 that he threw his hat in the ring by stating that, while he was not a conspirator and he would wait patiently, he was sure he would be called to the throne. He advocated complete neutrality in the war. During 1943 he broadened the basis of his appeal by convincing Rodezno that he was sufficiently traditionalist and the veteran Liberal Romanones that he was sufficiently constitutionalist.

That summer, agitation began to grow for a restoration: twenty-six prominent men signed a petition to Franco, but this had no effect but to lose some of them positions in the government. In September eight senior generals addressed a letter to the Head of State, discreetly reminding him that they were 'the same ... who placed in your hands seven years ago in the Salamanca aerodrome the supreme powers of military command and of the state',[12] and suggested that it was time to restore the monarchy. Franco's view, however, was that he represented the most broadly based regime possible, and that the monarchy was only the regime of a party in spite of Juan's non-involvement with the Civil War, on which Franco had insisted on the grounds that 'if there is a King, he will

[11] In April 1931, Alfonso had merely 'suspended the use of his prerogative.'
[12] Payne: *Politics and the Military*, p. 433.

195

have to come as a pacifier and should not be numbered with the victors'.[13] He was confident of the strength of his position and made no concession to Monarchist opinion at all, simply letting Juan become impatient and make mistakes. On 28 January 1944 the Pretender released to the press a letter he had written to Franco strongly condemning the regime. Immediately he realised the error he had committed, but his attempt to retrieve it with a conciliatory telegram failed.[14]

Juan's next important public act was to issue the Lausanne manifesto in March 1945, in which he called for a speedy restoration of the monarchy as the only means to avoid strife in Spain. It had been hoped that monarchists would refuse to continue to serve the Franco regime, but in the event the only important resignation was that of the Ambassador in London, the Duke of Alba de Tormes. (His resignation was not accepted and he was obliged to remain at his post throughout the summer.) A number of monarchists felt that the threat from the left was too present to break ranks with the coalition which had won the civil war. The veteran monarchist Antonio Goicoechea for example, leader of the orthodox monarchist party Renovacíon Española under the Republic, called the manifesto 'ill-timed, ill-advised meddling ... without previous consultation inside Spain'.[15] Nevertheless Franco thought that it would be prudent to treat with the Pretender, and in early May he sent José María de Areilza to Switzerland to see him. Juan refused to meet him as an official representative; he felt now that he must dictate the terms of the game, and many Monarchists were confident. Rumours in Madrid had it that prominent Monarchists were refusing offers of cabinet posts, but in Lausanne Juan was less confident; he told Ramón Garriga in April that 'Franco will always find somebody to tell him he is right and to justify his remaining in power'.[16]

Indeed, it seems that at this time Hungary under Admiral Horthy, a Kingdom with a Regent but no King, was the parallel

[13] *ABC* (Seville) 18 July, 1937, quoted in Ramón Sierra: *Don Juan de Borbón* (Madrid 1965), p. 95.
[14] Hughes, op. cit., pp. 181–4.
[15] *New York Times*, 18 April 1945.
[16] Garriga, op. cit., p. 386.

of which Franco was thinking. He was also planning the Spaniards' Charter and the municipal reforms, which he hoped would make his regime more acceptable, and which, on 17 July, he claimed gave Spaniards 'the maximum liberties compatible with order'.[17] It was not until the end of August that he again made a serious attempt to sound Don Juan. Even then Franco cannot have had much hope of agreement, for Juan had been reported as saying that he did not wish to 'inherit a ready-made Primo de Rivera',[18] while he himself is said to have remarked that he did not intend to become 'Queen Mother'. There was in fact no agreement, but Franco probably felt obliged to try in the face of the Potsdam declaration and of the meeting in Mexico of the Republican Cortes. On 28 August Martín Artajo, who had replaced Lequerica as Foreign Minister in the cabinet reshuffle in July, told the American Ambassador that he believed that Franco now realised he must step down.[19] But Franco's avowed principal aim was to avoid taking any step that would result in disorder or would endanger the victory over 'anti-Spain' he had won in 1939.

The constitution of a Republican Government in exile under José Giral, which on 26 August 1945 followed the meeting of the Republican Cortes, did not pose any direct threat to Franco, but it did provide both his Spanish Republican opponents and his foreign enemies with a focus for their support. The Giral cabinet was broad-based but it had strong critics both to left and to right. On its right were those like Miguel Maura and Indalecio Prieto[20] who realised that some contact must be made with moderate Nationalists, while on its left Negrín and the Communists thought that it was too hesitant to use force. Giral's Foreign Minister Fernando de los Ríos tried in December to elicit positive support from the American State Department by threatening otherwise to include the Communists in the cabinet, but the United States would not be drawn,[21] and in April 1946 a Communist did enter the cabinet.

[17] Franco: *Textos*, p. 23.
[18] *New York Times* 19 July 1945. Juan naturally repudiated the remark.
[19] FRUS 1945, Vol V, pp. 687–8.
[20] Maura was a Catholic Right-Wing Republican, and Prieto a moderate Socialist. Both had been prominent ministers under the Republic.
[21] FRUS 1945, Vol. V, pp. 704–5.

The Republicans were showered with goodwill by the democratic powers and of course by the socialist states, but they could not elicit any direct political action to match.

Conversely, the Franco government tried in vain to find out from the Americans what measures would be sufficient to abate their official hostility. Franco did not after all wish to do more than the minimum. While at the end of November 1945 he sent Truman the message that 'he is working honestly and loyally for evolution on liberal lines', the following day Martín Artajo added the gloss that 'much as Franco and many of his supporters would regret a worsening or a break in relations with other governments, they would prefer this rather than to compromise themselves or to take premature action here which might result in grave disorders or civil war'.[22] In fact Franco had come to believe that he could not pay the American and British price. This was, if not his own departure, at least the disappearance of the Falange. The Falange was mentioned as a source of displeasure in Churchill's reply to Franco, in Roosevelt's instructions to Armour and frequently in the press and in the Ambassador's official conversations. In response, Franco removed Arrese from the cabinet in his July reshuffle and left his post as Secretary of the Movement vacant. (The Falange was not now referred to as a party.) He also repealed the 1937 decree which made the raised arm salute official. But he would not consider dismantling the Falange altogether. It was a vital component of his political system.

The existence of the Falange was the primary justification for Franco's assertion that his was, more than the Monarchy could be, the regime 'which divides us least'. The Falange preferred him to Don Juan. So of course did the Carlists, except for the not insignificant number who had become reconciled to Don Juan; but the Carlist Regent, Prince Javier of Bourbon-Parma, a veteran of the French Resistance and of a German concentration camp, announced on 12 September 1945 that his followers would not fight for Franco in the event of another civil war. Falangists of the old guard were also resentful of Franco, in particular of his failure to attack monopoly capitalism and of his reliance on the old oligarchy for so many of the key posts in government. But they were

[22] FRUS 1945, Vol. V, pp. 694-5.

vulnerable, and in the last analysis they had no choice but to stand by Franco, who was at least their ally against Don Juan.

They had collaborated with Franco in the fabrication of an alternative monarchism with the obscure Carlos of Habsburg-Lorraine[23] as its figurehead; this had been used as a squib to distract the orthodox monarchists in 1943 and was resurrected for the same purpose in the autumn of 1945. They were also most useful to Franco as predatory wolves to which he could threaten to throw the capitalists and the Church if they did not behave. It was not Franco who was apostrophised in blood-curdling 'clandestine' publications of the Falange like the one which in 1943 asked 'you, respectable Señor, who can eat, smoke, and live well because the Falange has pulled your chestnuts out of the fire . . . have you thought what the Falange would be in the opposition? Have you thought of the effect of a Falangist company shooting its way into a meeting of the conservative party?'[24] And it was not Franco with his efficient secret police who was worried by rumours that the Falange were making contact with Barcelona anarchists as a precautionary measure.

These threats were a little extravagant, for the Falange had long lost its revolutionary élan in the comfort of profitable offices, but when the Falange came on to the streets of Barcelona at the beginning of August in protest against the removal of the old guard Civil Governor, Correa Veglisón, they pointed up the nature of Anglo-American concern with the Falange. Correa had looked after Barcelona's interests well as Civil Governor, and despite his blue shirt he had found favour with Sir Samuel Hoare.[25] His successor,

[23] Don Alfonso Carlos, the last living descendant of Don Carlos (see p. 108) in the male line, died in 1936, and this Carlos was the son of his niece. But Carlist succession rules do not permit descendants in the female line to succeed, and the next heir according to Carlist rules was in fact Don Juan. Yet hard core traditionalists found excuses to exclude him, and followed Don Javier whose own claim to the throne was very remote, but who as yet only aspired to the Regency for which Alfonso Carlos had designated him. For this whole complicated question, see Aronson, op. cit., pp. 218–19; Guy Coutant de Saisseval: *Les maisons impériales et royales d'Europe* (Paris 1966), pp. 48–56, 189–241, 387–411; Román Oyarzún: *Historia del Carlismo* (Bilbao 1939), pp. 578–80.

[24] Foltz, op. cit., p. 256.

[25] Templewood, op. cit., p. 145.

Colonel Barba, was an inveterate enemy of liberalism who had attempted, with considerable success, to damage and discredit the Republic from the moment of its inception. Yet the change was welcomed in the English language press as a sign of liberalisation in the regime.

Monarchists like the Duke of Alba de Tormes, oligarchs like Juan Ventosa, prominent men like General Aranda who had on personal grounds failed to get their estimate of their desserts under Franco realised that the Caudillo was a liability. The British and American governments were concerned that Spain should remove the symbols that connected her with the fallen regimes in Germany and Italy. These were the Falange, so many of whose attributes were, for all its denials, copies of Fascism or of National Socialism, and Franco. Franco it was who symbolised the Nationalist victory, brought about, it was believed, solely by fascist intervention. Franco it was who was photographed greeting the Führer with every appearance of cordiality on the station at Hendaye. If Franco were to go, the very focus of the idealist Left's campaign would be removed, and the hostility to Spain would die away without the regime having to change fundamentally. After all, as Lequerica had pointed out to Lord Templewood in December 1944, it was hypocrisy to pretend that it was the lack of democracy in Spain that Britain and America objected to; they had been able to maintain good relations with Stalin and with Getúlio Vargas of Brazil, and he might have added others.[26]

The problems which arose for those who were convinced that Franco must go were the succession and the mechanics of the change-over of power. One might arrive at a consensus that the Monarchy should be restored under Juan, but only a minority of those who agreed to this preliminary would further agree either to a real democratic parliamentary government or to a Spain in which the King really ruled. And if neither the King nor the people was to be sovereign, who was to be the strong man or the ruling clique? It seems that Aranda had contemplated organising an Army coup in 1944. General Kindelán's outspoken monarchism probably concealed a desire to be the power behind the throne. Ventosa was spoken of as a possible Prime Minister; his admirers regarded him

[26] Doussinague, op. cit., p. 338.

as a potential economic miracle-worker on the Salazar model. But nobody dared to make a first move against the regime for fear that they would do so alone, and such was the disunity of the Nationalist opposition that their fears were well-founded. Disunity was likewise the besetting weakness of the émigrés and Republicans. They managed to patch up a formal alliance inside Spain, but their common programme hardly went beyond the slogan: 'Neither Franco with the Falange, nor the Falange without Franco, nor Franco without the Falange'.

The difficulty of seizing power was tacitly recognised by all parties, for every group seemed concerned that somebody else should oust Franco, and that they should then exploit the situation. In September 1945 Juan reaffirmed what he had said in March, that: 'I incite no one to rebellion', and de los Ríos said it would be easy to change the government by peaceful means.[27] The Communists realised the need for force, but they recognised that they could not destroy the regime alone, and criticised Republicans for their refusal to provide their indispensable co-operation.

This division in the Republican ranks was seized on by the French government opponents of interference in Spain, specifically by Georges Bidault the Foreign Minister, as an important support for their case. In Britain and the United States further reasons for staying out of Spanish affairs were advanced. The Americans wished to maintain relations to safeguard against the hiding of Germans and German assets in Spain. The British thought that interference in Spain would serve to bolster rather than to weaken the Franco régime. In the post-war age of shortages, economic sanctions would be a dangerously two-edged weapon, while an Allied military intervention was quite out of the question. It was not only Hitler who had learned from Napoleon's experience how expensive and difficult it is to invade Spain. On 16 September the British Foreign Secretary, Ernest Bevin, made it clear in a speech that his government regarded Spain as a problem to be solved by the Spaniards. It was now clear that Franco need only retain a cool head to remain undisturbed in power, for his

[27] *Journal de Genève* 22 March 1945; *New York Herald Tribune* (European edition, Paris) 24 November 1945.

principal enemies had given notice they would not make war on him.

Franco was a man unlikely to become flustered. He had, and knew that he had, more widespread personal support than any other man on the Spanish political scene. He was, in his own words, 'the sentinel who is never relieved, the man who receives the unwelcome telegrams and dictates the solutions; the man who watches while others sleep'.[28] To a wide section of the middle class, particularly the younger middle class, he was the hero who had saved them from the chaos and revolution which had threatened them in 1936. To the young men who had fought with enthusiasm as Nationalist junior officers in the civil war, many of whom had stayed in the Army after 1939 with permanent commissions, he was the legendary military commander. These men were now the captains and majors, against whose will no military coup could succeed the men of whom General Yagüe was thinking when he pledged the 'most firm and indestructible support' of all his colleagues.[29] It was in deference to their feelings and to the feelings of the many civilians who thought like them that liberal monarchists were at pains to pay tribute to Franco even as they called upon him to resign.

As the quotation in the last paragraph makes clear, Franco was self-confident. The more strident grew the chorus of execration from abroad the more convinced he became that he was a symbol of Spain, and that the Communists and freemasons with their devilish cleverness had realised the paramount importance to Spain of the Caudillo's mission. It would therefore be the worst treason to desert his post. And of course it was true that Communists (perhaps freemasons too) believed that the Nationalist coalition would not survive Franco, and calculated that they would find opportunities for the advancement of their cause in the fluid situation which would ensue from his departure.

This was not the whole picture, however. Franco was not a symbol of Spain to the international left; he was a symbol of vesti-

[28] Galinsoga, op. cit., p. 9. Speech at the Army Museum in Madrid, 9 March 1946.
[29] *ABC* (Madrid), 20 September 1945.

gial fascism. He overestimated the importance which the world attached to Spain by supposing that the Allied fear of Spain in 1945 was of the same order as, say, their fear of German resurgence. Steeped in the history of Spain's golden past, conscious of the 'black legend' propagated abroad about Spanish history, he believed that the history of the world since the eighteenth century revealed a subtle conspiracy to prevent a revival of Spain's power. The motive for this conspiracy was anti-Catholic, fear of Spain as a sword arm of the Catholic Church. The ostracism of Spain after 1945 was, in Franco's view, simply an intensification of a vendetta of centuries' standing. It was politically convenient for him to dwell on the ancient origins of this hostility to Spain, for it removed from him any portion of blame for them, while giving him the part of Spain's champion in a noble cause. But he played the part with such skill and conviction because he believed passionately that it was true.

'Spaniards know what they can expect from abroad,' Franco told the newspaper *Arriba*, 'and as history teaches them, ill-will against Spain is not something which began today or yesterday.' Again he told the Cortes in May 1946: 'We should have to renounce our independence and sovereignty or surrender to anarchy and demagogy if we wished the noise of these campaigns to die out'.[30] This was an assessment of the political situation which appealed to his people. For every Spaniard who looked up to Franco as a hero there was at least one who saw him as a necessary evil, the only alternative to anarchy. If he were to step down, the future would hold all sorts of dark possibilities, which the terrifying experiences Spain had undergone in 1936 made more nightmarish still. Franco was in a position to call himself 'the devil you know', a point illustrated by an oft-told joke. One man says to a friend in a bar: 'Did you hear Franco's fallen?' 'Hombre!' says the second man, 'That's good news.' Then he pauses, and adds in a disturbed tone: 'Who's in power now then?' 'Oh, Franco again,' says the first. At which his friend breathes a sigh of relief.[31]

Franco had in a sense blackmailed his way into an impregnable situation, for by making it clear that he would 'defend the regime

[30] *Arriba*, 18 July 1946; Franco, *Textos*, pp. 46, 66.
[31] One version of this story is in Galinsoga, op. cit., p. 411.

to the last',[32] he threatened war if anyone should attack him. As long as he was known to have followers who would resolutely take the sword in his defence, he deprived his militant opponents of the support of the mass of Spaniards, for whom war was the ultimate evil.

He never lacked this positive support. And it considerably increased in the course of the propaganda onslaught on Spain in 1945 and 1946. Just as the memory of the Civil War was kept constantly in the public eye in order to hold together the Nationalist coalition with fear of Republican revanchists, so the media of communication used foreign attacks on the government to arouse the greatest possible measure of xenophobia. There were plenty of actions in this international campaign that were calculated to rouse the passions of Spaniards who, without being very politically minded, were proud of Spain and resentful of foreigners. No great gift of writing and no great distortion of the facts were required to rouse indignation when Frenchmen attacked a trainload of Spaniards returning home from Switzerland and Germany, and caused several fatalities and many injuries among them. Likewise, Republicans in France did their cause no service by broadcasting in great detail stories of uprisings against the government which were manifestly not taking place.

Most aggravating of all perhaps was the arrogance with which the United Nations presumed to sit in judgement on Spain. With its façade of a parliamentary assembly masking a shop for political horse-trading, the United Nations represented all that Franco found most hypocritical and degrading in the liberal democratic system. So, when in December 1946 the General Assembly of this body condemned Spain and recommended its members to withdraw their ambassadors from Madrid, Franco held a rally to demonstrate Spanish unity in the face of this affront. Every facility was given to Spaniards to attend in the Plaza de Oriente in front of Madrid's royal palace, but there is no doubt of the genuineness of the ovation Franco received from a crowd which must have been hundreds of thousands strong to fill the square as it did. Even at the cinema Franco's picture on newsreels began to evoke spontaneous applause. Spain withdrew into herself, and salved her

[32] Speech to his classmates at the Infantry Academy, 26 October 1945. *New York Times*, 29 October 1945.

pride and her self-esteem with what would in England be called the 'Dunkirk spirit' of defiance. And Franco, though hardly an orator, was cast in the role of Churchill.

The United Nations were obeyed by most members, except Argentina, who hastened to fill the vacancy at her Madrid embassy; but the embassies continued to function under *chargés d'affaires*, and the resolution proved predictably to be only a pinprick, painful but harmless—indeed, a positive benefit to Franco in internal politics. Meanwhile, the opposition was crumbling. During 1946 Juan, seeing little prospect of becoming King through the evolution of the Franco regime, turned gingerly towards the Left, opening negotiations with the Anarchists. The Bases of Estoril, which he issued at the end of February 1946, included a tentative commitment to decentralisation, which was anathema to Franco, and the promise of a plebiscite on the institutions of the new regime. His overture was taken up in July when the ANFD,[33] the clandestine non-Communist Republican organisation inside Spain, agreed to such a plebiscite, even if the Giral 'government' held fast to its Republican legitimacy. In February 1947 Giral resigned and was replaced by Rodolfo Llopis, a Socialist, whose cabinet decided to negotiate with the monarchists. But in the meantime Franco had decided to solidify the structure of his regime.

During March 1947 Franco communicated to the Pretender his project for a law of succession to be submitted to the Spanish people in a referendum in accordance with a law of October 1945, which had been a show piece of the evolution towards liberalism. It embodied the principle of Monarchism, but it offered very little comfort to Juan, for it established Franco in office for as long as he chose to say, and allowed him to designate as his successor anyone he pleased. If he felt that a King was desirable he might choose any mature person of royal blood, and if not, he might nominate another Regent. Juan lost no time in announcing that the proposed law 'is vitiated substantially by its origin', and that it had no right to interfere with the laws governing the royal succession. All the opposition parties combined to predict that the referendum ballot would be rigged, and urged abstention on 6 July. 'If you vote Yes, you vote for Franco. If you vote No, you vote for Franco. If you

[33] Stands for *Alianza Nacional de Fuerzas Demócratas*.

don't vote, they'll vote for you, but they won't get your vote. Don't vote!' was the advice of the Anarchists.[34] Left-wing propagandists also pointed out that a large number of former 'reds' had been judicially deprived of civil rights, including of course the suffrage.

Nevertheless 14,145,163 'Yes' votes were cast out of 15,219,563 voters, and an electorate of 17,178,812. The majority was very substantial, and seemed to observers to be fairly arrived at. Both then and in the 1966 referendum it was widely believed by electors particularly in country districts that their ballot would not in fact be secret, but it is only fair to add that this cynicism about the democratic process is of long standing. Franco, after nearly eleven years in power, could at last give the lie to the calumniators who claimed that he was without popular support.

Franco was now politically wholly secure within Spain, but he continued to be beset with difficulties in the world beyond. For the most part they were economic. The effect of continuous wartime difficulties from 1936 to 1945 was to intensify the poverty of Spain from year to year. Not only was there a perennial shortage of almost all goods, but also the distribution system was frequently near to a standstill. This was due both to the inadequacies of transportation which stemmed from the American-induced petroleum famines, and to the disappearance of so many goods into illicit trade. Although the official cost of living index rose little in the years 1941–1944, in 1940 it had gone up by thirty per cent, and black market prices tended to rise continuously as the government became more worried about and more watchful of its operations. It could never be eliminated because there were too many people, many of them important, involved in it, and because one of the major sources was never policed, namely the official stores where government personnel of one kind or another were able to buy larger than average rations at ration prices. Corruption was furthermore universally accepted as necessary and even good.

After a comparatively good year in 1944 the weather in 1945 was unprecedently bad. From February to June there was insufficient rain throughout most of Spain, and in northern areas, where the

[34] Handbill reproduced in I. Fernández de Castro & J. Martínez: *España Hoy* (Paris 1963), p. 12.

drought was less serious, an unseasonable frost in May did grave damage. Drought in Spain affected not only food grains and other agricultural crops, but also industry, which in Spain was almost exclusively supplied with power from hydroelectric plants. Even Spain's minerals did badly in 1945 for with the end of the war the world market price of several of her most important minerals collapsed.

In addition to these natural calamities, Spain's unfriendly relations with foreign powers had their economic repercussions, in many cases in spite of the governments concerned. Faced by demands for rupture of relations with Spain, de Gaulle told a news conference on 13 October 1945, that 'pyrites has no party', and after de Gaulle's departure Bidault continued to point out that France would lose more than Spain by the cessation of economic relations. Nevertheless, the frontier was closed at the beginning of March 1946 and remained closed for two years. The same month there was a brief attempt to impose a worldwide boycott on the handling of Spanish goods in the ports. In Britain and the United States officials and ministers alike were constantly reassuring the public that they had no sympathy with the Spanish government. The United States, for example, publicly announced that Spain was at the end of the queue for scarce American exports.

On the other hand, Spain in those days, because of her geographical protrusion into the Atlantic, was a vital link in air communications on the southern route between America and Europe. So the United States was prepared to invite Franco's representative to the International Civil Aviation Conference at Chicago in October 1944 even though this meant that the Soviet Union refused to attend, and later, despite the official announcement of American disapproval, Spain was allotted Hercules transport aircraft earmarked 'for friendly nations'. Where the United States' vital interests were concerned, her moral stance against Spain was not unnaturally overborne.

For one country, moreover, Spain's bad relations with the United States were a positive recommendation: Perón's Argentina. Even before Perón's rise to power, the two countries had had important links, for from the beginning of the Second World War Argentina had been Spain's most important source of wheat. These ties could only be strengthened by the mutual hostility of Argentina and the United States, since Argentines needed some link with the rest of the world and preferred to nod to Spain as their cultural progenitor than to bow to the Anglo-Saxons as their economic overlords; while Spain badly needed the credit which Argentina could provide out of her huge wartime trade balances. In such a liaison Argentina could be the equal, indeed the dominant partner, the United States as it were to Spain's Great Britain, for she had acquired virtually all Spanish investments in her country in exchange for the grain needed by Spain during the war. Immediately after the war Spain obtained a credit of 30 million pesos[35] in return for which she was to supply ships built in Spanish yards. But she did not supply them for want of capacity, and the imbalance continued. In October 1946 Argentina concluded a massive credit agreement under which Spain was to receive a credit of 350 million pesos, plus a loan of 400 million pesos to meet outstanding debts, and to guarantee to buy most of her grain out of Argentine surpluses up to 1951, supplying Argentina in return with manufactured goods.

Argentina's terms, including the interest rate, were extremely generous, so it was no wonder that when Eva Duarte de Perón, wife and political right hand of the Argentine President, made an official visit to Spain in June 1947 she received a rapturous welcome. Spain, meanwhile, was still unable to keep her trading account with Argentina in balance; her manufacturing industry simply did not have the capacity, particularly in a time of electricity shortage. Once again Perón bailed Franco out in what was known as the Franco–Perón protocol and was signed on 9 April 1948. Franco now promised in return for overdraft and extended credit facilities to provide materials and land for the Argentine to set up a free port in Spain through which their exports to Europe would be distributed. The project was an ambitious one and would have been mutually beneficial in the long term, but Argentina was running out of money to go on supporting Spain. Perón had an expensive social programme to finance at home, and he could not overlook the fact that meat brought more profit per acre than the grain Franco primarily needed and was still failing to pay for. After

[35] There were about 16 Argentine pesos to the pound sterling at that time.

Above Franco welcomes Hitler, October 1940: from Ribbentrop's album (Associated Press)

Below Franco welcomes President Eisenhower, December 1959

Franco at the wheel of his yacht *Azor*, circa 1950 (United Press International)

one further round of financial adjustments in 1949, Perón's charity was exhausted and deliveries from Argentina were finally discontinued amid insults and recriminations at a personal level.

The loss was felt less keenly than it would earlier have been, for accommodation with Spain was by now increasingly advocated in the United States. For all his defiant contempt for outsiders, Franco was extremely concerned for his public image in that country. Argentine credits had been a lifeline but they had not been a foundation for economic growth. If this was to be achieved Spain must receive aid from a nation rich in capital, so it was to the United States that Spain addressed the bulk of her considerable propaganda efforts. As the 'cold war' set in, with the Greek civil war, the Prague coup and the Berlin airlift creating a cumulative fear of the Soviet Union through 1948, the climate of opinion in the United States became more receptive towards the regime in Spain, whose anti-Communism was beyond reproach. In 1948 Franco sent the former Foreign Minister Lequerica to the United States to coax the Americans to relent towards him. At home he himself gave frequent press interviews to foreign correspondents, spreading the word that 'Spain has been perfecting her regime and is all the time giving Spaniards greater participation in the life of the nation,' but that 'democracy is something which has many meanings and which cannot be bound to the views of any one sector'.[36]

In March 1948 during the debate on the Foreign Assistance Bill, which authorised the huge capital aid programme to Europe known as Marshall Aid, the House of Representatives passed an amendment that Spain should be included in the scheme. But Truman and Marshall, his Secretary of State, were anxious that the Europeans should themselves administer American aid, and they knew that they were as hostile to Franco as the President was personally. At his insistence the amendment was 'stricken out'. The Export–Import Bank were permitted to consider Spanish applications for loans, but when one was submitted in May they rejected it because it asked for 1,275 million dollars, more than the entire funds of the bank. Private banks subsequently made loans of 20 and 25 million dollars but these were for current trading and for

[36] Franco: *Textos*, p. 241. Interview with the Vice-President of United Press, 27 June 1947.

buying out existing American investments and not for developmental purposes. Similarly, in 1948, trade with Britain and France was substantially increased under agreements signed in May, but these countries did not lend, did not even have funds to lend, for the capitalisation of the Spanish economy.

1949, however, brought further progress towards Spanish–American rapprochement. When, in May, Spain's Latin American friends proposed that the United Nations authorise its members once more to send ambassadors to Madrid, the American delegate abstained from voting on the issue, but he was severely criticised for so doing both by the Republican Senator Vandenberg and by the Democratic Senator Connally. And they were elder statesmen who did not form part of the regular Spanish lobby. This pressure group, well managed by Lequerica and by a professional American lobbyist, was able to draw together a wide body of legislators and public men friendly to Spain. Most of them were, it is true, Catholic, but the most important factor in the growth of support for Spain was the consideration of American strategic interest. American admirals, in particular, were looking to Spanish ports to free their Mediterranean fleet from dependence on British base facilities. When the explosion of a Soviet atomic bomb in September 1949 brought about a reassessment of the strategic position, an increasing number of Congressmen saw advantage in bringing Franco's Spain within the framework of Western defence and in taking up the offer of bases that Franco had made the previous November.[37]

The opposition to a rapprochement with Spain was led by President Truman himself, but he encountered the hostility of Congress and gradually found himself obliged to give ground. In September 1949 he permitted American warships to visit Ferrol and a number of American flag and general officers to pay Franco an 'informal but official' call at his Galician summer home. In January 1950, Secretary of State Dean Acheson committed the Administration to supporting a revocation of the United Nations' ban on ambassadorial representation in Spain. In September, Truman signed a bill appropriating 62·5 million dollars for aid to Spain, but, even

[37] Arthur P. Whitaker: *Spain and the Defense of the West: Ally and Liability* (New York 1961), p. 36.

though the Korean War had now broken out, he announced that he considered the appropriation as an authorisation and not as a mandate.

Similarly, when on 4 November his representative duly voted for the successful motion in the United Nations to lift the boycott on Spain, the President said that he did not envisage naming an ambassador 'for a long, long time'.[38] In the event, he decided before the end of the month to appoint Stanton Griffis, though his own personal hostility to the Franco regime was as strong as ever. It was largely religious in origin, for as a good Baptist, he had found Spain's attempt to deny discrimination against Protestants unconvincing. 'Do you know', he asked Griffis, 'that a Baptist who dies in Spain must even be buried in the middle of the night?'[39] But he finally allowed his personal feelings to be overridden by the advice of the Defense Department. On 16 July 1951 Admiral Sherman, Chief of Naval Operations, visited Franco for preliminary discussions about the leasing of bases in Spain.

The governments of Western Europe were hostile to this initiative. 'It is the view of His Majesty's Government', the House of Commons was told, 'that the strategic advantages of establishing any closer association between Spain and the West are outweighed by the effects which such an association would have on the morale of other members of the Western community'.[40] Indeed, there was a noticeable effect on morale. Fears were, for instance, expressed in the French press that the Americans had decided that the Pyrenees were more defensible than the Elbe and that the French were too 'soft on Communism' to be a reliable ally. The North Atlantic Treaty Organisation, which required unanimity in its political decisions, would certainly never admit Spain under its present government, but then Franco thought a bilateral arrangement much more satisfactory. If the United States would count Franco a friend, the hostility of the rest of Europe was surely of little account indeed.

[38] *New York Times*, 6 November 1951.
[39] Stanton Griffis: *Lying in State* (Garden City 1952), p. 269, quoted by Theodore J. Lowi in *American Civil-Military Decisions* (Birmingham, Ala., 1963), p. 691.
[40] Parliamentary Debates, House of Commons, 5th Series, Vol. 491, col. 440. Statement of Mr Ernest Davies, 25 July 1951.

9 Towards Prosperity

Admiral Sherman's visit to Spain not only promised the relief of Franco's diplomatic isolation but also raised hopes that his Spain might become a land flowing with the milk and honey of Marshall Aid. These prospects were opened at a most opportune time, for prices were rising and with them unrest and criticism. In March an official gathering of workers' representatives raised a welter of complaints against the rate at which rising prices were outstripping wages, and on the 11th Pope Pius XII broadcast a message to Spanish workers in which he reminded them that 'just wages and a better distribution of resources constitute two of the most pressing demands in the Church's social programme'.[1] It was no coincidence that there was a general strike and boycott of transport in Barcelona on the 12th. This seems to have caught the government unawares, but a show of force the following day easily restored order. Here was no revolutionary situation, and illegal strikes in Vizcaya in April and in Pamplona and Madrid in May did not present any serious direct threat either. They did, on the other hand, cast doubts upon the regime's reputation for the maintenance of order and tranquillity, and so upon the necessity of retaining the regime.

The alternative was of course a restoration of the monarchy, and monarchism was gaining ground. It was with Juan's consent that in August 1949, under the patronage of Bevin, the British

[1] *Discorsi e Radiomessaggi di Sua Santità Pio XII*, Vol. XIII (Vatican City 1952), p. 7.

Foreign Secretary, Gil Robles had negotiated a common minimum programme with the Socialist leader Prieto, but the Pretender had nevertheless moved closer to the regime. He saw now that evolution was more feasible than revolution, and, even while his representatives were negotiating with the Socialists, he met Franco at sea on the Caudillo's yacht *Azor*, where it was arranged that his sons should be educated in Spain to fit them for their possible royal role in the future. This limited endorsement of the regime worried the socialists, just as the Gil Robles–Prieto conversations worried the more conservative monarchists, but when on 10 July 1951 Don Juan wrote to Franco in a bid for an early restoration he moved his position considerably to the right. He denied responsibility for Gil Robles' actions, and called reports that he was not identified with the National Movement 'antimonarchical propaganda'. 'Let us come to an agreement to prepare a stable regime', he proposed.[2] He was discomfited by Sherman's visit a week later, and by the renewed optimism this kindled in supporters of the regime.

There was a widespread feeling that the worst was over, that after so many years of running hard to remain in the same place, Spain might now enter a phase of rapid economic development. The harvest in 1951 was a good one; the level of the reservoirs was rising. The tone of Franco's message for the New Year on 31 December 1951 was one of high optimism. 'Those clouded, crazy years which surrendered whole families of peoples in Europe and Asia to Communism and which repaid Spain's neutrality in the coin of hostility have passed,' he said, and went on to say that they had not been in vain, for 'while they were passing, we have taken the opportunity to forge the instruments of our national resurgence.'[3] All was now ready for a great leap forward. Juan Antonio Suanzes, who had returned to the Ministry of Industry and Commerce in 1945, left the cabinet in July 1951 and devoted himself full time to the Instituto Nacional de Industria (INI), a gigantic holding company of which he was the virtual founder, through which the government participated in industrial development particularly in backward and strategic sectors. This institution was to

[2] *New York Times* 5 August 1951, p. 1.
[3] Francisco Franco: *Discursos y mensajes del Jefe del Estado, 1951–1954* (Madrid 1955), p. 122.

play a dominant role in the economy of the fifties and, as if to emphasise its importance and its independence from the Ministry of Industry and Commerce, that ministry was divided into two when Suanzes left it.

The task of strengthening and industrialising the Spanish economy was one close to Franco's heart, for the starting point of his economics was the need for a strong and independent Spain. This included a Spain in which growing prosperity would remove the poverty on which the class war fed, but in the circumstances of 1939 and of the subsequent decade, the paramount objective was military strength. The admirers of Franco the economist cite as his first virtue the fact that he did not believe in 'the myth of gold'. He had, for example, disapproved of Calvo Sotelo's battle to save the peseta in the twenties, and thought that by 1931 orthodox monetary theory had proved itself bankrupt.

He seems to have been impressed by the example of Schacht in Germany, and he drew from it the conclusion that possession of raw materials is the crucial factor in economic and hence strategic strength. His optimism about Spain's potentialities derived from the consciousness of Spain's mineral wealth, and probably from underrating the importance of capital and technology. The industries which he sought to build up during the forties were steel, shipping, aircraft, motor vehicles and chemicals, most of which had military uses. During 1940 he gave a lot of thought to the design of mortars which could be easily and cheaply produced and could reduce Gibraltar without the need of foreign specialists.[4] INI itself was founded in September 1941 to cut through the difficulties which the expansion of Spanish shipbuilding was facing. The fact that petroleum was the one vital commodity of which Spain then had practically no home supply made Franco the more ready to believe in the Austrian who claimed to be able to produce aviation fuel from river water, and to give to this man's firm priority status in fiscal and commercial matters.[5]

The purpose of becoming independent of foreign suppliers, of

[4] Detwiler, op. cit., p. 85.
[5] Foltz, op. cit., pp. 258–260; *Boletín Oficial del Estado*, 7 December 1940.

the policy of autarky favoured in the early years of the 'new Spain' was to make possible the independent foreign policy, the great role in the world, which was the Nationalists' great constructive goal. But the practice of such an economic policy entailed the most rigid controls on the part of government, controls which were from the first highly unpopular with the business community. In February 1940, Carceller, not then a member of the cabinet, pointed out that not only was 'a controlled economy, which sacrifices the individual, supposedly to the collective interest,' largely Marxist, but also that Spain was bound to fail in her pursuit of autarky. There was no true comparison with Germany, for that country already had tremendous industrial capacity, and could negotiate bilateral agreements from a position of strength to which Spain could not aspire.[6] Yet, however true Carceller's remarks might be, government intervention in the economy was vital. The scarcity of currency and of shipping, not to mention the controls exercised by foreign countries, made it highly undesirable for import and production priorities to be determined by market forces.

The problems which faced those responsible for the regulation of Spanish trade and production were all the same formidable. The autarkist leanings of young economists and the ever-present anxieties of the government over the shortage of currency led inevitably to the scrutiny of every project in terms of foreign exchange cost. And, in the absence of reliable statistics for the recent past, quotas could be based only on the consumption figures of 1935 or on yet more irrational considerations. The result broadly was to retain the unsatisfactory fragmented industrial structure of 1935, except where new import-substitution schemes were grafted on to it.

Import substitution was very fashionable, and pursued to an extent which the sensible allocation of resources did not justify. Because of the vast unknown factor which the length and outcome of the war represented it was difficult to make an intelligent assessment of future requirements and only too tempting to assume that the capital cost of developing home production would inevitably be recouped. In these ways the government was sometimes led into absurdities. A Basque manufacturer was refused an import licence

[6] *New York Times* 29 February 1940, p. 3.

for a $300 stand-by machine to insure the production of a large factory against months of idleness if the main machine should break down.[7] Attempts were made to extract oil from shale and bituminous coal, which even in the conditions of World War II were uneconomic, and could not be done on a scale which would give any relief from dependence on petroleum imports.

Other industries encouraged by the government were entirely new manufacturing industries requiring great capital investments, considerable expertise, and in some cases involving important economies of scale. They included cellulose, paper, chemicals of many kinds, aero engines, motor vehicles and heavy munitions. The last three of these required in addition an infrastructure of special steels, and to add to the problems they were to be produced in hitherto non-industrial areas in order to favour regions other than Catalonia and the Basque country. Technical assistance was to be provided by the Axis powers, but it was not, and in fact these industries failed to receive in practice the priority treatment which Franco had decreed for them. Not until 1950 did industrial chemical production regain even the low level of the 1929–1931 average.[8] Similarly, although the home production of motor vehicles and aircraft was frequently promised, the first wholly Spanish transport aircraft did not fly until 1949 and only 8,900 motor vehicles (over 8,500 of them motor cycles) were made in Spain in 1951.[9]

This was doubtless a disappointment to Franco. The brave promises for the future he had made in the early days were sadly unfulfilled. But then over-optimism is a common failure of politicians, and it was not surprising that Spain should have failed to pull herself up by her bootstraps, should have fallen short of the level of capital formation necessary for sustained economic growth. After all, she had had no help from outside, and Franco admitted the disadvantage that this was. He had by the end of the war abandoned the pursuit of self-sufficiency along with most of the rest of his German legacy. He publicly lamented that Spain's economic progress was held back by her exclusion from Marshall Aid, and he

[7] Thomas J. Hamilton: *Appeasement's Child, the Franco Régime in Spain* (New York 1943), p. 104.
[8] *Anuario Estadístico de España* (Edición manual), 1952, p. 265.
[9] ibid., pp. 237–238.

and his ministers began to speak of the economic controls which hampered Spanish trade as evils which were unfortunately unavoidable for the time being. Grasping the nettle Franco spoke of Spain as a poor country when he addressed Asturian miners in May 1946. He attributed Spain's lower standard of living to the fact that unlike other nations Spain had no colonies to exploit. This at least gave her a position of moral superiority, poor but honest. 'Nobody in the universe works for Spain,' he said. 'Spaniards earn their bread by the sweat of their brow.'[10]

1951 was the year in which Spain began to recover perceptibly faster. Industrial production and exports both rose by thirteen per cent over 1950, and the level of imports fell.[11] This was not of course due directly to American help to Spain. It owed more to good weather and the beginnings of an expansion in world trade, which brought about a general recovery in Europe. Spain's industrial growth had in fact progressed proportionately faster since 1929 than the countries of formerly occupied Europe.[12] Her fear had been that, when other countries moved into a new expansionary phase, Spain would be left behind by the effects of a continuing political discrimination. It required the gesture of American goodwill and interest which Sherman's visit represented to persuade Spanish business, and indeed government circles, that Spain would not be left out, that her importance to the West was recognised.

In the end, the progress of Spain's rapprochement with the United States turned out to be very slow. Sherman died in Naples a week after his interview with Franco, and Truman was in no hurry to come to any definite agreement. Economic and military missions were sent to investigate Spain's needs and possibilities, but the President told his press conference on 7 February 1952 bluntly that he was 'not fond of' General Franco.[13] It was not until the Eisenhower administration came into office in the following January

[10] Franco: *Textos*, p. 421.
[11] *Anuario Estadístico de España* (Edición manual), 1960, pp. 360–1; 1962, p. 179.
[12] AEE (Ed. manual), 1962, p. 179; OEEC: *Industrial Statistics 1900–1955. Addendum* (Paris 1956), p. 3.
[13] *New York Times*, 8 February 1952, p. 2.

that the White House and State Department became really interested in a bases agreement. James Dunn, a senior member of the Foreign Service, was sent to Madrid as ambassador, and spoke of 'the cordial relations existing between our two countries'.[14] After a long summer of intensive negotiation Dunn and Martín Artajo signed the Pact of Madrid on 27 September 1953. This consisted of agreements for arms supply and economic aid to Spain in return for the use of bases.

The actual location and nature of the facilities had not been agreed upon, but they were to be under Spanish nominal control. On the other hand, a large part of the 'counterpart funds' which were used in the Marshall Aid countries for the economic development of the recipient nation were to be used in Spain for the construction of the bases. 'The time and manner of war-time utilisation of said areas and facilities will be as mutually agreed upon'[15] according to the text of the agreement, and no public elucidation was offered. A furore arose when the American Secretary of the Air Force, Talbott, explicitly stated that atom bombs would be stockpiled in Spain, and again that the United States would definitely use the bases in time of war. Retractions were issued, but the existence of secret clauses had been cautiously admitted in Madrid, and it seems probable that the Spaniards conceded, or that the Americans thought they conceded, more than they were prepared to admit in public.

The fact was that the agreement with the United States met with widespread opposition in Spain. For a start, Spaniards were unwilling to appear as suppliants, or as satellites of the Americans. Martín Artajo in presenting the agreement went out of the way to emphasise that it was the Americans who were the returned prodigals of the anti-Communist household. The negotiators felt it necessary moreover to write into the Pact strict rules of conduct for American personnel in Spain in order to avoid any provocation to the strong anti-Americanism in Spain. This was at root mostly cultural. For many Spaniards, the North American was a being with more money than manners who presumed to lord it over the centuries-

[14] *New York Times*, 10 April 1953, p. 11.
[15] The published texts of the agreement are in the *Department of State Bulletin*, Vol. XXIX, pp. 436–42 (Washington), 5 October 1953.

old civilisation of Europe. Worse still, he often allied his materialism with Protestantism. Cardinal Segura, the Archbishop of Seville, issued a pastoral for the Lent of 1952 in which he warned against the danger of selling Spain's Catholic values for American money. Admittedly, Segura was rigidly hostile to all forms of government except the monarchy, and having lost the see of Toledo when his hostility to the Republic was so extreme as to embarrass the Vatican, he was now pursuing a vendetta against Franco and his government. Yet, in his outspoken manner, he was giving voice to an attitude that was deeply felt in Spain and particularly in the Church.

Not only the hierarchy but organised Catholicism as a whole had been one of the strongest props of the Nationalists during the Civil War, and despite its distaste for the Falange, had generally supported the regime. It was impossible for churchmen not to feel gratitude for their deliverance from communistic atheism or not to recognise the privileged place which they had been assigned in Franco's scheme of things. On the other hand, the Holy See was reluctant to commit itself too deeply to the regime, for to set the seal of Papal approval on an institution which might prove to be temporary could seriously compromise the Church. So, though the Holy See recognised Franco's government in 1938, it did not hasten to regulate Church–State relations by the conclusion of the new concordat which Franco earnestly desired. Relations became strained. When Serrano Súñer was in Rome in October 1940, he did not seek an audience with the Pope, and the Vatican newspaper publicised this fact.[16] In the interests of the Church's pastoral work, however, the Vatican came to a *modus vivendi* in 1941 by which Franco would make the final choice in the appointment of bishops from a list of those selected by the Pope from a longer list (of six) agreed between the Nuncio and the Spanish government. A comparable compromise was reached over presentation to deaneries and canonries in 1946; in 1947, Spain was again permitted her special Rota Tribunal, independent of Rome, for the adjudication of petitions for marriage annulments and similar questions; in 1950, the Holy See appointed an archbishop-in-ordinary to the Spanish armed forces.

[16] *Osservatore Romano*, 6 October 1940, p. 5.

Rome was extending its blessing to Franco piecemeal, but Franco still looked forward to the formal Concordat, which was signed after long negotiations the month before the American Bases Agreement. For the most part it confirmed rights which the Church already had in practice, but it did underline the freedom of the Church to speak and act for itself. If priests were to be bound daily to pray for Franco, they were also to be allowed freedom to publish 'any ordinance relating to the government of the Church', and Catholic Action groups were to be allowed 'freely to carry out their apostolate'.[17] These freedoms enabled the Church to become not less but more detached from the regime than they were before, while in return Franco received little more tangible than the Supreme Order of Christ.

Both before and after the Concordat, the Church found a good deal to deplore in the ways in which Spanish society was changing, and a good deal to deplore in the ways in which it was not changing. The years between 1945 and 1951 had seen an even steeper rise in the official cost of living index than had the Second World War period. Wages had not kept pace, and churchmen complained in print of the high cost of living, blaming it implicitly or explicitly on corruption and profiteering. 'By paying the minimum legal wage one may escape the justice of men, but one does not escape the justice of God, unless there is some excuse like the genuine inability of the firm to pay more,' said the Archbishop of Valencia in 1951.[18] But the fault did not lie only with the employers. It was the government which regulated wages, and the money supply. In the forties, when the road to recovery was painful, the progress that was made was made at the expense of the working classes, for it was their incomes which were fixed in money terms while the value of money declined.

When the tempo of economic growth quickened in the early fifties, however, wage rates did not rise significantly. But there was more overtime to work, and the cost of living index was lower on average in 1952 and 1953 than it had been in 1951. If there was not

[17] An English text of *The Concordat between Spain and the Holy See, 27 August 1953* was published by the Oficina de Información Diplomática in Madrid.

[18] *Ecclesia* (Madrid), 1 December 1951, p. 608.

a bonanza for the workers, there was apparently none for share-
holders either. If increased profits were distributed rather than
reinvested in businesses, they were handed out clandestinely in
order to avoid the tax on dividends. Certainly the profits of the
booming economy were unevenly distributed, just as the pace of
the expansion was unevenly distributed, but most of them went
into capital investment. Spain was suffused with the sensation of
growing wealth. If in the forties the poor man might have felt that
the black market spiv was enriching himself at the expense of the
community, in the fifties he would have complained rather that he
was being left behind in a gold-rush. The Church condemned the
Spanish businessman for giving his heart to Mammon, while the
Communist Party turned from terrorism to trade unionism, making
common cause with the many Falangists who were hostile
to capitalism. The fat years stored up almost more political
trouble than had the lean years, for they built up expectations,
and nothing is more politically explosive than an unfulfilled expectation.

For unfulfilled the expectations were, and the feeling of well-
being to a certain extent illusory. No changes had been made in
the structure of the economy, or in the protectionist nature of
Spain's external trading policy. Spain was a high cost country.
She took insufficient steps to effect economies of scale in some
areas, while in others her industry was controlled by monopolistic
cartels or by the enormously powerful banking community. Her
labour market was inflexible, and her capital market little developed. All this made her liable to experience severe consequences
from comparatively minor setbacks. In 1955 these appeared in the
shape of a poor cereal harvest and a sharp rise in the visible trade
deficit. The cost of living index rose substantially for the first time
since 1951.

Meanwhile, INI continued to invest heavily in new projects, but
in so doing only contributed to inflation by issuing paper which the
Bank of Spain was legally obliged to rediscount on presentation by
the commercial banks. The government was unable to counteract
this by deflationary tax increases. There was a limit to what they
could raise by increases in indirect taxation without occasioning
serious social unrest, and the attempt by a law of 1954 to rely more

heavily on income tax was rendered largely ineffectual by monumental evasion.

The economic situation was serious, but it was not in itself
nearly as threatening as it had been on many occasions in the past.
What was much more disquieting for Franco, was the political
atmosphere, in which real tension was apparent for the first time in
ten years. When Franco attended the celebrations at El Escorial
marking the nineteenth anniversary of José Antonio's death, he
was insulted by the indiscipline of militant Falangist youths who
threw off their red berets, symbol of the link with Carlism, and
shouted 'Down with capital'. There was unrest also among university students. In November 1955 a Congress of Young Writers,
which would have reflected growing hostility to the government
among young intellectuals, was banned as a Communist front. In
February 1956 at the elections of student representatives to the
official University Syndicate (SEU) demands were made for a
free and truly representative syndicate, and a group of students
broke up the SEU's offices. There followed a clash between left-
wing students and Falangists whose preserve the SEU was, in
which a young Falangist was seriously wounded. His comrades
became highly excited and threatened that if he died, his death
would be avenged by the murder of a hundred of their prominent
opponents.

These were serious incidents and those who bore the responsibility for them lost their jobs. The head of the Falange Youth
Front went in November; the Minister of Education, Ruiz Jiménez, went in February. The malady was not so easily cured, however, nor were the incidents more than symptoms of it. Only a
minority of students were political activists, but most of them
found their middle-class social environment stifling, and sought to
demonstrate their independence of its assumptions. Most of them
held the political and social establishment in contempt as hypo-
crites and cynics whose spiritual development had been arrested in
1936, and who hoped to stop the clock at that date. They were too
young to have personal recollection of the Civil War, and they did
not judge the ideas of writers by their attitude to the Republic and
to that conflict. University students came to liberal ideas if not to

liberal politics with all the freshness of a new discovery. That they were able to do so was in part owing to Ruiz Jiménez's belief that it was undesirable altogether to suppress heterodox philosophies if university education was to achieve its purposes.

Similarly young Falangists owed their beliefs to the careful instruction in the thought of José Antonio which they had received from the Movement's representatives. But they saw this thought without the spectacles of those who had had to compromise. They understood that José Antonio castigated both left and right, and, seeing that the left was now overthrown, they turned their venom against the forces of reaction, capitalism, monarchism, which presented the more actual threat. They realised that the Falange was not all the élite spearhead of social change that its founder had envisaged, and that as monarchism gained ground it would soon lose what little chance remained of its ever becoming so. It was this realisation which now led young Falangists to join older left-wing 'old shirts' in their last attempt to storm the heights they had hoped to reach in the aftermath of the Civil War.

While this attempt could not be allowed to succeed, Franco was concerned to retain something of the Falange, at least as a framework for labour relations, so he would not let its 'young Turks' ruin it in a head-on collision with the conservatives and capitalists. At the insistence of his senior military colleagues he arrested some of the Falangist sabre-rattlers involved in the events of February, and he dismissed Fernández Cuesta, the Secretary-General of the Movement, from the cabinet along with Ruiz Jiménez. But in his place he appointed José Luis de Arrese, whom he charged with the drawing up of proposals for a redefinition of the Movement's place in the political structure.

Arrese was a Catholic and a *franquista* before he was anything, but he had also been connected with the Falange since before the Civil War, had drawn up proposals for the constitution of the Cortes in 1942 and had written voluminously on the political theory of Franco's national syndicalist state. His appointment suggested that concessions would be made to the Falange, and he set up a committee which worked on that assumption and which included the recently replaced Youth Front leader, Elola. While it

rejected the drastically democratising proposals of Luis González
Vicén, and agreed to bowdlerise the more fascist aspects of the
Movement's original statutes, it proposed to give increased power
to the Cortes and greatly increased power to the National Council
of the Movement. Of course the National Council contained a
higher proportion of true Falangists than most areas of the Spanish
establishment, but even so it was not dominated by them. The
creation of a totalitarian party-state was not threatened even
remotely by the proposals, but when they were circulated in the
autumn of 1956 they were denounced by the conservatives, especially by the generals, as giving too much power to the Falange and
too much encouragement to democracy, whose growth Arrese's
committee regarded as an 'irreversible trend'.

The popularity of the Falange among conservatives was not
enhanced by the wage rises sponsored by José Antonio Girón, the
other Falangist member of the cabinet. Girón had made his name
as a militia leader during the Civil War, and after it he became
head of the veterans' organisation. In May 1941 he became
Minister of Labour, and over fifteen years built the reputation of
being genuinely concerned for the welfare of the workers. (A Communist even told a Belgian journalist in 1946 that Girón should
have been one of his party.[19]) In the Spring of 1956 he was able to
achieve a general increase in wages to maintain the workers' standard of living. To be implemented in two stages, the first on 1 April
and the second in November, the rise was to vary between twenty-
five and seventy per cent. This was a considerable concession,
which it was hoped would quieten the home front at a difficult
moment in Spain's external relations, and which represented at the
same time a blow for the Falange against its opponents. Unfortunately the increase was a disappointment to many workers, and
strikes for more broke out over much of Northern Spain in April and
May, the most widespread since the corresponding period in 1951.
In October the archbishops, in a joint pastoral, also demanded that
greater increases be awarded, while the employers were infuriated
by the size of those already granted. Many of them made little
effort to absorb their cost, even raising their prices out of proportion to the increased cost of labour. The only effect of the increases,

[19] R. A. Francotte: *L'heure de l'Espagne* (Brussels 1947), p. 83.

therefore, was to accelerate the pace at which the currency was inflated.

By the autumn of 1956 even the Minister of Commerce spoke of the widespread lack of confidence in the Government's economic policy, so there was no escaping its failure. The Americans had always favoured a more *laissez-faire* approach by the Spanish government, and had written into the Pact of Madrid a Spanish commitment to create or maintain internal financial stability, to discourage cartels and monopolies and to encourage competition. In this they had growing support from those Spanish economists who were anxious to introduce into industry the discipline of foreign competition and to develop trading links with the rest of Europe. Meanwhile, the military had had their faith in the regime shaken by the sudden loss of the Moroccan protectorate, and all conservatives were worried by the labour disturbances and, even more so, by the unrest among the students, their own children.

Franco inevitably came in for some criticism, bearing as he did the ultimate responsibility for all government policy. He would surely have to bring his critics into the cabinet in place of some of his present ministers before the errors of his government were visited on him personally. As a first step he reversed his policy of promoting the Falange and in January 1957 told Arrese to withdraw his proposals for constitutional change. Arrese thereupon resigned and circulated a clandestine pamphlet exonerating the Falange from responsibility for the situation of the country on the grounds that less than five per cent of important public offices were held by 'old shirts'. The political crisis had come to a head and was resolved by the removal of ten of the cabinet, and their replacement by twelve new ministers, the most extensive government reshuffle since Franco came to power.

It had in any event been five and a half years since the previous major change in the government, so another had been about due. The ministers of longest service were replaced, not only Girón, tainted with Falangism, but also Blas Pérez, of undoubted loyalty but perhaps blamed for the continuing civil disturbances. He left the Ministry of the Interior to General Alonso Vega, an old subordinate of the Caudillo's in the Legion, indeed a friend from his boyhood in Ferrol, a classmate at Toledo and a colleague in the Regiment of Zamora. In the Ministry of Public Works, too, a civilian (Vallellano) gave place to a general (Jorge Vigón), so there were five generals in the new cabinet of eighteen as opposed to three in the old one of sixteen. Head-counting was not a reliable index of strength, however, for although there were more 'old shirts' in the new cabinet than there had been in the old, the changes were regarded as a blow to the Falange. Both Girón, who publicly insulted his successor, and Arrese were replaced by men of far less standing, and the latter was denied any room for political manœuvre by his appointment to a new Ministry of Housing. His architectural training and his interest in the reconstruction of Málaga when he was Civil Governor there after the Civil War led him to accept the post, but his ambitious schemes found no finance in the economic climate of these years, and he resigned finally in 1960.

But the most noted of all the changes of February 1957 were those at the Ministries of Finance and Commerce. Both the new ministers were 'technocrats' of acknowledged competence. Navarro Rubio, a lawyer and banker, came from second place at the Ministry of Public Works to the Ministry of Finance. Ullastres came straight from a professorial chair of economic history to the Ministry of Commerce. Significantly both were members of an organisation whose star was rising in the sky, the Opus Dei.

Members of Opus Dei, like freemasons, form the sort of semi-secret, loosely organised body that everybody who is not a member regards as a conspiracy or as a mutual benefit society. Formally, the Opus is a secular apostolic institute authorised by Pope Pius XII in 1947, and founded by a Spanish priest, Mgr. José Escrivá de Balaguer, some years before that. Its members must devote themselves to apostolic work, but they must do this in the world, and can do it best by demonstrating the excellence, efficiency and integrity of God's servants. For full membership, several years of theological studies and a very high academic standard is essential. From the first Escrivá was concerned with the universities, and from the forties the Opus had great control over the purse strings of government research. It was axiomatic for Escrivá and his followers that the clever and powerful were the most important to convert, and it is difficult to acquit them of intellectual snobbery. But naturally their intellect was a recommendation for high office, and although the Opus no more had a political programme than did freemasonry, like freemasons its members shared a broadly similar social outlook. The Opus outlook was in tune with Franco's. It believed in probity and in professionalism, it believed in technical progress but in political and religious conservatism; it was hostile to *aggiornamento* in the Catholic Church, and rejected democracy on the grounds that equality is a dangerous myth, that 'only the truth has rights'.[20]

It was not surprising that Ruiz Jiménez had been hostile to the Opus, and in 1957 this added to the appeal it had for Franco. Navarro and Ullastres were no more delegates of the Opus in the cabinet than Martín Artajo had been a delegate of Catholic Action or Vallellano of the Pretender, but it was the Opus which had formed their world outlook, and their world outlook which had caused Franco to entrust them with portfolios (Gual Villalbí, the orthodox spokesman for Catalan business, had entered the Cabinet but without portfolio).

Throughout this difficult period Franco made it clear that he did not intend to relax his grip on the situation, that he would weather the storm. At the same time he laid emphasis on the flexibility of the regime. Not for nothing, he insisted, was the political structure in Spain known as the National Movement. It did move forward with the times: the constitution was not a closed one, but one open to change in the light of circumstances. The moral was that everybody should remain within the framework of permitted political activity, and hope that their point of view would find favour. Divisions in the Movement must be avoided for they could only help the enemies of Spain. 'I understand the just indignation of many Spaniards about the shamelessness of political charlatans who make use of loopholes in the law to try their light-footed manœuvres with a view to polarising the sympathy of the discontented,' Franco told the National Council of the Movement in

[20] This phrase was actually used against religious toleration by Mgr. Granados, not an Opus member, but it encapsulates a general Opus attitude. Cf. Pierre Jobit: *L'Eglise d'Espagne à l'heure du Concile* (Paris 1965), p. 140.

July 1956.[21] He went on to assure the Council that the laws would be inexorably enforced, and in 1957 some of the loopholes in the law were indeed closed. Those charged with offences against the Head of State were no longer to be allowed bail, and in illegal political gatherings without obvious leaders the oldest man present was to be regarded as primarily responsible.

In his speech to the National Council in 1957 Franco stressed the need for his successor to subscribe to the principles which were enshrined in the National Movement, and lest anyone might suppose that he would soon be stepping down, he went out of his way in his broadcast the following New Year's Eve to refer to the lifelong nature of the office conferred on him by the 1947 referendum. In May of the following year, the Declaratory Law of the Principles of the Movement added a preamble to the rudimentary constitutional structure provided by the Law constituting the Cortes, the Succession Law, the 1938 Labour Charter and the Spaniards' Charter of 1945. Defining the Movement as the 'community of Spaniards in the ideals which gave birth to the Crusade',[22] the law added little that was new.

Franco's steadfastness in the constitutional field was not matched by success in dealing with the economic situation. The country's gold and currency reserves continued to dwindle in 1957 and 1958 in spite of the reforming legislation of the new government. Within two months the system of multiple exchange rates, which had so complicated foreign trade, was officially abolished. In December 1957 a new tax law was introduced and the following year laws were brought forward for the stimulation of medium and long-term credit. The most portentous step was perhaps the introduction in the spring of 1958 of the principle of collective labour agreements, whereby under the aegis of the Syndicates bargaining was to take place between employers and employees. This decentralisation was widely saluted by supporters of the regime, for while many employers and economists hoped it would make Spanish industry more supple, the Syndicates hoped to gain in authenticity, to become accepted by the workers as their genuine representatives. Valuable as these measures were for the longer

[21] *ABC* 18 July 1956, p. 35.
[22] *Boletín Oficial del Estado* 19 May 1958.

term, their implementation could not be rushed, and in the meantime the pressing problems of short-term economic management remained.

Not all the increases in government expenditure nor all the piecemeal reintroductions of special rates of exchange could be laid at the door of the INI, but that body nevertheless did much to nullify the deflationary aspirations of the economic ministers. It was, of course, independent of the ministries, and continued to be supported by Franco. The majority of its schemes were well conceived in themselves, but its continued, ever-quickening expansion was quite at variance with the cabinet's monetary policy. Inflation could hardly be checked while INI might borrow hundreds of millions of pesetas at a mere three quarters of one per cent from the Bank of Spain, and the fact that savings institutions were obliged to place at least half their funds in INI stock did not help the development of the capital market which Navarro Rubio so earnestly desired.

Between 1957 and 1958 the cost of living index rose by thirteen per cent and the level of money supply by twenty per cent. On official figures, the balance of payments also worsened somewhat, but the official figures did not show the extent to which money was being illegally exported from Spain to safe havens like Switzerland. Of course, this drain had never been entirely closed, but the flight was believed to have become headlong during 1958. In December, a Swiss courier was arrested and found to be in possession of papers incriminating, it was reported, a number of highly placed Spaniards in exchange control offences. This provided anti-capitalist elements with a handy weapon, but at the same time it did demonstrate a collapse of confidence which would somehow have to be remedied. There was mounting pressure on Franco to look for foreign loans and foreign capital investment and to make the concessions to foreigners which this must entail.

Franco had already moved towards a more internationalist position by taking the Opus members into his cabinet, for they both favoured greater European economic co-operation. The issue of Spain's attitude to the rest of Europe was indeed becoming increasingly important, for 1958 saw the coming into operation of the new European Economic Community, whose tariff walls would eventually threaten Spanish exports. A first step to bring Spain closer to Europe was taken in January 1958 when she became an associate member of the Organisation for European Economic Co-operation. In July of that year she also joined the International Monetary Fund, and so prepared the ground for large-scale financial support should it become necessary. During the winter of 1958–1959, Franco received a good deal of strongly worded public advice on the conduct of the economy. The Bank of Spain spoke up for cuts in government expenditure and an open door for foreign capital, while the Banco de Bilbao raised the matter of European integration.

It was becoming clearer and clearer that Spain must have foreign capital, and the OEEC countries and the IMF made it clear that this would only be forthcoming under conditions. Franco seemed reluctant to accept this. He pressed ahead with long-term measures like the Law on Medium and Long Term Credit', and he allowed a 'National Investment Programme' to be published in the spring which presupposed an influx of foreign capital. Yet he was not willing to be rushed into opening Spain's economy to the exploitation of foreign capitalists.

The second quarter of 1959 was a disaster for the Spanish economy. By June Spain's credit was exhausted, and the crisis had arrived. The only solution appeared to be a devaluation of the peseta against the dollar, and large credits from overseas on whatever terms were offered. It was a humiliation. Franco was forced to do what he had been unable to decide to do willingly. He is said to have agreed to the inevitable with an exasperated 'Do whatever you like' to his economic ministers. With the agreement of the OEEC and the IMF they introduced a package of economic measures whose keynote was 'stabilisation'. The peseta was devalued from 42 to the US dollar to 60, and a savage deflation was imposed at home further to divert goods into exports. For example, an import deposit scheme was introduced, bank credit to the private sector severely restricted and prices of public services raised. From the end of July foreigners were permitted to subscribe up to fifty per cent of the capital of a firm instead of the previous maximum of twenty-five. They were also allowed freely to repatriate dividends of up to six per cent. In return, Spain was admitted as a full member of the OEEC and 200 million dollars of foreign loans were immediately forthcoming.

The winter of 1959–60 was a gloomy one for the workers of Spain. It was estimated early in 1960 that loss of overtime had led to workers taking home a quarter to a third less than before the Stabilisation Plan. Small employers were also hit, and there were a number of bankruptcies. But the deflation most certainly worked; 'a complete success' the OEEC Report called it. By the early summer the government was able to begin the reactivation of the economy through an easing of interest rates. Early in 1961, at the invitation of the government, an economic mission sponsored by the World Bank arrived in Spain to study the economy and to advise on the outlines of a development plan for the country. The World Bank's outlook is one of classical liberalism tempered by common sense, so the mission was likely to advise—and did in fact advise— a much more detached role for the government in the economy and much more reliance on market forces. Assuming that the government would implement the mission's report, the mission's arrival signed the death warrant of economic statism in Spain. The great INI would have its wings clipped and Spain would never again aspire to go it alone in economic development.

During 1961, however, bureaucracy and legal restrictions were still discouraging foreign investment, quota restrictions on imports were still offending the liberal economists, and the rate of re-activation of the economy was not sufficient to satisfy the workers. Then 1962 was a year of industrial unrest on a scale unknown since before the Civil War. There was a large strike at Bilbao in February, and a massive wave of strikes started in the Asturian mining area in April. It followed the failure of the Syndicates to move towards the more 'authentically' representative form which had been suggested at their congress in March. It started at a time when the announcement of a wage settlement under the new collective agreements procedure was imminent. The aims of the strikes were certainly more than simply economic, for they returned again and again to the question of authentic labour unions. On the other side, some large employers seemed to welcome a showdown hoping perhaps that they might escape paying the previously negotiated wage rise. If so, their hopes were vain, and in August a large rise was decreed in the national minimum wage.

Indeed, it was most notable how gently Franco and his government reacted to the strikes, which were after all easily within the regime's definition of military rebellion. Franco did not succumb to the temptation of using military force, but sent José Solís, the Minister and Secretary-General of the Movement, to Asturias to talk to the strikers. Solís actually met leaders of men who were in revolt against the government, and even after he failed to persuade them of their folly the relatively soft line was continued. A number of arrests and dismissals did arise out of the strikes, but so also did government concessions. A law of 14 July provided for workers' representation in the boardroom and for management representation on the workers' syndical committees, and a law of 20 September recognised the possibility of genuine collective grievances not conjured up by clever foreign agitators, and provided machinery for their satisfaction. In a cabinet reshuffle of 11 July, Sanz Orrio and Arias Salgado, who were the principal civilian conservatives, were replaced. Franco certainly seemed to have mellowed.

Of course, Franco was influenced by the fact that Spain's image abroad was particularly important at this time, but another partial explanation of his attitude certainly lies in the part which sections of the Church played in encouraging the strikers. Several prelates had made specific wage demands on behalf of workers, and the Primate himself gave his guarded approval to this clerical support. Throughout the sixties HOAC (Catholic Action Workers' Fraternities) continued to countenance their activities, partly as a hedge against a shift to the left in Spain after Franco's death. The Caudillo is undoubtedly hurt by this lack of confidence in him, but an open break with the Church would undermine the credibility of the regime's Christian posture. And this would be much more damaging than any industrial unrest which has yet been stirred up by the young socially conscious priesthood.

When the Church magazine *Ecclesia* defended the right to strike, *Arriba* called on it to 'render unto Caesar the things which are Caesar's'.[23] It was not an unreasonable riposte to the political pretensions of the Church. The Abbot of Montserrat had gone so

[23] *Arriba*, 18 May 1962.

far as to say that 'the Church always speaks the truth. If this truth is not welcome to those that govern, then it is up to them to change.'[24] Franco has not, however, parried these blows, but rather deflected them. Commenting on Pope John XXIII's radical encyclical on social policy *Mater et Magistra*, he claimed that 'we welcomed it joyfully because we had been leading up to it for twenty years',[25] implicitly daring the hierarchy to contradict him. This pretence of like-mindedness has been very successful in papering over the cracks, though priests who have become too active in, for example, Basque nationalism have soon discovered that it is maintained only within certain limits.

1963 was the beginning of the boom years. Controls on prices were lifted. Quotas on imports began to be lifted. A new taxation system more progressive than heretofore was introduced, and an anti-trust law was passed. Already in April 1962 the government had obtained a greater degree of control over the private banks. At the end of 1963 the proposed Four-Year Development Plan for 1964–1967 was published after a gestation of more than a year supervised by Laureano López Rodó, a ranking member of Opus Dei whom Franco appointed in 1962 and raised to cabinet rank in 1965. Most of the Plan's goals were not in fact new: development of industry with particular attention given to metallurgy, chemicals and machine tools, irrigation in the countryside, development of the fishing industry, dispersal of manufacturing industry into less developed areas. More emphasis than before was now laid on mechanisation of agriculture and on road building, but the innovation of the Plan was its concern with broad outlines and its comparative unconcern with details. The model was the 'indicative planning' which laid the groundwork for the recovery of France after the Second World War. The goals of government policy were now set out coherently in public, and their progress would be open to commentary by the public, and to adjustment where required by the government.

The Plan met with considerable enthusiasm, and also with

[24] Quoted by Angelo Del Boca in *L'altra Spagua* (Milan 1961), p. 146.
[25] *ABC*, 18 July 1962, p. 32.

considerable success, but old problems did not vanish. The government has not always given the firm lead that was expected of it, perhaps because it has not always held a firm opinion. Monopolistic practices were deeply rooted in the Spanish economy and continued to manifest themselves from time to time, most notoriously in the distribution of foodstuffs. Even INI remained independent of ministerial control until March 1968, although its influence had declined after the departure of Suanzes, who had held Franco's ear. Lobbyists of all kinds campaigned for special dispensations to protect them against the cabinet's continued liberalisation of imports, which was an article of faith both with Ullastres and, after he had gone to Brussels in 1965 as Ambassador to the EEC, his successor García-Moncó. There were also frequent complaints of wages that were not keeping pace with the steeply rising cost of living, for inevitably some industries remained static as others forged ahead. This meant a much greater mobility of labour than before, and particularly a flight from the land into the big cities, where the influx produced serious housing and social problems. In September 1966, a forty per cent increase in the minimum wage relieved the very poor, but the compensating deflationary package aggravated the growing number of skilled workers and *petits bourgeois* affected by such devices as hire purchase curbs.

The following year did not bring the full recovery which had been hoped for and in this the failure of the government to cut back public expenditure sufficiently was an important factor. The slowing of growth in productivity as the most obvious cases of underemployment were dealt with, and perhaps an excessive reliance on monetary rather than fiscal measures of deflation, may also have contributed to the disappointing result. All the same, it was unfortunate that Franco should have chosen 16 November 1967, to make a rather self-satisfied speech to the Cortes about the economy. Two days later the British government devalued sterling. The Spanish government decided that, although British markets and British tourists were by no means of overwhelming importance to Spain, additional burdens could not easily be absorbed, and that they could best escape recriminations by devaluing in the wake of the British. In the deflationary package which they introduced to bolster devaluation, the government aimed their hammer blows at their own expenditure, making exemplary cuts in civil service personnel and in the use of official cars. They took legal powers, backed by awesome sanctions, to freeze all consumer prices. Yet inflation was not conquered, and a disappointing rate of productivity growth continued to worry the government. By 1969 the outlook was brighter, but it is impossible to overlook the long-term problems which beset the Spanish economy in its voyage towards a Northern European standard of development.

The most worrying weakness is Spain's dependence on sources of foreign exchange which are liable to severe fluctuations from causes beyond her control. Pre-eminent among these sources is tourism. From 1958 to 1968 Spain had a favourable balance in visible trade in only two years, and was able in the others to run considerable deficits because of the massive inflow of tourist money. Of course, a great amount of it has been reinvested in the tourist industry, and it has had inflationary effects, but it is not far-fetched to attribute to the tourist boom much of the difference between the economic successes of the sixties and the long run failure of the fifties. In gross terms, tourist receipts dwarf foreign capital inflow, and much of the capital has been attracted by a growth in the Spanish market itself partly attributable to the tourist boom. And this boom began precisely in 1959, when the number of tourists rose by forty-six per cent to over six million and receipts (in terms of US dollars) by sixty-four per cent over the previous record year to 159 million dollars. Numbers rose in every year thereafter until in 1969 more than twenty-one million tourists were expected to bring in at least 1,200 million dollars. But the growth of earnings is beginning to level off, and Spain remains vulnerable to undercutting from, for example, Eastern Europe, and ultimately to changes of fashion in Northern Europe.

Other important foreign exchange sources are also insecure, and foremost among these are émigré remittances. Over the past ten years or so there has been an enormous emigration of Spaniards overseas, particularly to West Germany. It has become an increasingly recognised means for a young man or woman to save up money and to broaden his or her outlook at the same time. The remittances of émigrés amounted in 1967 to as much as 320 million dollars, but this source of exchange is more vulnerable even than tourism. Indeed Spaniards abroad are mostly on short-term labour permits, and their numbers are now dropping dramatically as they return and are not replaced.

Further anxieties surround Spain's *aperitivo y postre* exports. While tariffs on food imports gain ground abroad, wine, olive oil, tomatoes, above all oranges, still make up the greater part of Spain's export earnings. Progress is being made in the diversification of Spanish exports, but it is slow. The government's efforts to accelerate the process have been cautious and modest. If at the end of the Civil War Franco may have felt that Spain was on the brink of economic greatness, over the years he has come to believe more and more in the inevitability of gradualness. 'It is necessary that everybody should understand', he told the National Council of the Falange in 1956, 'that half a century of neglect cannot be repaired in a few years, that great chasms are bridged not at a leap but by means of ramps and steps.'[26]

It is perhaps in his agrarian policy that this caution has been most evident. Spanish agriculture not only suffers from the hardness of its physical context, but has its fill of structural problems also. The large holdings, *latifundia*, of much of the south are both wasteful of manpower and resistant to innovation, dependent as they are on a large pool of unskilled casual labour. The converse problem, especially typical of Galicia, is of fragmented holdings too small, despite good soil and climate, to be economically viable.

Under the Republic plans for agrarian reform counted on the expropriation of the great landowners who were held responsible for the evils of *latifundismo*. Expropriation began in 1932 and was largely completed in the revolutionary turmoil of 1936. Meanwhile, the property rights of the tiny smallholders, staunch Republicans, remained mostly undisturbed by any government scheme for concentration or collectivisation of holdings. Not surprisingly, the victorious Franco government entirely restored the pre-Republican situation on the great estates, but gave its attention to the consolidation of smallholdings through the Servicio Nacional de Concentración Parcelaria. For the social problems of the *latifundia* and of the dry farming areas Franco has prescribed only indirect remedies. Irrigation works on a grand scale have been carried out,

[26] *ABC* 18 July 1956, p. 35.

pre-eminently in the valley of the Guadiana, and these have increased both productivity and the level of employment. The development of industry since the Second World War and the growth of foreign emigration since the mid-fifties have drained some of the surplus manpower from rural areas. Laws even provide for the eviction of landlords and the collectivisation of estates. These laws are the nearest Franco has come to dealing directly with the social problems of rural capitalism, but they have in practice remained without effect. Landlords can be evicted only in the interests of better utilisation of the land, and the implementation of agrarian policy is in the hands of the employing class to an extent that industrial policy never has been. The fact is that in Franco's view peasant ownership is unlikely to solve any more economic problems than it creates, for all the enthusiasm that some Spanish economists publicly express for it. Patience, not energy, is required, he believes. And the economic judgement is buttressed, if not conditioned by his concern to maintain property rights and the present social order substantially unchanged. Franco is no social engineer.

Nor is he a professional economist, and probably has about the same level of skill and interest in economics as those other political leaders today who have no professional grounding in the subject. The interpretation of statistics, the regulation of demand, the management of foreign exchange he has mainly delegated to those whose speciality it is. Characteristically he has interfered from time to time, so sustaining his reputation for attention to detail, but such month-to-month developments he looks on as tactical rather than strategic. His function as *generalissimo* is to plan for the long term, and it is surely no coincidence that he has taken an interest in the re-afforestation of Spain, a long-term project *par excellence*. Of course, it would be unreasonable to expect his strategic plan to have remained unchanged over more than thirty years, but a biographer has used of him the phrase from Goethe 'unhasting, but unceasing, like the star',[27] and such consistency is a part of his mystique. So it is perhaps right to point out that Franco's economic outlook has gradually moved with the trend of fashionable economic thought. In 1938 he spoke as a disciple of Schacht, the wizard of German

[27] Galinsoga, op. cit., p. 289. From Goethe: *Sprüche in Reimen. Zahme Xenien II.*

economic recovery; in 1967 his account to the Cortes of the economic state of the nation was concerned with rate of economic growth and with the 'take-off' of the Spanish economy. All that had not changed was his reluctance to bore the audience with statistics, a sure sign of the unashamed amateur, which is in the last analysis what Franco the economist is. He can draw more satisfaction from involvement in foreign affairs, which requires less technical expertise, and to which he brings many natural gifts.

10 In Search of a Role

The central problem of Franco's foreign policy was to define Spain's place in the world, and the roots of this problem lie in 1898, for it was the loss of Cuba, Puerto Rico and the Philippines in that year that severed Spain's last link with the empire of the Golden Century. There was no denying the shock this gave the country, so politicians and public men of every hue taking an optimistic view suggested that the disaster might have a purgative effect on Spain. Some simply hoped for a rebirth of Spain's glorious Catholic past. 'Spain evangeliser of half the planet: Spain the hammer of heretics, the light of Trent, the sword of the Pope, the cradle of St Ignatius. This is our greatness and glory: we have no other,' said the Catholic philosopher Menéndez y Pelayo.[1] Others aspired to a new empire in Africa to replace the one lost in America.

Many of them looked to a future as glittering in some respects as the past had been, and refused to cast a nation once capable of such grandeur in a role in which there was nothing exceptional. To them, to suggest that Spain might never regain such heights was to display a despicable lack of patriotism, if not an allegiance to sinister internationalism or petty regionalism. The disaster of 1898 had loomed large in Franco's childhood, and the glory of Spain was the oratorical currency of his whole environment. When the reins of foreign policy were placed in his hands, he was as little prepared as anyone to cut Spain down to size. Although he has

[1] Quoted Raymond Carr: *Spain 1808–1939* (Oxford 1966), p. 355.

travelled very little, having since 1941 left Spanish territory only for two brief visits to Portugal, his interest in foreign affairs has always been very close. Indeed, he might be called the leader of Spain's search for her international significance, for the special talent which can rekindle respect for her in the world and in herself.

The most obvious direction which Spanish resurgence could take would be the acquisition of a new territorial empire, a new geopolitical power. Enthusiasm for Spanish involvement in Morocco stemmed from this will to empire, which grew in intensity as the political Darwinism of Spengler became influential in Spain. Even under the Republic, Colonel Capaz, who brought Spanish administration to the little enclave of Ifni, was hailed as 'the last of the conquistadores'. Empire was always a watchword of the Falange. 'The world is once again tending,' José Antonio told the newspaper *Ahora* in 1934, 'to be directed by three or four racial entities. Spain can be one of these three or four.'[2] The hope of young patriots during the Second World War was that this prominence could come to Spain from an Axis victory. The hope was by no means confined to Falangists of the old school. Franco himself shared it, and of the authors of *Reivindicaciones de España* (Spain's claims), the blueprint for a new worldwide Spanish empire published in 1941, neither was an 'old shirt'.[3] But the victory of the Allies and the emergence of two super-powers which dwarfed even Britain killed any hope of Spain becoming a Great Power in anything like the accepted sense. She ceased to strive for any addition to her territory beyond Gibraltar, and that is an irredentist rather than an expansionist ambition. For the rest, Spain would have to be conspicuous not for size and power but for some special talent or example that she could offer the world.

Naturally, her special contribution would have to be consonant with her history, and fortunately her history had certain obviously special features. Her language and culture were far-flung. Seventeen republics in America spoke her language and had ties of blood with her; the Philippines owed much to her culture; in the

[2] José Antonio Primo de Rivera: *Obras completas* (Madrid 1954), p. 165.

[3] The authors were Fernando María Castiella, Minister of Foreign Affairs, 1957–69, and José María de Areilza.

Franco on holiday with his grandchildren, September 1958 (Associated Press)

Prince Juan Carlos of Bourbon and his wife in the Cathedral at Santiago de Compostela with the Francos soon after his nomination as successor to the Spanish throne (Associated Press)

Eastern Mediterranean Sephardic Jews clung to the Castilian language as it had been spoken four centuries earlier when they had left Spain. General Primo de Rivera was the first political leader to foster Spanish pride in being the centre of this *Hispanidad* (Spanishness), but it became an ideal of Franco's regime, in particular of the Falangists. Serrano Súñer set up a whole structure of organisations to strengthen the links with Spanish America, but there was little flesh on their bare bones. So far as they had life it was as centres of virulent anti-Yankeeism, often actively engaged in collecting intelligence for the Axis powers, and they tended to alienate the South Americans by giving the impression that Spain might again aspire to political suzerainty in the area.

After the Second World War any such ambitions had resolutely to be cast aside, and, speaking on Columbus Day 1946, Franco said that there were two kinds of empire, 'the empire that takes and ... the empire that gives'. The Spanish empire was of the latter kind, a cultural empire, and he would not have it otherwise. 'If at one point in history Spain stood first by virtue of her power, and demonstrated in her crusade the strength of her faith, her courage and her virtues, with the coming of better times, she puts before these her spiritual, social and cultural works.'[4] But it was becoming increasingly difficult to pretend even to cultural authority, and Spain from the fifties has posed more as a bridge between America and Europe, an interpreter of the one to the other.

Reaching still further back into its history, Spain could also claim to be a bridge between Europe and the Arab world. Spain, after all, had seen a flowering of Islamic culture which could not be claimed by Sicily or by the Balkans, the other European areas where Islam had penetrated. At the same time as Spain looked back with admiration to the reign of Ferdinand and Isabella, and took their yoke-and-arrows emblem for the symbol of the Movement, she began also to claim for her own the medieval cultures of Jews and Moors, which the same Ferdinand and Isabella had done their utmost to destroy.

It was, in fact, largely as a result of the circumstances of the Civil War that Spain had become concerned to parade her link with the Arab world. The Moors were a most important element in the

[4] Franco: *Textos*, p. 377.

I

Nationalist armies, and their adherence to a Christian crusade had to be rationalised—and consolidated. Doubtless the majority of Moorish volunteers were simple mercenaries, attracted by pay and conditions. But the Jalifa, the Sultan's representative in the Spanish zone, expressed support on the basis of the common theism of Spaniards and Moors in contrast to the atheism of Communism. 'I am proud,' he told German visitors in 1938, 'to aid Spain in its battle against those who believe in no God.'[5] Moreover, as a practical demonstration of brotherhood between Spain and Morocco and in order to neutralise a possible source of trouble, concessions were made to Moroccan nationalist feeling. Arabic language newspapers were allowed. Abdelkhalek Torres, leader of the nationalist party al-Islah, was even taken into the administration of the Protectorate. Such concessions were more than the Republicans, anxious for French goodwill, felt able to promise, and they split the Moroccan nationalist movement between co-operators in the Spanish zone and subversives in the French zone.

Later, it is true, the freedom of action granted to Moroccan nationalists declined; Torres had left the administration before the end of the Civil War. In 1945, the drought which afflicted Spain affected Morocco also, and when the resulting hardship led in 1946 to unrest, the High Commissioner, General Varela, reacted sharply. Torres and other nationalist leaders retired into exile. But Franco was still anxious for Arab goodwill, and in December he proposed to the Arab League that he should conclude a cultural agreement with the League on behalf of the Jalifa's government. The League, however, declined to conclude such an agreement before independence and the next couple of years saw little progress in Hispano–Arab relations. Early in 1948 Varela even promised the French Resident, General Juin, that he would give no shelter to Moroccan nationalist refugees from the French zone, an unusual departure from the often voluble hostility of Franco–Spanish relations at that time. Nevertheless, Spain remained a more sympathetic protecting power than France, if only because in

[5] Erich Raeder: *Mein Leben* (Tübingen 1956), Vol. II, pp. 87–8. Cf. Robert A. Friedlander: 'Holy Crusade or Unholy Alliance? Franco's National Revolution and the Moors' in *The South-western Social Science Quarterly* (Austin, Tex.), Vol. 44, No. 4 (March 1964), pp. 346–56.

her zone she had no large *colon* class to claim her special consideration.

By the end of the forties relations between Spain and the Arab world had significantly improved, largely because of Franco's support for the Arabs in their struggle against Israel. He had not recognised the new state when it came into being in 1948, and he became positively hostile to it when its representative at the United Nations voted in May 1949 for the retention of the boycott on Spain. Franco was hurt by the Israeli suggestion that he had harmed the Jews by supporting Hitler. In fact, his diplomatic representatives had, at his instructions, extended the protection of Spanish nationality wherever possible to Sephardic Jews, and he now had the Ministry of Foreign Affairs publish a booklet detailing these good deeds.[6] He also invited the King of Transjordan, who was at war with Israel, to be the first foreign Head of State to visit the country since the Civil War, a valuable demonstration of mutual solidarity.

Meanwhile, the standing of other Western European powers in the Islamic world became lower and lower. The British, blamed for the existence of Israel, found their occupation of the Suez Canal zone more and more arduous to maintain, while in 1951 the nationalisation of their Iranian oilfields extended the scope of their troubles. The French faced mounting unrest in North Africa, particularly in Tunisia, while the Americans were considered the patrons of Israel, regardless of attempts to keep their distance. So, by the time Spain was knocking seriously at the gates of the Western bloc, Franco could with conviction claim that he had better relations with the Arab world than any other Western power, and could hint that his good offices might be of value to his European neighbours.

At the time when perhaps Britain's difficulties in the Middle East were reaching a new peak, the spring of 1952, Franco sent his Foreign Minister Martín Artajo on a tour of Arab countries, accompanied by a large retinue which included Spain's Moorish general, Mohamed ben Mezián. A fruitful crop of cultural and economic agreements followed, and the question of political development in the Spanish zone of Morocco was tactfully left on one side. The

[6] *L'Espagne et les Juifs* (Madrid 1949).

Secretary-General of the Arab League, Azzam, said that the question could be settled in a friendly manner. Indeed, although both Torres and his principal rival Mekki Neciri had in 1951 subscribed to the independence programme of the Moroccan National Front, and although the new High Commissioner, García Valiño, had condemned 'fanatical Arab nationalism', nationalism was given a great deal of scope. This was of course particularly so as long as it was directed against the French, who were increasingly faced in Rabat with the impossibility of governing against a coalition of the Sultan and the Istiqlal (Independence) party. It was also used to Spain's advantage in Tangier, where native agitation succeeded in having Spain restored to an equal share in the administration of the international zone in September 1952.

In 1953, Spain was able to take full advantage of the discomfiture of the French in Morocco. She offered sanctuary to exiled nationalist leaders like Balafrej and al-Fassi, and strongly denounced the deposition of the Sultan, which the French staged on 20 August. In 1947, the French had arranged for the Sultan to visit Tetuán and Tangier, hoping that an enthusiastic reception would demonstrate the loyalty of the Spanish zone to the French-protected symbol of Moroccan unity, and so embarrass the Spanish authorities. In 1953, it was Spain's turn to take a trick off her rivals with the trump card of loyalty to the Sultan. She followed it up by permitting Moroccan nationalists to use her zone as a base area for terrorist activities inside the French zone, with the result that the French had to station troops on the inter-zonal border. Meanwhile, Moroccan participation in the administration of the Spanish zone made some progress, with Abdelkhalek Torres and two of his party being given senior posts, but Spain's policy of encouraging nationalism was one fraught with a grave risk. So long as the French were willing and able to contain nationalism, Spain could continue to win the sympathy of the Arab world by denouncing them, could pose as a model protectorate power by making moderate concessions, and could enhance the value to the Americans of bases in Spain by calling in question the security of those in French Morocco. But Franco seemed not to envisage the possibility that France might give in to the Istiqlal.

And this was precisely what did happen. In September 1955

the puppet Sultan, Mohamed ben Arafa, left the country, and on 6 November the French Government promised rapid progress towards independence. There was a responsible Moroccan cabinet in Rabat by December. Franco was highly alarmed. He began to claim his right to be consulted on such fundamental changes in the constitution of the country, but he received little sympathy from the French Premier, Faure, who had bitterly denounced Spanish aid to the rebels in a powerful speech to the Chamber on 9 October. Franco was not anxious to see an independent Morocco, because he feared that it would mean only that France would exchange overt colonialism over a part of Morocco for a more subtle economic and financial control over the whole of a nominally autonomous Morocco, the Spanish zone included. He was not, therefore, prepared to Moroccanise the administration in Tetuán as rapidly as was being done in Rabat, 'precisely', he said, 'because we know and love the Moroccan people'. Besides, the arguments which he and his comrades had deployed against the Dictator's proposed withdrawal in 1924 were still valid. Could he, could his powerful military supporters, forget how much Spanish blood had been invested in the Protectorate?

Agonising though it was, however, sentiment had to give way to realism in the face of the unrest that was now spreading through the Spanish zone. On 14 January 1956 Franco publicly recognised the imminence of Moroccan independence. The French signed the independence agreement on 2 March, and in the following fortnight Franco made up his mind that nothing could prevent Spain from following their example. He decided that at least he would bow out with a good grace, and the Sultan came to Madrid in person to accept the retrocession of the northern part of his kingdom on 7 April. Professions of goodwill were made on all sides. García Valiño even claimed that the independence parade in Rabat was the high spot of his service in Morocco. But clouds still hung over Spanish relations with Morocco, for Spain retained not only her ancient *presidios*, but also the enclave of Ifni and the territory of Cabo Juby in the extreme south of Morocco, which Morocco claimed as her own. The quarrel would later lead to bloodshed and damage beyond repair the picture of Spain as the Arab's special friend, but by then Franco would largely have cast off that image,

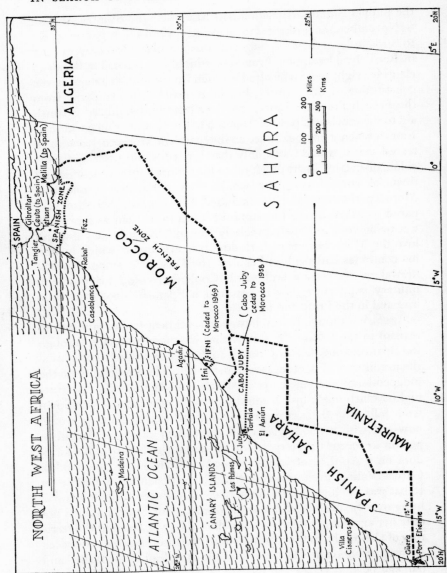

together with the Foreign Minister largely responsible for projecting it.

Not only the fiasco in Morocco but also the darkening clouds of the Middle East contributed to the interment of Spain's Arab policy. When Nasser nationalised the Suez Canal in July 1956, the Spanish press took a pro-Egyptian line, and the invitation of Spain to the London Conference in August was felt to constitute a belated recognition of Spain's role as bridge between the Arabs and the Western world. But the increasing involvement of the Communist bloc in the Middle East could not but worry Franco, since anti-Communism, the cement of the Nationalist cause in the Civil War, the stimulus to Spanish patriotism in the days of the boycott, was a more natural if a less idiosyncratic element in his policy than friendship with the Arabs. One of the principal objectives of this friendship had been to exemplify a distinction between anti-Communism and imperialism, and so to win Arab co-operation against the Soviet menace. If Morocco had damaged Spain's non-imperialist image, the Suez affair killed any residual hope of an Arab alignment against Communism. The Spanish generals could see no purpose in continuing to support the Arabs once the Protectorate was lost. The Americans were asking Franco to show his solidarity with the West, and the French were holding out an olive branch. No wonder that by the spring of 1957 the course of Spanish foreign policy had significantly shifted.

Franco's new-found friendship with France was soon to be of service in Africa. In November 1957, the enclave of Ifni was attacked by a force of Moroccan nationalists, who were strongly but unofficially supported by the Rabat Government. Initially, the Spanish Government was in some difficulties for communications between that desert area and the nearby Canary Islands were poor, and the United States strongly requested that military equipment supplied by her should not be used in the operations. But the French Government was worried about the threat to Mauretania and to Saharan Algeria, both areas of great and so far untapped natural resources, so the first Franco–Spanish joint operations since 1926 were mounted, and by the middle of February 1958 had met with complete success.

Franco was strongly opposed to further territorial concessions, but in the end he agreed that the area known as Cabo Juby should be ceded to Morocco, while Ifni and the Saharan territories should be bound closer to Spain by receiving in January 1958 the status of provinces. Since then Morocco has made further claims on Spain, has even raised the question of sovereignty over Ceuta and Melilla, but relations with Spain have not again descended into violence. (In 1963, when Morocco came to blows with newly independent Algeria along her southern frontier, Spain even offered military assistance.) But pressure has increased, and in 1969 Spain gave further ground by the cessation of Ifni, an economically useless enclave, hoping thus to buy security for the richer province of Sahara.

Spanish Sahara has only 24,000 inhabitants, and most of the indigenous people are nomadic. Its value lies in its mineral resources even though the high hopes for petroleum fields both under the province and offshore have not yet been fulfilled and phosphates remain the principal resource exploited. Since the General Assembly of the United Nations passed a resolution in December 1960 declaring that colonialism is a denial of the human rights of indigenous peoples, Spain, like other colonial nations, has been under growing pressure to take 'immediate steps' towards decolonialisation. The constitution of her colonies (the two equatorial colonies as well as Ifni and Sahara) into overseas provinces was originally a manœuvre copied from Portugal with the purpose of avoiding the obligation to supply to the UN information about colonial development, but Spain conceded after only a year that she would supply information *ex gratia*. Indeed, if Spain has not followed the dictates of the Special Committee on Colonialism with indecent haste, she nevertheless voted in December 1968 for self-determination for Ifni and for an UN referendum in Sahara. She is presumably fairly confident of a victory for the *status quo*, particularly since she has two mutually hostile rivals for possession of the territory, Morocco and Mauretania.

Besides her territories in the Maghrib, Spain had colonies in Equatorial Africa: 10,000 square miles of mainland between Cameroon and Gabon, surrounding the river after which this Territory is named, Río Muni, and also a number of islands in the

Gulf of Guinea, of which Fernando Póo, the seat of their administration, is the largest. The population of these colonies was both more numerous and more settled than that of Ifni and Sahara, so they were obviously more viable as independent states than the desert territories. The call of the United Nations to Spain in September 1963 to speed up decolonisation was followed in December by a referendum in Río Muni and Fernando Póo, as a result of which a single internally autonomous administration was set up for the whole of Spanish Guinea. Africans took a greater part in government than before, acting as ministers as well as mayors, but agitation for full independence continued in the United Nations and to a perhaps lesser extent in Río Muni. Throughout the spring of 1968 a conference took place in Madrid on the nature of an independence constitution. It presented the difficulty of reconciling the island minority, many of whom wanted either separate independence or retention of colonial status, with the mainland majority, many of whom demanded an unacceptably unitary constitution. The result was that full independence which had been expected by the end of June 1968 did not in the end take place until 12 October.

Trouble followed shortly, for President Macias of the new state of Equatorial Guinea resented the pervasiveness of the remaining Spanish presence. Spain continued to contribute technical and economic advice generously, and her flag continued to wave over her advisers' offices, an irritating reminder of colonial days. The riots which developed from this irritant were countered in March 1969 by an attempted *coup d'état* by the Foreign Minister, who realised Guinea's vital need for continued Spanish aid, a need which had in all probability been pointed out to him on a recent visit to Madrid. Macias, at all events, lost no time in bloodily suppressing the rising, and in accusing the Madrid Government of responsibility for it. The Spanish seemed to regard the charge only as evidence of Macias' paranoia, but although the independence of Guinea unburdened the Spanish budget, Franco and his deputy, Carrero, certainly intended to protect the interests of private citizens there, and had retained a force of Civil Guards there specifically for their protection. They were not in fact used, and Spain turned appropriately to the United Nations for help in evacuating the vast majority of her citizens from the ex-colony. It was after all to a great extent for the sake of United Nations' approval that Spain had decolonised it.

Spain's concern with approval from a body which had merited such contempt and odium from Franco in the first years of its existence is at first sight surprising, but the General Assembly provides a useful forum in which Spain can air her own anti-colonialist grievance—Gibraltar. Of course, the existence of such a grievance guarantees Spain a measure of sympathy from the dozens of emergent nations for whom colonialism is the greatest evil in the world, and for all Franco's pride he remains anxious for sympathy. Sympathy can lead to influence after all. Nevertheless, it would be a self-deception for Englishmen and Gibraltarians to regard Spain's obstinate campaign for the retrocession of the Rock as disguising the pursuit of some ulterior motive. It is as true of Gibraltar as of any other political issue that most people do not regard it as of the greatest personal importance, but it is hard to find the Spaniard who does not believe in the justice of his country's claim to the Rock. British possession of Gibraltar affronts Spanish pride, and is often described as a thorn, painful even if not dangerous. The Spanish Red Book on Gibraltar is right to point out that, while there may be few things on which Spaniards can agree, Gibraltar is one of those few. 'It is not worth a war,' Franco told an interviewer in 1959, 'but it destroys the sincerity of a friendship.'[7] Yet Britain and Spain are not prepared to settle the dispute.

Gibraltar was captured by the English under Admiral Rooke in 1704. At that time England was supporting the Austrian claimant to the throne against the French claimant in the War of the Spanish Succession, and when the war ended with the Treaty of Utrecht in 1713, the town and fortress of Gibraltar were ceded to Great Britain. During the course of the eighteenth century Spain attempted several times by force of arms to recover the fortress, but without success. On the other hand, Britain has broken the Treaty of Utrecht by allowing both Jews and Moors to settle in Gibraltar. In the course of time, furthermore, they have extended

[7] *Pueblo* (Madrid), 30 April 1959. Translated as Document No. 62 of *The Spanish Red Book on Gibraltar* (Madrid 1965).

the area of their jurisdiction by the matter of a square mile or two, in which the weak Spanish governments of the past more or less acquiesced. The final encroachment by the British was made during the Spanish Civil War when on agreed neutral ground they built an airfield, described at first as an 'emergency landing strip' but destined later to play an important part in the Second World War. The Gibraltar problem in fact does not derive only from Rooke's occupation and from the Treaty of Utrecht, but also from Spain's weak acceptance *de facto* of British encroachments over the years. At moments when Spain has felt less weak *vis-à-vis* Britain, in 1940 for example, and now that she has the backing of a large segment of world opinion, she has made efforts to reverse her cessions, but as yet with little success.

In the summer of 1940 the British indicated that the status of Gibraltar was negotiable, as they had done in similarly dark moments of the eighteenth century. In recent years too they have been prepared to enter into discussions, and now that Gibraltar is no longer so vital a strategic base for Britain, progress might have been expected. But no talks have made any important progress, because, while Spain is interested only in discussing the special treatment to be given to Britain and her subjects under the Spanish flag, Britain will not consider the transfer of sovereignty unless it can be demonstrated that the inhabitants of Gibraltar wish for it.

That the inhabitants of Gibraltar do not wish for it is abundantly clear and was confirmed by a referendum held by the British in September 1967, so the British stand firm despite the support which Spain has from the third world. They stand the firmer because Left and Right are united in their support of the Gibraltarians. Buttressing their concern for the wishes of the people is the Left's determination to cede no territory to fascism, and the fact that for the Right the Rock is a symbol of their Augustan Age, one bastion of empire where old-fashioned loyalty to the British Crown is not a joke or a dirty word.

The arguments used by the Spanish Government have inevitably strengthened the Gibraltarians' enthusiasm for the British connection. Although Spain offers dual nationality and all manner of guarantees for job security and personal freedoms, she will not recognise the reality of the Gibraltarians' domicile. The Spanish inhabitants of 1704 mostly fled inland, taking with them the town's records, and founded the village of San Roque. Their descendants, according to Spain, are the real people of Gibraltar, and the Maltese, Genoese and other immigrants are, despite their many generations of settlement, 'an artificially constituted human group'. Much is also made of the large part played by smuggling in Gibraltar's economic history. 'The economic life of Gibraltar,' according to Franco, 'has always been artificial and parasitical, feeding on contraband against our country.'[8] It is on this pretext that from October 1964 greater and greater restrictions were placed on commerce and communications between Gibraltar and Spain, until in the summer of 1969 they were altogether halted. It is pointed out that in the Treaty of Utrecht all commerce was forbidden except in emergency. The Treaty also gave Spain the first option on Gibraltar should Britain ever wish to dispose of it, so every step towards the self-government, if only in internal matters, of the colony has been denounced by Spain as a move by Britain to alienate the Rock to a third party without permission, so violating the Treaty.

The Gibraltar issue has become particularly embittered since the question of decolonisation has arisen at the United Nations, and it is by no means softened by the mutual hostility of Franco and the British Labour Party. Franco has perhaps realised that, despite the fears he expressed during the Second World War,[9] the Labour Party is not communist; but Harold Wilson still resolutely labelled Spain 'a fascist country' in a campaign speech as Leader of the Opposition in June 1964.[10] Franco furiously cancelled the frigate building contract whose imminent signature Wilson had denounced, and when a UN resolution favourable to Spain coincided in October with the inauguration of a Labour government in Britain, he immediately put into force restrictions at the Gibraltar frontier.

Later, however, he supplemented his restrictive economic pressure on the Rock with an economic policy for the hinterland

[8] *Spanish Red Book*, loc. cit.
[9] FRUS, 1942, Vol. III, p. 291.
[10] *The Times* (London), 17 June 1964.

(*campo*) of Gibraltar which would develop it to the point where it would no longer need Gibraltar as a source of employment, and where its standard of living would attract Gibraltarians towards integration with Spain. Early in 1965 the Gibraltar area was given the status of a 'development pole' which meant *inter alia* that companies wishing to set up in the area would be given ninety-five per cent tax rebates, and would have land compulsorily acquired for them by the Government. It was planned that there should be a petrochemical plant and large dry-dock and bunkering facilities in Algeciras Bay, but to date, progress has been somewhat disappointing; and, though a few 'doves' have already emerged among Gibraltarians anxious to co-operate with Spain in developing the area as a whole, it looks as though it will be many years before the prosperity of the *campo* might tempt a majority of Gibraltarians to follow them.

The sympathy of the third world, and especially of Latin America, for Spain over the Gibraltar issue is of service to Franco in the propagation of yet another facet of Spain's image, that of the bridge between the rich countries with developed industry, and the developing countries, many of whose problems Spain shares and consequently understands better than other Europeans can. This view of Spain is not altogether a new one, for it calls to mind explanations of Spain's backwardness expressed in the forties. Since the appeal is largely to Latin America, it also represents an updating of *Hispanidad*, which necessarily entails a degree of competitiveness against the United States, even of anti-Americanism. This does not of course take the same virulent form as in the 1940s, but it serves to rebut the charge of Franco's enemies that the Caudillo is a puppet, now manipulated by Uncle Sam where once Hitler pulled the strings. When in 1965 Spain offered to Latin America a large development loan, it was widely seen as a *riposte* to the Washington-sponsored Alliance for Progress.

The best illustration of Franco's independence, however, is his relations with Castro, which, if they cannot be called warm, do at least exist. There was a period of rupture shortly after Castro's accession in 1959, which was largely attributable to Franco's close links with the former Batista regime, but there was considerable sympathy in Spain with the Cubans against the Bay of Pigs invaders. Spain naturally supported Kennedy during the missile crisis the following year, but in 1963 commercial relations were resumed with Cuba in spite of American disapproval and threats of sanctions. Spain bought sugar, and sold trucks. She also maintains a direct airline link with Havana, and allows sympathetic accounts of the Cuban regime to appear in her newspapers. All this reflects an undercurrent of hostility to the United States which is not confined to competition for the friendship of Latin America.

The misgivings of many over the Bases Agreement of 1953 had increased rather than diminished with the passage of time, and by the end of 1957 the Government itself was somewhat disillusioned with the Americans. Semi-official sources condemned the niggardliness of American aid to Spain in comparison with Marshall Aid. United States largesse to the United Kingdom or France up to 1951 alone was of more than four times the amount which Spain received throughout the fifties, and even the Americans' former enemies, the Italians, benefited much more than Spain.[11] On the other hand, Spanish sources did not always resist the temptation to blame domestic inflation on the influx of that American money which was thought at the same time to be insufficient. Disillusionment came to a peak with the realisation that, by alignment with the USA, Spain had not found safety in a winning side but rather committed herself to exposure in the front line.

This realisation can be dated to 4 October 1957, when the Soviet Union, by launching the first Sputnik satellite, conclusively proved its capacity for delivering Intercontinental Ballistic Missiles. With major American airbases within a few miles of her capital and of three other important cities (Cádiz, Seville and Zaragoza), Spain naturally felt uneasy. Communist propaganda broadcast from Prague on Radio España Independiente made much of the danger, but there was little that could be done to remove it short of evicting the Americans. Tentative requests for resiting of the bases were advanced, but received no satisfaction; Spain would simply have to

[11] The many different forms which aid took make accurate figures of comparison impossible, but see US 82nd Congress: *13th Report to Congress of the Economic Cooperation Administration* (Washington 1951), pp. 114–15, 127, and Whitaker, op. cit., pp. 241–2.

hope for the best. In the meanwhile she could perhaps loosen a little her links with the United States.

Tentative steps were already being taken towards a normalisation of relations with the Communist bloc, and these were continued with renewed vigour. The political content of this policy was, however, less important than the commercial, and the emphasis in Spain's diplomatic policy was on developing greater integration with the Western defence system. In December 1957 the American Secretary of State, Dulles, visited Franco to brief him on the outcome of NATO discussions. Two years later President Eisenhower himself, after a brief session of talks, publicly embraced Franco at Madrid airport, but this sort of gesture of confidence could not alter the fact that for Spain multilateral links with the West were now preferable to her present bilateral connection.

General Barroso, the Spanish Minister of the Army, told the Cortes in December 1957 that Spain had much to offer NATO, and it was a fact that some members of the alliance, notably the Germans, were anxious that Spain should be asked to join. On the other hand the smaller and more left-wing governments, such as the Belgians and the Norwegians, were strongly opposed; so Franco considered the possibility of a Southern European or Mediterranean grouping which would overlap with NATO and would join him with Portugal, France, and Christian Democratic Italy. Unfortunately, as France became more and more deeply embroiled in Algeria, this idea also broke down.

But even if Spain was not in the immediate future to be integrated into the Western defence system, an army which could be of real use in NATO remained highly desirable. The Spanish Army was still structured and deployed for a political garrison role, for which in the 1950s it was no longer required, and reform was made all the more urgent by the loss of the Moroccan protectorate, which rendered the substantial forces previously stationed there redundant. In 1958 Barroso brought out a plan whereby the manpower of the Army was to be reduced by one quarter, and the savings effected used to improve its equipment. Like much of Franco's military policy, the enhancement of the NCO's status for example, this scheme was one whose principles would have gladdened the reviled Azaña. Like Azaña, however, Barroso was short of money for the implementation of his plans, which were ambitious enough to envisage the acquisition of tactical nuclear weapons, besides the very latest in personal weapons and conventional artillery.

The Spanish Army hoped for United States help in supplying their deficiencies, but has been somewhat disappointed, since their requests arrived at a time when the Americans were beginning to look carefully at what came later to be called the cost-effectiveness of their military aid, even to impeccable anti-Communists. During 1959 Spain explored the possibilities of military co-operation with the German Federal Republic. Germany could provide money and technical expertise, and Spain wide open spaces for training manœuvres and installations. But unpleasant publicity accusing them of creating a neo-fascist axis led the Germans quietly to turn their attention to Portugal. Today, certain crack Spanish units have been fully modernised (though in no case supplied with nuclear weapons), and they take part from time to time in well-publicised joint manœuvres, usually with the French or the Americans. But Spain remains on the margin of Western European defence.

It is not only in the military field that Spain has looked for integration into Western Europe, and received more promises than performance. Economically and politically too, Franco's Spain has sought close association with Europe, although Franco himself did not approve of the European movement in its early days. If many of its leaders were, like Schuman, staunchly anti-Communist and good Catholics, others, like Spaak, were socialists and old enemies of Nationalist Spain. All were firmly attached to liberal parliamentary institutions, which of course Franco regarded as unsuitable for Spain, while the idea of supranationality was profoundly repugnant to him. It also inspired in him the deepest scepticism: he neither hoped for nor expected the success of the European idea. 'These ambitious aspirations towards some United States of Europe are chimerical,' he told the Spanish people in his 1956 New Year's Eve message. 'The old nations of the West have formed their personalities over centuries, and these cannot be erased.'[12]

The entry of the Opus economic ministers into the cabinet in

[12] *ABC* (Madrid), 1 January 1957, p. 37.

1957 was a step towards the Europeanisation of Spain—and even of Franco. Ullastres and Navarro did not of course intend to submerge Spain's identity, but they were acutely aware of the economic lead which France, Germany and the Benelux countries had over Spain. They felt that closer economic links with more developed countries and a gradual liberalisation of Spanish trade would provide much needed stimulus to Spanish economic growth. Particularly after the coming of de Gaulle and the consequent waning of the political dynamism of the Common Market, the Spanish 'Europeans' had grounds to hope that they could derive economic benefits from Europe without paying an unacceptable political price. Nevertheless, Franco himself remained hostile and continued to attack 'Europeanism' as late as 1961. In the end it was not the positive benefits associated with joining Europe that brought him to court the EEC, but rather the more and more apparent dangers of remaining outside.

So long as the Community was comparatively small and the common market policy restricted to industrial goods, Spain could remain relatively unconcerned. But, in July 1961, Greece concluded an agreement of association with the EEC, which gave its agricultural exports a more favourable position than competing Spanish products. In the autumn of 1961 applications for membership from the United Kingdom, Ireland, Denmark and Norway threatened to make the Community an overwhelmingly powerful economic force, from which Spain would be excluded to her discomfiture. The potential discomfiture grew when, in January 1962, the Community's Council of Ministers hammered out a common agricultural policy. Now Spain was threatened with a tariff wall against her wine, olive oil and fruit exports, which could shut her out of most of her export markets. On 9 February 1962, the Spanish Minister of Foreign Affairs wrote a letter to the Secretary-General of the EEC Council of Ministers asking for the opening of negotiations with a view to Spain becoming associated with the Community.

The news of this approach intensified the controversy over Spain's economic future, which was allowed considerable scope to rage in public, probably because it reflected uncertainties within the government itself. Most Spaniards favoured a closer connection with Europe, even if they often feared the consequences of it. Like Franco, they had come to regard it as an ineluctable necessity, a necessity heartening or disheartening depending on whether or not one was eager for a closer political similarity to Europe. Everybody either hoped or feared that the EEC would demand a political price for economic concessions. The democratic opposition loudly adjured European statesmen not to admit Spain under her present government, and a large and prominent group, including such luminaries as Gil Robles and Dionisio Ridruejo, attended a Congress of the European Movement at Munich in June, at which they issued a liberal programme, which they suggested the EEC impose on Spain. It was one difficulty more for Franco in a difficult summer, and he reacted strongly, giving the returning oppositionists the choice between exile and confinement to the arid island of Fuerteventura in the Canaries. The European press reaction to these events was not sympathetic, and EEC circles were not greatly impressed by Franco's explanation of his bad press by the fact that 'it is unusual for an organ of opinion not to be suffering from the infection of Soviet gold'.[13]

At all events the application has made slow progress, primarily because all the members of the EEC were happy to give a matter as controversial as the Spanish application a low priority on their agenda. If during 1962 it was reasonable for the British application to take priority, the continued failure of the EEC to give adequate consideration to Spain's approach began afterwards to give offence. During 1964 an alternative link with the Latin American Free Trade Association was canvassed, and during 1965 fears that the Community would ruin the Spanish citrus trade by an exorbitant 'countervailing duty' on imports exacerbated resentments. Only after strenuous lobbying by Ullastres, who was in 1965 sent to Brussels as Ambassador to the EEC, did the Council of Ministers in December 1966 instruct the Commission to brief them on the subject. In April 1967 the Council of Ministers decided to open negotiations, offering gradual progress towards an industrial free trade area, and the possibility of full integration later if it should appear practicable. Since then detailed negotiations have proceeded

[13] Speech in Valencia, 16 June 1962. Francisco Franco: *Discursos y mensajes del Jefe del Estado, 1960–1963* (Madrid 1964), p. 402.

at a somewhat leisurely pace, and large reductions of duty on EEC imports of Spanish manufactures, sherries and Malaga wines have been proposed, in return for accelerated liberalisation of the Spanish tariff. In September 1969 a reduced rate of duty on Spanish citrus fruits was conceded, but no comprehensive agreement had by then been reached.

As within NATO, so with the EEC individual members have forged stronger links with Spain than has the organisation as a whole. France and West Germany are much better disposed towards Franco than are the Benelux countries or Italy, for, while Benelux is seriously concerned by Franco's authoritarianism and Italy sees Spain as a rival agricultural exporter, France and West Germany see Spain primarily as an important and rapidly expanding market for manufactured consumer products and capital goods. The seemingly perennial labour shortage in the Federal Republic gives Spain further importance to the Germans as a pool of unskilled labour. But German interest is not confined to this context of economic colonialism. Germany is interested also in a partnership with Spain in Latin America, where Spanish goodwill and lack of language barriers would marry well with German technical skills, and could capture important sections of the trade and commerce of the area from the North Americans.

This was indeed the public theme of Chancellor Kiesinger's talks with the Spanish Government in Madrid in October 1968, but their incidental object for Franco was to remind the Americans that he had other friends in the world. During 1968–1969 the Spanish Government was carrying on tough negotiations with the United States for the renewal of their lease on the Spanish bases set up under the 1953 Agreement. The last renewal had been in 1963, and then too Franco had taken care to point to alternatives to the American connection. Then it had been de Gaulle whom Franco was anxious to court. At the beginning of the year, General Alonso Vega agreed with his French opposite number that Spain should cease to harbour and secretly to encourage leaders of the OAS right-wing opposition to the Fifth Republic. In return it was understood that France would favour closer collaboration in other fields, including the military and financial. The signature of the financial agreement was, however, delayed by the unfavourable climate created by the Grimau affair in April.

Julián Grimau García, an underground Communist leader and a Republican police official during the Civil War, was on 18 April 1963 condemned to death by a military tribunal, partly for murders committed during the Civil War. Despite the numerous intercessions for Grimau's life made from all over the world, notably by Khrushchev, Franco allowed his cabinet's narrow majority recommendation against commutation to stand, and Grimau was shot on 22 April. It brought the worst publicity the Spanish Government had had for years, but Franco clearly agreed that he could not be dictated to by the bigotry (as he saw it) of the world's press. He regarded the consequent departure from Madrid of the French Finance Minister, Giscard d'Estaing, without signing the financial treaty as a lesser evil, however regrettable.

The treaty was in fact signed the following November, but by that time the renewal of the Bases Agreement with the United States had been signed, so, to the extent that *rapprochement* with France had been intended to influence these negotiations, the Grimau affair had damaged Spanish diplomacy. In fact, neither the execution of Grimau nor the Spanish Gaullist policy much altered the realities of the situation. The United States wanted to retain the bases, and made concessions of form rather than of substance to secure Spanish agreement. Franco wanted to retain, indeed was happy to intensify, relations with the United States, so he entrusted negotiation to diplomats, who would be satisfied with a closer public identification of the United States with Spanish interests, rather than to the military, who were interested in more concrete goods and services.

In 1968 the situation was much more difficult. Spain was seriously worried by the extent to which the Americans were cutting back their overseas expenditure, but they felt it tactically best to take a strong line, throwing out hints, for example, of their displeasure at the Americans' lack of support for their claim on Gibraltar. Unfortunately, despite growing Soviet strength in the Mediterranean, the Americans now felt able to do without their Spanish bases. An agreement in principle to renew was indeed reached within hours of the moment in March 1969 when the previous lease would have expired, but the final American offer of aid to Spain remained scarcely more than half the minimum Spain was prepared to accept. The agreement eventually reached in June 1969 provided only two years' extension of the lease, and it is problematic whether any further renewal will take place.

Like the United Kingdom and the Federal Republic of Germany, perhaps even to a greater degree, Spain must be more concerned about her relations with the United States than about any other element of her foreign policy. Today they are in a state of flux. As long as Spain was militarily useful to the Americans, they gave their friendship and support without demanding a political price which Franco felt unable to afford in terms of internal disturbance. Now that the bases are of less strategic value, more weight is attached to the susceptibilities of senators like Fulbright who do not wish to continue patronising authoritarianism. Even so, the United States is still more understanding than the Western Europeans, the only other group with which Franco might align himself. A genuine integration of Spain into Latin America, or into a 'non-aligned' grouping, is highly improbable. Spain is economically and spiritually part of Europe and not of any other continent, and not only its present regime but also much of the opposition is far from being 'uncommitted' in world politics. Isolationism would hardly suit her, if only because of the world's continuing suspicion of Franco's authoritarianism. Nobody wants the 1940s back again.

Therefore, unless and until Spain can become fully integrated into Western Europe, it is essential for her to remain in good relations with the United States, for on these good relations very largely depends her place in the comity of nations. She is fortunate that she is now making some progress into Europe, and thus obtaining more room for diplomatic manœuvre. But this could be only most indirectly placed to Franco's credit, for it is at bottom an economic more than a political development; the political nature of Franco's regime, and his own image, are the strongest factors which delay Europeanisation, and Franco himself long worked against it. If Spain does not have the significance on the world stage for which Franco has searched, her influence surely does not fall short of what one might expect of a nation of her size, her stage of economic development and her geographical situation. That it does not exceed it, that it does not reflect, let alone live up to her great past, may be explained by the fact that, for all Franco's interest in the world stage, diplomatic advantage has on occasion necessarily been subordinated to internal political security.

11 Pater Patriae

It is the preservation of peace and order at home which is Franco's most important and most praised achievement. At the beginning of April 1969 Spain celebrated thirty years of internal peace. Over all these years Franco has presided, and he has now been longer in office as political leader of an independent country than anybody else in the world.

Not all his years of office have been blessed with prosperity, but Spain now enjoys under him greater and probably better distributed prosperity than ever before in her history. Yet when Franco's nomination as Head of the Government was announced in Burgos on 1 October 1936, prosperity and peace were not the objects of policy he had most in mind. Apart from the immediate object of victory, he looked then for social justice certainly, but for justice with the emphasis on common sacrifices on behalf of national greatness. In December 1966, the referendum campaign for the acceptance of his constitutional proposals dwelt almost solely on the beating of swords into ploughshares, and on the prospect of unbroken material progress. 'You are Spain; yours is her progress,' the posters told the people. 'Don't put a stopper on progress: Vote Yes.' Franco claimed the credit for peace and prosperity, and the electorate, by turning out on a spring-like December day to vote 'Yes' in their millions, endorsed the claim. The peacemaker of Franco's current self-image (he is said to have compared himself with Abraham Lincoln) is more in harmony with the present time than the empire builder he asked God to make him at the Victory *Te Deum* in 1939. He is also more in harmony with the wishes of the Spanish people as reported by virtually every observer of the last thirty years.

Franco's adjustment has taken place gradually and probably largely unconsciously, as he has discovered that to make Spain 'as great again as she was of old' is not something that can be achieved hurriedly—even in a lifetime. Gradually he has discovered the immensity of the problems which he has inherited from the past, and he has certainly never underestimated the damage which jealous foreigners, Communists and other workers can still do in Spain. So he has come to realise that it would be an achievement of greatness simply to bequeath to his successors a peaceful, prosperous and united Spain. It is an achievement which he confidently believes to be within his reach, and it might be admitted to be within his grasp were it not for the dangerous uncertainties of the situation which will follow his death. There are, of course a thousand complex social and economic problems outstanding in Spain, and Franco's Olympian exterior must hide many nagging political worries; but it is nevertheless instructive to compare, as apologists for the regime do so often and so lovingly, Spain in 1969 with Spain at various points in the past. The comparative lack of passion today is startling.

Liberal democrats do not find it difficult to name the price which Franco has made Spain pay for this calm. Government influence over the press is vastly greater in Spain than in Britain, let alone than in the United States. Freedom of organisation is denied the workers, who have no effective legal right to use the withdrawal of their labour as a bargaining counter. Political action is similarly circumscribed, since no organisation may be set up with the aims of a political party. Criticism of the government is potentially dangerous, and the consequent political conformism sometimes seems to have spread into social behaviour. Spain is often spoken of as a cultural desert, whose best talents work either on the fringes of the law or in exile. Not one of these criticisms would pass, however, without being dismissed by Franco and his supporters as either untrue or unimportant. Picasso is an often cited cultural exile, but while his hostility to the regime could hardly be questioned, it was not because of the Franco regime that he left Spain. Better examples are men like Buñuel and Juan Ramón Jiménez, but then Pío Baroja returned to Spain in June 1940. If foreigners or exiles scorn the ability of young artists in Spain, it is easy for a Spaniard to reply in kind, and examples of official philistinism and censorship are by no means confined to Spain.

Other criticisms too Franco would meet either by attacking the genuineness of the freedoms which exist in so-called free countries, or, in a more charitable mood, by denying their suitability for Spain. For example, he would argue that the press outside Spain is not a genuine expression of popular opinion, but the voice of its proprietors, occasionally garbled because of Communist penetration. It is therefore the duty of a wise government to regulate the journalistic profession, to preserve it from undesirables, and to ensure that the criticisms made in the press are constructive. It is the destructiveness of most political criticism which justifies the outlawry of political parties. Franco, in common with many military men, has always regarded politicians as an idle and parasitical lot of people, and politics as a quite unnecessary and indeed harmful activity. Political parties serve to polarise differences of opinion rather than lead to a constructive consensus, and the same criticism is levelled at trade unions on the British pattern. Franco believes that polarisation of differences is the very last thing which Spain wants since 'every people is haunted by its familiar demons, ... and Spain's are an anarchistic spirit, negative criticism, lack of solidarity, extremism, and mutual hostility'.[1]

In April 1967 Franco told an audience in Seville that adequate opportunities for the expression of differing opinions existed in syndical and municipal government. No more could be asked for.[2] Moreover, despite the political apathy or conformism of so many people, there has of late years been an increasing amount of debate, sometimes acrimonious, in the Cortes. In fact, there is scope for considerable politicking, provided that the views propagated do not conflict with the basic principles of the Movement—do not, in other words, offend the constitution. It is simply indispensable to

[1] Franco's speech to the Cortes, 22 November 1966. *Documentos Políticos, No. 7: Referéndum 1966, Nueva Constitución* (Madrid 1966), p. 33.
[2] Francisco Franco: *Discursos y mensajes del Jefe del Estado, 1964–1967* (Madrid 1968), pp. 282–3.

believe in the irreversibility of the Nationalist victory in the Civil War; for, while Republican people may be redeemed, 'red' views can never become acceptable. Constitutional law in Spain will not tolerate so wide a spectrum of political views as the British, American, or other Western European constitutions, but one should not underestimate the differences between a radical, anti-capitalist Falangist 'old shirt' and an aristocratic monarchist banker. Both are free to express their views in Franco's Spain, although they are perhaps less free to deal in personalities than they would be in other countries.

The heart of the matter, however, is the distribution of political power. As long as this remains concentrated in so few hands, freedom of expression is of comparatively modest importance. While the elective element in the Spanish constitution was considerably extended by the institution under the Organic Law of 1966 of 'family' representatives in the Cortes, this has not constituted progress towards one man, one vote, but rather towards one man, one voice. Under Spanish constitutional law the Head of State is obliged to listen to advice from the Cortes, and also from his ministers and from the Council of the Realm, but he is not formally obliged to heed it, and very little constitutional leverage can be applied to make him do so. He can only be prevented from courses of action, and that only in a small number of cases. Supporters of the regime can point to the alienation that exists in parliamentary systems between the people and their elected representatives, and conclude that democracy in its literal sense (power in the hands of the people) does not exist anywhere. Yet it is significant that the Spanish people is not even supposed to have any power, and that this formal disenfranchisement is justified by the immaturity of the people, which is widely accepted as a fact both by Spaniards and foreigners. For fear of where their demons might lead them the Spaniards have, for the most part willingly, entrusted power to a single man, Franco. An increasing degree of freedom of political expression has been allowed partly as a safety valve, partly in order to generate ideas for the resolution of problems. Yet however many people propose, it is Franco who disposes.

All the same, Franco sets great store by the necessity to consult his ministers. He even said once that it made him less a dictator

than the President of the United States. This was perhaps disin-
genuous, yet if in Britain and the United States the legislature does
not in practice fully exercise the brake which it can constitutionally
put on executive action, in Spain Franco's theoretically unlimited
power is restricted in practice by political considerations. He has
always been careful to balance the various interest groups within
his government. It was expedient that no group should be so far
alienated as to put it into resolute opposition, and equally that
none should be so fully satisfied in its aspirations that it might feel
able to dispense with Franco as arbiter of political life. For one
who always affects to despise politics Franco has played politics
extremely sure-footedly. Throughout his thirty-three years of
power he has built up his personal position. The longer he be-
strides Spain like a colossus the more difficult he becomes to
remove, for by now he has become more than a convenient link to
bind together the coalition which won the Civil War. When he
became Head of State he was a political tyro, though obviously
one of great natural talent. Today he is the most experienced political figure in Spain, and it is unlikely that any of his ministers
would speak of him, as Serrano Súñer used to do, 'as one would
of a moronic servant'. As Franco has grown older, the flattery
with which he is constantly surrounded has become more sincere.

The praise which is heaped on the Caudillo through every
medium of communication and on every possible occasion sometimes appears so extravagant as to be ludicrous. Yet it is not really
difficult to find parallels for it, even in societies which would consider themselves politically more mature than Spain. Winston
Churchill and Charles de Gaulle also had virtually superhuman
qualities attributed to them, and in Spain itself Azaña and Largo
Caballero were provided by their supporters with personality cults
whose evanescence makes them now seem almost pathetic. What is
most striking about the Franco cult is its close association with
Catholic Christianity and the extent to which he himself orches-
trates the hymns of praise. Like de Gaulle he identifies himself
with his country: 'I am the sentinel who is never relieved,' he has
said, and, 'I am the captain of the ship.'[3] Unlike de Gaulle he is

[3] Speech at Valencia, 16 June 1962. Franco: *Discursos y mensajes 1960–1963*, p. 399.

specifically described on coinage as 'Caudillo of Spain by the Grace of God', and has often explicitly referred to God's intervention in recent Spanish history. 'The suffering of a nation at a point in its history is no chance,' he said in 1940; 'it is the spiritual punishment which God metes out for a corrupt life, for an unclean history.'[4] The good fortune of his rise to power, so often commented upon, he himself ascribes to the finger of God. He has no doubt that God answers his prayers in moments of political stress, and even that the timely death of a German Ambassador was providential. It is this confidence in his mission which enables him to accept what a group of Basque priests in a letter to their bishop called 'the almost idolatrous cult of the Head of State'.[5]

It is also this belief in his mission which allows him to rationalise his personal aloofness and his sensitivity to personal criticism. It is of course a crime in Spain to criticise the Head of State, and it requires political courage to give unwelcome advice. Franco is prepared to listen, and even to accept, such advice, but he has seldom rendered any political favours to those who have disagreed with him. He has surrounded himself with a comparatively small circle of admirers, and has regarded those outside the circle as advisers to be retained or not according to the proven quality of their advice, or to the value of their political support.

Apparently in 1939 he considered acquiring a house in the embassy quarter of Madrid, and only decided to live in the former royal palace of El Pardo, outside Madrid, when he was persuaded that the town house he had in mind was insecure. Nevertheless, his seclusion in the country, his aloofness from the political currents of Madrid, has been commented on ever since with exasperation by those—like the belligerents' ambassadors during the Second World War—who wished urgently to see him. And when Franco is not in El Pardo, he is usually either at his country estate in Galicia, Pazo de Meirás, which was presented to him by the people of Galicia; or on

[4] Speech at Jaén, 18 March 1940. *Palabras, p. 157.*
[5] An English translation of the letter is printed as an appendix to the International Commission of Jurists report: *Spain and the Rule of Law* (Geneva 1959).

board the yacht *Azor*, on which he has finally gratified his first ambition, to be a sailor. Since he is served by an efficient personal intelligence system, his distance from the political hurly-burly has done him no harm. Indeed, since his directing hand has been largely unseen, he has remained untarnished by any political scandal or by any failure of policy. The heads of subordinates have rolled for errors which may have been as much his own; frequently they have read of their dismissal in the official gazette, and have so been denied even the opportunity to reproach their chief for his ingratitude. The satisfactory final result for Franco is that he has almost ceased to be a controversial figure in current Spanish politics. He has become a symbol, and is respected or despised not for what he is but for what he has come to represent, just as a king, regardless of his personality, might be loved by monarchists and hated by republicans.

A king, indeed, is what Franco is, in all but name. Since 1947 Spain has been nominally a kingdom, and Franco possesses, and exercises, the right to create titles of nobility and grandeeships. On public occasions the honours paid to him are those due to a king, and (some would say more significantly) those paid to his wife befit a queen consort. The ceremonial and protocol of his court is said to be more elaborate than that of any other in Europe, even if it has lost something in splendour since 1958 when his gorgeous Moorish guard was dismissed. Apart from his relations, a surprisingly large number of his close companions are noblemen, and men who share his pleasure in the aristocratic pastimes of shooting and fishing. His daughter, Carmen, was married into an aristocratic family in 1950, though her husband, Cristóbal Martínez Bordíu, Marqués de Villaverde, far from being a typical nobleman, is a prominent surgeon, and in 1968 carried out Spain's first heart transplant. The Cortes by special dispensation in 1954 allowed the Caudillo's new-born grandson, Francisco, to use the surname Franco as if it were his patronymic, and so enabled the Head of State to found a dynasty even though the blessing of a son had been denied him. This was a great pleasure to Franco, who is by common consent a very proud and affectionate grandfather.

Indeed, his private as opposed to his public morality has never been seriously impugned. Though his official emoluments as Head of State are not as great as, for example, the Queen of England's, they are none the less substantial. He can shoot and fish on a grand scale, besides running a yacht, and pursuing less expensive hobbies like golf and painting. Yet he is not a collector of priceless *objets d'art*, and he is far from lavish in his general manner of life, eating and drinking little, and smoking not at all. It would be difficult to know what he would have done with an illegitimate fortune had he used his undoubted opportunities in public life for acquiring one. He has sometimes been compared in his coldness and conscientiousness with King Philip II of Spain, whose monumental monastery at El Escorial he seems to have hoped to outmatch with the astounding underground war memorial basilica at the nearby Valle de los Caídos, which is rumoured to be his intended mausoleum. But unlike Philip II his life as ruler is apparently a pleasure to him as well as the fulfilment of his inescapable duty. Despite what would appear a very full working schedule, he has had leisure since the end of the Civil War to pursue hobbies like painting for which he had little or no time before. And, even during the anxious days of the Second World War, he found time to write not only a military text but also a vaguely autobiographical screenplay, romanticising patriotic sacrifice and Duty with a capital D.[6] 'I do not find the burden of rule heavy,' he told Don Juan in 1954, 'Spain is easy to govern.'[7]

Juan was left to comfort himself, as all Franco's opponents have comforted themselves since he named himself Head of State for life in 1947, with the thought that the man cannot live for ever. Juan calculated that, since he was twenty years younger than Franco, he should rightfully be able to look forward to the throne after the Caudillo's death. He was after all the next in line of the House of Bourbon; while lacking personal involvement with the regime he had in the fifties publicly committed himself to its broad principles. On the other hand, impatience had already seriously impaired his chances. His repeated criticisms of the regime during the forties, his public espousal of policies sharply differentiated from those of the Caudillo had already led Franco to regard him as a

---

[6] *Raza* (Madrid 1942), published under the pseudonym Jaime de Andrade, but never produced.

[7] Benjamin Welles: *Spain, the Gentle Anarchy* (New York 1965), p. 354.

personal opponent as well as a dangerous liberal. So, to become king, Juan would have to appear the only suitable candidate for the succession, when the time came. If Franco was unlikely to choose him, he must at least choose no one else.

For many years no choice was in fact made. Franco was always so careful to keep his options open that he refrained from naming an heir even though he could, at will, withdraw the nomination; his death or incapacitation might well have found Spain without an heir apparent. In that case, a Council of Regency comprising the President of the Cortes, a senior prelate and the senior general would take over the reins of government while the Council of the Realm, comprising these three and a number of other prominent members of the Cortes, and the cabinet would join together in continuous session to select a royal personage to become King. Alternatively they might select another Regent to preserve the institutions of Franco's monarchy until a time when one of the Bourbons might be found worthy of the throne. Any ruler selected would have to be male, over thirty years old, Catholic, of Spanish nationality, acceptable to a majority of the Cortes and prepared to subscribe to the principles of the Movement.

The context of power struggle among the upper échelons of the Movement which is likely to follow Franco's death always made it unlikely that a candidate for the Regency could be agreed on. Two of Juan's principal rivals were excluded by the criteria of constitutional law. Although Carlos Hugo of Bourbon-Parma is a flamboyant politician with a considerable following of loyal Carlists, he is of French nationality, having held a Spanish diplomatic passport for some time only by one of those bizarre courtesies to which the Franco regime is prone. His father, Javier, is more French still, and their petition to be granted Spanish nationality in due form has remained unattended to since 1963. While the Carlist pretenders were the representatives of an outmoded traditionalism, whose appeal was limited to Navarrese and Basque romantics, they had little prospect of the throne, and Franco was prepared to tolerate them. But in 1964 Hugo's marriage into the royal family of the Netherlands brought them not only publicity but also, reputedly, wealth. By 1968 they were broadening their appeal by outbidding the senior branch of the Bourbon family in commitment to liberal democracy; in December of that year they were deported from Spain, and their political fortunes had ebbed lower than ever.

This was no comfort to Juan, however, for by this time he had a very much more serious rival in his own son, Juan Carlos. This tall, athletic young man, born in 1938, had lived mostly in Spain since 1948, when Franco had agreed that he should complete his secondary education in Spain. Subsequently he trained for the Spanish armed forces, studied political economy at the University of Madrid, and served a general apprenticeship in the administration of the various ministries. He was apparently being groomed for the succession by Franco, but in his own rare statements of his political standpoint he continually emphasised his loyalty to his father. Then in 1968, the year in which he became constitutionally eligible for the throne in his own right, Juan Carlos moved sharply away from his father politically, a move which some attributed to the influence of his mother-in-law, Queen Frederika of the Hellenes. In June of that year he let it be known in the diplomatic corps that he was prepared, if Franco willed it, to supplant his father.[8] In January 1969, he gave a carefully prepared interview to the Spanish news agency, Efe, in which he said that 'the political situation which has made the reinstitution of the monarchial principle a possibility was achieved with the assistance of many monarchists and at the sacrifice of hundreds of thousands of Spanish families. It follows that the most faithful maintainers of dynastic principles should also accept the sacrifice of some of their aspirations.'[9]

The challenge to his father was patent. Juan must at this point have realised that his position was grave, for his son, without any noticeable heterodoxy of views, was a much more acceptable choice for the Franco regime. Juan's hope had rested on the continued loyalty of Juan Carlos to the principle of dynastic legitimacy, but now the publication of a letter written by father to son in October 1968 only pointed up Juan Carlos's newly found independence from his father. Juan had warned that if he divided the royal family Juan Carlos would be 'a king tarnished from his origins by a lack of dynastic correctness', and reminded him that 'having reached the

[8] *New York Times* 10 July 1968, p. 5.
[9] *Pueblo* 7 January 1969.

age of thirty must not in any way, modify your loyal and disciplined position.'[10] Yet the young prince had gone right over to Franco's camp, and, since no one credited him with a political line of his own, the succession question resolved itself into a struggle for the King's right hand after Franco's departure.

It is a struggle which is unlikely to be resolved in Franco's lifetime, unless he becomes clearly physically incapable. It is difficult to picture the abdication of one who has so clearly enjoyed the exercise of power[11]. His injury in a shooting accident at Christmas 1961 may have been responsible for his nomination in 1962 of General Muñoz Grandes as the first Vice-President of the Government since 1939. His failing health in 1966 may have led him to promulgate the new constitutional proposals, which differentiated more clearly the functions of Head of State and President of the Government. Franco had combined these offices since 1936, and it was widely supposed that he would now delegate the functions of the latter to a younger man.

He did not however do so, only replacing Muñoz Grandes by Admiral Carrero Blanco as Vice-President of the Government in September 1967, and there seems to be no particular reason to read significance into this. Muñoz, almost as old as Franco and in worse health, was under the terms of a new law ineligible for the cabinet by virtue of being the senior officer of the armed forces; Carrero was the senior member of the cabinet, and Franco's close political associate, having been under-secretary to the Presidency of the Government continuously since 1940. Franco might like to see Carrero succeed to the first place in political life, but the admiral has many enemies, if only because of his closeness to the Caudillo, so it would be foolhardy to predict that he will in fact succeed. Every year that passes increases the relative importance of the generation who were still boys during the Civil War. The position of the Opus technocrat López Rodó in particular was greatly improved by the massive cabinet reshuffle of October 1969. Several of his former subordinates were promoted to the Cabinet, and his rival, the highly talented and pragmatic Manuel Fraga was removed

---

[10] *Nuevo Diario*, 17 January 1969.
[11] This was underlined by his end of year message in 1969. 'While God gives me life. I shall be with you, working for the fatherland,' he said.

K

273

from the Ministry of Information and Tourism. Besides, while the political importance of Franco's health is sufficient to make it a closely guarded secret, although he looks very old and suffers from involuntary shaking in his hands his general health seems to be good. Moreover, he is of a very long-lived family; Carrero himself was sixty-six in March 1969. One must wait and see what the next ten years bring forth.

The prospect of Spain without Franco is a frightening one for many Spaniards, and an exhilarating one for many more. He has become such a symbol of stability that those who are not satisfied with the stability of the status quo await his disappearance from the scene as the first possible opportunity at which any significant change may occur. There are many of them who have convinced themselves that a change of regime will be a panacea for all problems. If Franco's departure may be followed closely by a liberalisation, it is only too likely to be followed at a distance by a profound disillusionment. So many have nourished dreams over so many years, and when their aspirations cannot be satisfied overnight, those of them whose politics are at present moderate may all too easily take up more impatiently radical attitudes.

Already the waves of the new Left have washed Spanish opposition politics. The effects on student politics have led, as elsewhere, to student riots and university closures, violent police repression and so forth. Similarly, regionalism in the Basque country and Catalonia, which has been strongly repressed throughout the Franco era, has already led to the adoption of more extreme positions. Catalan nationalism seems to have strengthened as compared with Catalan regionalism, and the Basque direct action organisation ETA (Euzkadi Ta Askatasuna) appears to have gained a surprising amount of support. Franco, mellowed though he may be, does not offend either his own conscience or the scruples of his supporters by suspending constitutional guarantees and deploying the security police against movements of this kind. Yet they would trouble liberal successors to Franco as they troubled the Second Republic. As the history of the twentieth century has already demonstrated in the career of General Primo de Rivera and its aftermath, democracy is easy to destroy in Spain and hard to rebuild.

This is a lesson which has been learned in their own way by
Franco and by those who favour the present political configuration.
They attribute the disasters of the thirties to the attempt by the
monarchy to reintroduce parliamentary democracy after the fall
of Primo de Rivera. They do not intend to allow this mistake to be
repeated, and are frightened by the prospect of political change,
which might bring with it retribution for crimes or imagined
crimes of the past third of a century. On the other hand, they are
not a very coherent group, and consequently may become weakened by internecine struggles for political advantage. They may
not be constrained to the same extent by pressures of the kind
which ensured Caetano's smooth succession in Portugal in 1968.
Yet the Army, though its political attitudes are as much guessed at,
probably as diverse, and much less well known than they were in
the 1930s, is likely to retain its concern for public order. Officers
were doubtless as disturbed as other governmental circles by the
events of May 1968 in France. This proof of the speed with which
a revolutionary situation can develop certainly influenced the
introduction of a 'state of exception' into Guipúzcoa in the summer
of 1968, and into all of Spain for part of 1969. Will the fear of bush-
fire revolution, therefore, make for an iron regime once Franco has
gone? Or will pressures for Europeanisation and democratisation
be so great that the risk of disorder is run?

It is in the context of these fears and uncertainties that one
should probably see the actual nomination of Juan Carlos as heir
to the throne on 22 July 1969. A number of Franco's leading
ministers were worried at the confused situation which might arise
from the Caudillo's death or incapacitation without naming an
heir, and persuaded him that it would be better for Spain if he
delayed no longer in designating Juan Carlos. The timing of the
news for a moment when the summer holidays and the American
moonshot were distracting the world from politics will hardly have
been coincidental. Certainly the announcement came as a complete
surprise to everybody, including Don Juan, who, although he
refused to abdicate and reaffirmed his belief in political evolution
towards a more open society, realised that he could only damage
the monarchy by fighting a losing battle against his son. In Spain,
the news was greeted with scant enthusiasm. The nomination was

opposed in the Cortes only by a small minority of Carlists, Left Falangists and ultra-legitimist monarchists, but many members voted for it only out of loyalty to Franco, and outside government circles the monarchy is widely regarded as a laughable anachronism. Juan Carlos may indeed be the heir who commands most general support, but he would still be a much more controversial Head of State than Franco is.

The burden on his shoulders after Franco's departure will be enormous, since, despite the institutional structure Franco has created, he will remain the greatest power in Spanish political life. It is some index of his responsibilities that his personal role will approximate more closely to that of the Kaiser Wilhelm II in Germany than to that of his grandfather Alfonso XIII in Spain, and that he will probably start his reign with less goodwill than either of those sovereigns, both of whom ultimately lost their thrones. Of course the circumstances of his accession cannot now be prophesied—indeed, Franco could, if so minded, withdraw his nomination; and so far he has had little chance to display any great political talent, so it is impossible to judge the chances for his success as King. Until he is King, therefore, it will not be possible to judge the wisdom of Franco's most important decision. It will be then only that one may judge whether Franco has realised his great ambition. Will his regime 'succeed itself'? Will it be the foundation for Spain's new golden age? Or will it appear simply a paradoxical interlude in which one man was able by his transcendent position to impose peace and order on Spanish life?

Note on Bibliography

Although only a small number of more important sources and bibliographical works will be mentioned in this note, it is the duty of the biographer first of all to acknowledge his debt to previous biographers. There have been many studies of Franco which range from the frankly hagiographical to the virulently hostile. With the exception of Luis Ramírez's *Francisco Franco, Hijo de Dios* (Paris 1965), which contains some cruel insights, those in the latter category that I have seen are of no value. On the other side the hagiographies of Arrarás and Galinsoga, for all their cloying hero worship, contain many hard facts about Franco's career up to the Civil War, as does the excellent little work by Timmermans. More recently, foreign biographers (Claude Martin,[1] Crozier, Hills) have added to understanding of Franco both with new facts and, more importantly, by a more dispassionate appraisal.

For the bare and unvarnished facts of Franco's military career, see Esteban Carvallo de Cora: *Hoja de servicios del Caudillo de España* (Madrid 1967), Franco's own *Diario de una Bandera* puts some flesh on these bones for the 1920–22 period. Barea's *Forging of a Rebel* gives a less romantic view of military life in Morocco, but it must be stressed that the book is quasi-fictional, and that statements in it should not be accepted as historical facts without confirmation. Rupert Furneaux's *Abd-el-Krim* (London

[1] Claude Martin: *Franco, Soldat et Chef d'Etat* (Paris 1959). For the titles etc. of works cited only by author see List of Works Cited.

1967) gives a Berber view of the wars, and many other sources on the period are given in the monumental official work of Hernández de Herrera and García Figueras.

More general works on Spain as a whole abound, and range from works of historical scholarship to light travelogues with a historical flavour. From the historical point of view two works in English are essential reading for a background understanding of modern Spanish history. They are Raymond Carr's *Spain*, and Gerald Brenan: *The Spanish Labyrinth* (Cambridge, England 1943). Covering the early part of the twentieth century in more detail are M. Fernández Almagro: *Historia política de la España contemporánea* (1956) which deals with Spanish politics from the Restoration of 1874 to Primo's *coup d'état* in 1923, Gabriel Maura's *Bosquejo histórico de la Dictadura* (Madrid 1930) on 1923–30, and two more recent works: Víctor Fragoso del Toro's *La España de ayer*, 2 vols. (Madrid 1966–7) on 1909–36, and the first volume of Ricardo de la Cierva's *Historia de la Guerra Civil Española* (Madrid 1969) covering its antecedents from 1898 on. The Second Republic is dealt with from a right-wing standpoint in four volumes by Joaquín Arrarás, and in one by Gabriel Jackson, who is more democratic in outlook.

On the Civil War itself the literature is enormous, but fortunately bibliographical studies are now being undertaken on a corresponding scale. The Sección de Estudios sobre la Guerra de España at the Spanish Ministry of Information and Tourism has published under the direction of Ricardo de la Cierva a more or less comprehensive bibliography of separately issued printed books and pamphlets, entitled *Bibliografía general sobre la Guerra de España (1936–1939) y sus antecedentes* (Madrid 1968). This, however, is a standard work of reference and not a guide to further reading. More suited to that purpose is the work of the same team entitled *Cien libros básicos sobre la Guerra de España* (Madrid 1966) or the so far uncompleted series directed by Vicente Palacio Atard: *Cuadernos bibliográficos sobre la guerra de España, 1936–1939*. These works both supply critical analyses of the works listed. For a general account of the Civil War the best in any language remains, in my judgement, Hugh Thomas's, particularly in the paperback edition (London 1965) whence certain errors of the original edition have

278

been removed, but mention must be made of Bolloten, whose excellent work badly needs a sequel to cover the last two-thirds of the war. Among important works published since the appearance of the *Bibliografía general* are the posthumous *Memorias de guerra* (Madrid 1968) of Admiral Cervera, Franco's Chief of Naval Staff, and two more excellent military monographs by José Mª Martínez Bande.

For the political climate and structure of Spain in the forties the starting point for any student must be Stanley Payne's *Falange*. Unfortunately, his general survey of *Franco's Spain* (New York 1967) is a very slim volume, and for a general history of Franco's Spain up to 1961 one can probably do no better than turn to Sancho González's somewhat insipid *25 años de Historia*, 2 vols. (Madrid 1962)[2]. This must be salted with some of the large number of political 'travel diaries' written by diplomats and newspapermen. By and large the newspapermen are more interesting than the diplomats about the internal situation of Spain, though, as might be expected, the diplomats shed more light on foreign affairs. The best accounts for the Second World War period are Hamilton and Hughes, both hostile to the regime, and André Corthis, broadly favourable. Also of interest, particularly in view of the author's right-wing temperament, is Charles D'Ydewalle's *An Interlude in Spain* (London 1944), later published in the original French as *Geôles et bagnes de Franco*.

For the period of the late forties and early fifties see in particular another work by Brenan: *The Face of Spain* (London 1950), which is most evocative. The background to the *rapprochement* with the United States is dealt with in Arthur Whitaker and by Lowi. A more general portrait of the later fifties and early sixties appears from Benjamin Welles's very readable book. The turbulent years 1962 and 1963 are covered by Fernández de Castro and Martínez's book, which also contains a brief retrospect, from an opposition standpoint, of the twenty previous years.

The economic history of the Franco regime can be studied in the numerous works of Higinio París Eguilaz, and its general economic problems are assessed in the World Bank's report: *The*

[2] Or perhaps to George Hill's: *Spain* (London 1970), which goes up to 1969.

Economic Development of Spain (Baltimore 1963). An introductory work of human geography of great merit is that by Günther Haensch and others entitled *España contemporánea* (Munich 1968). Finally, Spain's present and future are the subject of many works, particularly of collected opinions, for example Salvador Pániker's *Converaciones en Cataluña* (Barcelona 1966) and *Conversaciones en Madrid* (Barcelona 1969), or *España: Perspectiva 1969* (Madrid 1969). Indeed, books on all aspects of contemporary Spain appear in such encouraging profusion that this bibliography will doubtless soon be out of date, and that must be my excuse for not making it more ambitious.

List of Works Cited

BOOKS, REPORTS, PUBLISHED DOCUMENTS ETC

La Academia de Infanteria en 1909 : Recuerdo (Toledo 1909).
AEE (see *Anuario Estadistico* ...)
Andrade, Jaime de (pseud.): Raza (Madrid 1944).
Anfuso, Filippo: *Roma, Berlino, Salò, 1936–1945* (Milan 1950).
Ansaldo, Juan Antonio: *¿Para qué? De Alfonso XIII a Juan III* (Buenos Aires 1951).
Anuario Estadístico de España (Madrid, various years): cited as AEE.
Aronson, Theo: *Royal vendetta; the crown of Spain, 1829–1965* (Indianapolis 1966).
Arrarás, Joaquín: *Franco* (San Sebastián 1937).
  Francisco Franco (London 1938).
  Historia de la Segunda República Española (Madrid 1956–68).
Azaña, Manuel: *Estudios de política contemporánea francesa: La política militar* (Madrid 1918).
Barea, Arturo: *The forging of a Rebel* (New York 1946).
Blond, Georges: *Pétain, 1856–1951* (Paris 1966).
Bolloten, B. H.: *The Grand Camouflage* (London 1961).
Calvo Sotelo, José: *Mis servicios al Estado. Seis años de gestión* (Madrid 1931).
Cantalupo, Roberto: *Fu la Spagna. Ambasciata presso Franco, Feb.-Apr. 1937* (Verona 1948).
Carr, Raymond: *Spain, 1808–1939* (Oxford 1966).
Charles-Roux, F.: *Cinq mois tragiques aux affaires étrangères (21 mai-1er. nov. 1940)* (Paris 1949).

Ciano's Diary, 1937–1938 (Translated by A. Mayor) (London 1952).

The Ciano Diaries, 1939–1943 (ed. Gibson) (Garden City 1946).

Ciano's Diplomatic Papers (ed. Muggeridge) (London 1948).

Cierva, Ricardo de la (compiler): *Los documentos de la primavera trágica; análisis documental de los antecedentes inmediatos del 18 de julio de 1936* (Madrid 1967).

Coles, S. F. A.: *Franco of Spain* (London 1955).

Collins, Larry, and Dominique Lapierre: *Or I'll dress you in mourning* (London 1968).

The Concordat between Spain and the Holy See, 27th August 1953 (Madrid 1953).

Cortés Cavanillas, Julián: *La Caída de Alfonso XIII, Causas y Episodios de una revolución* (5th edition, Madrid 1932).

Corthis, André (pseud.): *L'Espagne de la victoire* (Paris 1941).

Coutant de Saisseval, Guy: *Les maisons impériales et royales d'Europe* (Paris 1966).

Crozier, Brian: *Franco, a Biographical History* (London 1967).

Cruzada: see *Historia de la Cruzada Española*.

DDI: see *Documenti Diplomatici Italiani*.

Del Boca, Angelo: *L'altra Spagna* (Milan 1961).

Detwiler, Donald S.: *Hitler, Franco und Gibraltar: Die Frage des spanischen Eintritts in den zweiten Weltkrieg* (Wiesbaden 1962).

Deutsch, Harold C.: *The conspiracy against Hitler in the Twilight War* (Minneapolis 1968).

DGFP: see *Documents on German Foreign Policy*.

Díaz de Villegas, José: *La guerra de liberación* (Barcelona 1957).

Diez, José Emilio: *Colección de proclamas y arengas del Excmo Sr. General D. Francisco Franco* (Seville 1937).

Dimitrov, Georgi: *The Working Class against Fascism* (London 1935).

Documenti Diplomatici Italiani (8a & 9a Serie); cited as D.D.I. (Rome 1952).

Documentos Políticos, No. 7: Referéndum 1966, Nueva constitución (Madrid 1966).

Documents on German Foreign Policy, 1918–1945. Series D (London 1949–1964); cited as DGFP.

Doussinague, José María: *España tenía razón (1939–1945)* (Madrid 1949).

Du Moulin de Labarthète, Henry: *Le temps des illusions* (Geneva 1945).

Enciclopedia Universal Ilustrada (Madrid).

L'Espagne et les Juifs (Madrid 1949).

Feiling, Keith: *The Life of Neville Chamberlain* (London 1946).

Feis, Herbert: *The Spanish story: Franco and the nations at war* (New York 1948).

Fernández de Castro, Ignacio, and José Martínez: *España hoy* (Paris 1964).

Foltz, Charles S.: *The Masquerade in Spain* (Boston 1948).

Foreign Relations of the United States (Washington): cited as FRUS

Franco, Francisco: *Diario de una Bandera* (Madrid 1922)
    Discursos y mensajes del Jefe del Estado, 1951–1954 (Madrid 1955).
    Discursos y mensajes del Jefe del Estado, 1960–1963 (Madrid 1964).
    Discursos y mensajes del Jefe del Estado, 1964–1967 (Madrid 1968).
    Palabras del Caudillo, 19 de abril 1937 de diciembre 1942 (Madrid 1943).
    Textos de Doctrina Política. Palabras y escritos de 1945 a 1950 (Madrid 1951).
    See also Andrade.

Francotte, R. A.: *L'Heure de l'Espagne* (Brussels 1947).

Friedlander, R. A.: 'Holy Crusade or Unholy Alliance? Franco's "National Revolution" and the Moors' in *South-western Social Science Quarterly,* Vol. XLIV, no. 4 (Austin, Texas) March 1964.

FRUS: see *Foreign Relations of the United States.*

Galinsoga, Luis de (in collaboration with General Franco-Salgado): *Centinela del Occidente: Semblanza biográfica de Francisco Franco* (Barcelona 1956).

Garriga, Ramón: *Las Relaciones secretas entre Franco y Hitler* (Buenos Aires 1965).

Gil Robles, José María: *No fue posible la paz* (Barcelona 1968).

Gomá, José: *La guerra en el aire (Vista, suerte y al toro)* (Barcelona 1958).

González Ruano, C.: *Miguel Primo de Rivera* (Madrid 1933).

Griffis, Stanton: *Lying in State* (Garden City 1952).

Gutiérrez Ravé, José: *Gil Robles, Caudillo Frustrado* (Madrid 1967).

Halder, Franz: *Kriegstagebuch* (Stuttgart 1962-4).

Hamilton, Thomas J: *Appeasement's Child, the Franco Régime in Spain* (New York 1943).

Harris, W. B.: *France, Spain and the Riff* (London 1927).

Hayes, Carlton: *Wartime Mission in Spain 1942-45* (New York 1945).

Hernández de Herrera, C. and T. García Figueras: *Acción de España en Marruecos, 1492-1927* (Madrid 1929-1930).

Hills, George: *Franco, the Man and his Nation* (London 1967).

Historia de la Cruzada Española (ed. J. Arrarás) (Madrid 1940-44); cited as *Cruzada*.

Hitler's Table Talk 1941-1944 (ed. H. R. Trevor-Roper) (London 1953).

Hitler's War Directives 1939-1945 (ed. H. R. Trevor-Roper) (London 1964).

Hughes, Emmet J.: *Report from Spain* (New York 1947).

Iribarren, José María: *Con el general Mola. Escenas y aspectos inéditos de la guerra civil* (Zaragoza 1937).

Mola; datos para una biografía y para la historia del Alzamiento Nacional (Zaragoza 1938).

International Commission of Jurists: Spain and the Rule of Law (Geneva 1959).

Jackson, Gabriel: *The Spanish Republic and the Civil War* (Princeton 1964).

Jobit, Pierre: *L'église d'Espagne à l'heure du Concile* (Paris 1965).

Kelly, Sir David: *The Ruling Few* (London 1952).

Kindelán, Alfredo: *Mis Cuadernos de guerra* (Madrid 1945).

Kordt, Erich: *Wahn und Wirklichkeit* (Stuttgart 1948).

Lerroux, Alejandro: *La pequeña historia: Apuntes para la Historia Grande vividos y redactados por el autor* (Buenos Aires 1945).

Líster, Enrique: 'Lessons of the Spanish guerrilla war, 1939-1951' in *World Marxist Review*, Vol 8, No. 2 (Prague), February 1965.

Lomax, Sir John: *The diplomatic Smuggler* (London 1965).

Lowi, T. J.: 'Bases in Spain' in Harold L. Stein (ed.) *American Civil-Military Decisions, a book of case studies* (Birmingham, Ala. 1963).

McLachlan, Donald: *Room 39: Naval Intelligence in Action* (London 1968).

Madriaga, Salvador de: *Spain: A Modern History* (2nd ed., London 1961).

Maíz, B. Félix: *Alzamiento en España* (Pamplona 1952).

Mariñas, Francisco Javier: *General Varela* (*De soldado a general*) (Barcelona 1958).

Martín Blázquez, José: *I helped to build an army* (London 1939).

Martínez Bande, José María: *La marcha sobre Madrid* (Madrid 1968).

Medlicott, W. F.: *The Economic Blockade* (London 1952–9).

Menéndez-Reigada, Ignacio G.: *La guerra nacional española ante la moral y el derecho* (Salamanco 1937).

Miller, Webb: *I found no peace: The Journal of a Foreign Correspondent* (London 1937).

Organisation for European Economic Cooperation: *Industrial Statistics 1900–1955. Addendum* (Paris 1956).

Oyarzún, Román: *Historia del Carlismo* (Bilbao 1939).

París Eguilaz, Higinio; *Diez años de política económica en España 1939–1949* (Madrid 1949).

Parliamentary Debates: House of Commons (London).

Pattee, Richard F.: *Portugal and the Portuguese World* (Milwaukee 1957).

Payne, Stanley G.: *Falange: A History of Spanish Fascism* (Stanford 1961)
Politics and the Military in Modern Spain (Stanford 1967).

Pérez Madrigal, Joaquín: *Augurios, Estallido y Episodios de la Guerra Civil* (Avila 1936).

Peterson, Sir Maurice: *Both sides of the curtain* (London 1950).

Piétri, François: *Mes années d'Espagne, 1940–1948* (Paris 1954).

Pio XII: *Discorsi e Radiomessaggi di Sua Santità, Vol XIII* (Vatican City 1952).

Plenn, Abel: *Wind in the olive trees: Spain from within* (New York 1946).

Primo de Rivera, José Antonio: *Obras Completas* (Madrid 1954).

Queipo de Llano, Gonzalo: *El general Queipo de Llano perseguido por la dictadura* (Madrid 1930).

Raeder, Erich: *Mein Leben* (Tübingen 1956–7).

La Reconstrucción de España. Resumen de 2 años de labor (Madrid 1942).

Ridruejo, Dionisio: *Escrito en España* (Buenos Aires 1962).

Romanones, Conde de: *Notas de una vida, 1912–1931* (Madrid 1947).

Salvá Miquel, F., and J. Vicente: *Francisco Franco: Historia de un español* (Barcelona 1959).

Schellenberg, Walter: *The Schellenberg Memoirs* (London 1956).

Schmidt, Paul: *Hitler's Interpreter* (London 1951).

Serrano Súñer, Ramón: *Entre Hendaya y Gibraltar* (Madrid 1947).

Sierra, Ramón de la: *Don Juan de Borbón* (Madrid 1965).

Southworth, Herbert R.: *Antifalange; estudio crítico de 'Falange en la guerra de España' por Maximiano Garcia Venero* (Paris 1967).

The Spanish Red Book on Gibraltar (Madrid 1965).

Statesman's Yearbook for 1928 (London 1927).

Stein, Harold L. (ed.): *American Civil-Military Deicsions; a bok ofo case studies* (Birmingham, Ala. 1963).

Sweet, Escott, Bickham: *Baker Street Irregular* (London 1965).

Templewood, Viscount (Sir Samuel Hoare): *Ambassador on Special Mission* (London 1946).

Tharaud, J. & J.: *Spain and the Riff: Political Sketches* (London 1926).

Thomas, Hugh: *The Spanish Civil War* (London 1961).

Timmermans, Rudolf: *General Franco* (Olten 1937).

Torrent García, Martín: *¿Qué me dice usted de los presos? Contestaciones* (Alcalá de Henares 1942).

Trevor Roper, H. R.: see *Hitler*.

U. K. Naval Intelligence Division: *Geographical Handbook on Spain and Portugal* (London 1943) cited as UKNID.

US Department of State: *The Spanish Government and the Axis. Documents* (Washington 1946).

US 82nd Congress: *13th Report to Congress of the Economic Cooperation Administration* (Washington 1951).

286

Vicuña, Alejandro: *Franco* (Santiago de Chile 1956).
Vigón, Jorge: *General Mola (el conspirador)* (Barcelona 1957).
Welles, Benjamin: *Spain, The Gentle Anarchy* (New York 1965).
Whealey, Robert H.: *German–Spanish relations, January–August 1939: the failure of Germany to conclude military and economic agreements with Spain* (University of Michigan Ph. D. dissertation 1963; available on microfilm).
Whitaker, Arthur P.: *Spain and the Defense of the West. Ally and liability* (New York 1961).
Whitaker, John T.: 'Prelude to War: A witness from Spain' in *Foreign Affairs*, vol. XXI, no. 1 (New York), October 1942.
Whitaker's Almanack 1937 (London 1936).

NEWSPAPERS AND PERIODICALS

ABC (Madrid).
ABC (Seville) *El Adelanto (Salamanca)*.
Africa: Revista de Tropas Coloniales (Ceuta).
Arriba (Madrid).
Boletín oficial de la Junta de Defensa Nacional (Burgos).
Boletín Oficial del Estado (Burgos; afterwards Madrid).
El Carbayón (Oviedo).
Chicago Daily Tribune.
Claridad (Madrid).
Correo Gallego (El Ferrol).
Corriere della Sera (Milan).
El Debate (Madrid).
Department of State Bulletin (Washington).
Diário de Notícias (Lisbon).
Diario Oficial del Ministerio de Guerra (Madrid).
Ecclesia (Madrid).
Estampa (Madrid).
Extremadura (Caceres).
Figaro (Paris).
Frankfurter Zeitung.
Journal de Genève.
Il Messaggero (Rome).

LIST OF WORKS CITED

Le Monde (Paris).
News Chronicle (London).
New Statesman (London).
New York Herald Tribune (European edition, Paris).
New York Times.
Nuevo Diario (Madrid).
Nuevo Mundo (Madrid).
Osservatore Romano (Vatican City).
Pueblo (Madrid).
Sunday Express (London).
The Times (London).

This list contains only those works cited in the main text. For reference to some of the further works used, see note on bibliography.

Index

Index

NOTE ON SPANISH PROPER NAMES: A Spaniard has two surnames (sometimes joined by the particle *y*), the first of which is his (or her) father's patronymic, and the second of which is his (or her) mother's patronymic. Married women retain their surnames, sometimes adding one or both of their husband's after the particle *de*. Occasionally a person uses more than two surnames; e.g., he might add his grandmother's patronymic if it were more distinguished or unusual than his grandfather's. In accordance with Spanish practice, where more than one name is used in the text, the main reference is under the first patronymic.

INDEX

Towns underlined are
capitals of the provinces
bearing their names